Irony and Crisis

A Critical History of Postmodern Culture

Stuart Sim

CRITICAL HISTORIES SERIES

CONSULTANT EDITOR: NICOLAS TREDELL

ICON BOOKS UK TOTEM BOOKS USA

Published in the UK in 2002
by Icon Books Ltd., Grange Road,
Duxford, Cambridge CB2 4QF
E-mail: info@iconbooks.co.uk
www.iconbooks.co.uk

Sold in the UK, Europe, South Africa
and Asia by Faber and Faber Ltd.,
3 Queen Square, London WC1N 3AU
or their agents

Distributed in the UK, Europe,
South Africa and Asia by
Macmillan Distribution Ltd.,
Houndmills, Basingstoke RG21 6XS

Published in Australia in 2002
by Allen & Unwin Pty. Ltd.,
PO Box 8500, 83 Alexander Street,
Crows Nest, NSW 2065

Published in the USA in 2002
by Totem Books
Inquiries to: Icon Books Ltd.,
Grange Road, Duxford,
Cambridge CB2 4QF, UK

Distributed to the trade in the USA by
National Book Network Inc.,
4720 Boston Way, Lanham,
Maryland 20706

Distributed in Canada by
Penguin Books Canada,
10 Alcorn Avenue, Suite 300,
Toronto, Ontario M4V 3B2

ISBN 1 84046 369 4

Front cover image:
W/P Camera Press, London

CRITICAL HISTORIES series
Consultant editor: Nicolas Tredell
Originating editor: Duncan Heath

Typesetting: Wayzgoose

Printed and bound in the UK by
Biddles Ltd., Guildford and King's Lynn

Contents

Stuart Sim is Professor of Critical Theory in the Department of English at the University of Sunderland. He has published widely on critical and cultural theory, as well as on seventeenth- and eighteenth-century prose fiction. His most recent books are *Contemporary Continental Philosophy: The New Scepticism* (Ashgate, 2000), *Post-Marxism: An Intellectual History* (Routledge, 2000), *Lyotard and the Inhuman* (Icon, 2001), and, with Borin Van Loon, *Introducing Critical Theory* (Icon, 2001).

Introduction

The postmodern has been with us for some time now, and there is a very considerable literature both celebrating and attacking its features. Modernity may still have its supporters, but there is a general consensus that postmodernism is the new cultural paradigm,* the theory that now sets the ground for debate. Some will even argue that we have only really come to understand what modernity itself *is* since postmodernity has emerged to provide a basis for comparison. This volume is designed to trace the critical history of the new paradigm, giving some idea of the scope of the literature just mentioned – a literature both for and against postmodernism. In other words, we will trace the perception of postmodernism as it has developed over the course of the twentieth century and then into the twenty-first. The variety of viewpoints on the phenomenon is striking. For some thinkers, postmodernism is the liberation from an institutionally repressive culture; for others, it is an abdication of social and intellectual responsibility that is symptomatic of advanced cultural decline. One side wants to accelerate, the other to arrest this process. It is the concern here to track the various debates that have led us to this impasse – where postmodernists look back with irony on older paradigms, and their opponents accuse them instead of an unwarranted flippancy and destructive iconoclasm.

The volume is organised into five main sections, in which we work our way through the emergence, philosophy, sociology and politics, science and technology, and then finally the aesthetics of the postmodern. (A full list of all texts extracted in this volume can be found in the bibliography – see pages 263–73.) The objective is to communicate as much as possible of the richness of debate over the concept (as well as the passion that goes into it), and in so doing to reveal just what is at stake in current cultural discourses – who thinks there is a crisis; why they think there is a crisis; and why they react to that perceived crisis in the ways they do. We set out, therefore, to determine why irony and crisis have come to dominate the cultural scene in the West in recent times.

* See 'Glossary of Critical Terms' on pp. 279–89.

Postmodernism might be thought of as a challenge to the cultural assumptions of modernity – assumptions that we have almost come to regard as the natural order of things by our own day. The philosopher Jean-François Lyotard most famously described the 'postmodern condition' as a crisis in the authority of the 'grand narratives' of modernity. He argued that by the later twentieth century these narratives could no longer rely on our unthinking support, and without that support they were in danger of complete collapse. A grand narrative, or metanarrative, is in essence an ideology, and as with all ideologies it claims privileged status as the final authority on all social and political matters. Modernity has spawned several grand narratives, such as liberal humanism and Marxism, each purporting to hold the answer to humankind's problems. The source of modernity's grand narratives is to be found in what is called the 'Enlightenment project'.

The Enlightenment project is that movement in Western culture which, from the eighteenth century onwards, has striven for the liberation of humankind from material want and political oppression. Both liberal humanism and Marxism claim to provide the means for achieving these goals, although their methods of doing so differ. The Enlightenment project establishes some of what we now take to be the fundamental features of modernity – most notably, a commitment to technological progress and to democratic political structures. Great emphasis is also laid on the role of reason in creating the basis for liberation: Enlightenment is above all a rationalist-minded project aiming at the eradication of superstition from human affairs (older histories often refer to the Enlightenment as the 'Age of Reason'). Although very different from liberal humanism in its working methods, Marxism is no less committed to those ideals than its ostensible ideological opposite is; it is no less a child of the Enlightenment in its belief that rational solutions can be found to any human problem, if only we apply ourselves with enough dedication. Lyotard pictures a world in which the institutions set up to deliver those commitments have become dictatorial and oppressive, generating a widespread reaction against their authority. Over the course of the later twentieth century, significant numbers of people simply stop believing in the ideological systems they live under (as happened in the Eastern bloc in the 1980s, for example), and that, for Lyotard, projects us into the postmodern condition: 'I define *postmodern* as incredulity toward metanarratives.'[1] Postmodernity is one long series of declarations of incredulity towards metanarrative authority, in whatever form that authority chooses to assert itself.

It is important to see postmodernism as more than just an intellectual theory. It is also something we can see operative at grass-roots level in terms of the decline in respect for authority – both in the public and private sectors – that is such a notable and widely acknowledged feature of contemporary Western societies. This generalised scepticism *vis-à-vis* authority reveals itself in our everyday behaviour no less than in our cultural theorising in the academy. The green movement has been able to tap into this deep vein of scepticism to promote its campaigns against the environmental abuses perpetrated by governments and the multinationals, drawing support from both socialists and conservatives in the process. Respect for public figures is arguably at its lowest ebb in modern times in the West, with politicians, and the institutions they control, often being treated with outright disdain – especially in the mass media. Even the British royal family can no longer count on the deference of the British public to traditional authority, and finds its constitutional role increasingly under threat with some national newspapers conducting campaigns calling for the abolition of the monarchy and the foundation of a republic. These trends are at least as much a manifestation of postmodernism as the high-flown philosophical theories of a Lyotard, or any of his contemporaries in the poststructuralist movement. Postmodernism is to be understood as a theorisation of what is happening in more diffuse fashion in the general culture around us, of the incredulity that is becoming an increasingly regular feature of our daily lives. Some commentators even speak of the phenomenon of 'credicide', the death of belief, in our culture.

The pervasive quality of postmodernism, the way it has made its presence felt across the cultural spectrum, has been well captured by one of its major theorists, Charles Jencks:

> Post-Modernism is now a world-wide movement in all the arts and disciplines. Post-modern politics varies from the conviction politics of Margaret Thatcher and Tony Blair to the search for a new liberalism that can combine multiculturalism and universal rights; post-modern food varies from Cambozola (Camembert and Gorgonzola improved by combining) to California Cuisine (French plus Pacific Rim plus supposedly healthy). There are more books on Post-Modernism than its parent Modernism, which is not to say it is more mature or better, but just here to stay. We are well past the age when we can merely accept or reject this new 'ism'; it is too omnipresent for either approach. Rather we have to ask about its emergent possibilities, ask 'What is it?', and then decide selectively to support and criticise

> aspects of the movement. (Charles Jencks, *What is Post-Modernism?*, 4th edn, London: Academy Editions, 1996, p. 6.)

Tim Woods is another to express bemusement at the bewildering ubiquity of the concept.

> What connects the Duchess of York, Batman, the new MI6 Building, Bill Clinton and Blur? Well, they are all apparently postmodern. For among the tally of 'isms', the new password is 'postmodernism'. To adapt Wordsworth, we may say that the postmodern is too much with us; late and soon, getting and spending, we lay waste our lives before it. Books proliferate on the subject; newspaper journalists write articles on the phenomenon; it is bandied about on the radio; few self-respecting English departments ignore it … The term gets everywhere, but no one can quite explain what it is. In the midst of all this terminological mayhem, Harry Enfield recently mused as to whether there is a First Class Postmodernism and a Second Class Postmodernism, and whether it is all delivered by Post(modernist-)man Pat. (Tim Woods, *Beginning Postmodernism*, Manchester and New York: Manchester University Press, 1999.)

The message in both cases seems to be that whether we like it or not – and, as we will discover over the course of this study, a considerable body of commentators patently do not – we have now irrevocably passed over the threshold into the postmodern world. We have no real option, therefore, but to try to come to terms with it as gracefully as possible – loose and baggy though it may well be for the cultural commentator to deal with. Postmodernism is our destiny.

Postmodernism has manifested itself particularly strongly in the arts, where a significant backlash to modernism can be noted over the last few decades. Modernism's rejection of traditional models, and its cult of originality and experimentation, have been subjected to challenge across all the creative arts. Authors have returned to older forms of novel-writing, painters to representational art, composers to tonality, architects to premodernist building styles. In each case the older style has been given a particular twist when adapted for postmodernist purposes – it is not simply imitation that we are dealing with, but a recontextualisation. What is noticeable throughout the creative arts, however, is a desire to open up a dialogue with the past – a dialogue that modernism had largely banished from its practice.

Charles Jencks, the person who more than anyone has helped to popularise the term 'postmodern', has defined the postmodern appropriation of the past as 'double coding'. In his own field of architecture, Jencks argued that practitioners had a responsibility to appeal to the general public as well as to their peers – to 'double code' their buildings such that they did not alienate the general public, as the 'new brutalism' of modern architecture so obviously had done. The new brutalism, with its severe geometrical shapes and lack of ornamentation, tended to make the general public feel uncomfortable and, thanks to its extensive use in the public building projects of most Western societies in the post-Second World War period, it was a style that few of the populace could avoid coming into contact with in their daily lives. Along with tower-block office buildings, tower-block estates came to dominate the landscape of Western cities, and in most cases they were deeply disliked by their inhabitants, very often turning into vandalised slums within just a few years of their opening. Jencks saw the destruction of these unpopular estates as the birth of postmodernism, famously, and wittily, arguing that,

> we can date the death of Modern Architecture to a precise moment in time. Unlike the legal death of a person, which is becoming a complex affair of brain waves versus heartbeats, Modern Architecture went out with a bang. ... Modern architecture died in St. Louis, Missouri on July 15, 1972 at 3.32 p.m. (or thereabouts) when the infamous Pruitt–Igoe scheme, or rather several of its slab blocks, were given the final *coup de grâce* by dynamite. Previously it had been vandalised, mutilated and defaced by its black inhabitants, and although millions of dollars were pumped back, trying to keep it alive (fixing the broken elevators, repairing smashed windows, repainting), it was finally put out of its misery. Boom, boom, boom. (Charles Jencks, *The Language of Post-Modern Architecture*, 6th edn, London: Academy Editions, 1991, p. 23.)

The dynamiting of Pruitt–Igoe was for Jencks a highly symbolic act in that it represented an admission of failure on the part of the modernist architectural establishment (or, at the very least, an admission of failure on their behalf by those employing them). Henceforth architects were required to take popular taste into account, which modernism had adamantly refused to do, regarding that as a breach of its principles and the purity of its aesthetic vision. Similar moves were undertaken in the other arts, with painters gradually turning away from abstraction (the prevailing style in Western art for the greater part of the twentieth century), authors going back to nineteenth- and even eighteenth-century realism for their narrative models, and composers abandoning atonality and serial music (which had never found any substantial audience despite decades of effort) in favour of tonality. Whereas modernism had resolutely turned its back on the past, for postmodernism the past was to be appropriated as an integral part of the creative process. Pastiche became the dominant postmodernist artistic manner, with the ethos of double coding very much in evidence. Double coding served to undermine the grand narrative of modernism, and, by extension, the grand narrative of the Enlightenment project itself. Incredulity towards modernism became the norm and, by and large, the general public came to appreciate the impact this had on the arts.

At the heart of the postmodern project is the problem of our relationship to modernity – the metanarrative that has held sway over our culture for so long that we are hardly aware of its workings any more. There is still considerable disagreement as to whether we have left modernity and its works behind, with such high-profile cultural commentators as Jürgen Habermas and Fredric Jameson continuing to argue that we exist within a modernist frame of reference. Their sentiments will be echoed throughout the full range of intellectual disciplines. Even Lyotard concedes that modernity and postmodernity are symbiotically linked in many ways, and that the latter phenomenon is as much a change of emphasis as anything:

> As you know, I made use of the word 'postmodern': it was but a provocative way to put the struggle in the foreground of the field of knowledge. Postmodernity is not a new age, it is the rewriting of some features modernity has tried or pretended to gain, particularly in founding its legitimation upon the purpose of the general emancipation of mankind. But such a rewriting, as has already been said, was for a long time active in modernity itself. (Jean-François Lyotard, 'Rewriting Modernity', *SubStance*, 54, 1987, pp. 8–9.)

The impetus for postmodernity comes from within modernity itself – which leaves it open as to whether we regard this as a necessary or welcome development. Lyotard will also argue that modernity and postmodernity exist in a cyclical relationship to each other alternating over time, such that we can speak of both modernisms and postmodernisms in the past and can postulate the emergence of both again in the future.

As we will see in Chapter five, this has prompted several literary historians to argue for particular correspondences between eighteenth-century literature and the postmodern era, with the novelist Laurence Sterne, as a case in point, repeatedly being claimed for the postmodernist cause.

Certain recurrent features begin to reveal themselves as we work through the critical literature on postmodernism, with competing claims being made for the phenomenon's value by its supporters and detractors respectively. Supporters tend to claim that it is politically radical, anti-authoritarian, and that it marks a paradigm shift in our culture away from the objectives of the Enlightenment project and modernity. It is, they insist, a paradigm shift we should welcome in that it frees us from the repressions that mar later modernity, with its approved norms of behavioural and political practices. Another positive aspect of the development of postmodernism is that it enables us to reconstruct relationships with the past, with modernity being criticised for having consigned that past to cultural oblivion. The cult of originality and experimentation that had underpinned modernist culture is reclassified as a form of tyranny – a tyranny that, apart from its detrimental effect on creative artists (forced into following what amounted to a party line if they wanted to retain the respect of their peers), had succeeded in alienating the general public from the art world. There will be a deliberate blurring of the boundaries between 'high' and 'low' art in postmodern thought, with ever greater emphasis being put on the value of popular culture (the development of the discipline of cultural studies is a notable part of that process). The notion of a governing aesthetic is no more acceptable to the postmodern community than a governing political metanarrative is, although it will often adopt an attitude of irony in its dealings with the aesthetics of the past. If irony and crisis mark out the postmodern in general, then incredulity plus irony might well stand as a definition of the postmodern aesthetic.

Another metanarrative to be challenged vigorously is that of science, with its assumption of unbroken technological progress stretching indefinitely into the future. What is substituted in its stead is postmodern science, which is taken to reveal a world far less controllable and open to manipulation than modern science would want to believe. Modern science works on the principle that the material world can come to be known through rational methods of enquiry. Some scientists, taking their lead from figures like Einstein, even hold that if we pursue our rational enquiries into the physical world with enough rigour, we can come to construct a 'Grand Unified Theory' that will explain everything about how our universe works. Postmodern science, however, disputes this. It deals instead in ruptures, discontinuities and unbreachable limits, offering yet another challenge to the narrative of progress that is embedded in the Enlightenment project.

Detractors claim that postmodernism is politically conservative or, at best, that it unwittingly plays into the hands of political conservatives and neoconservatives, that it is intellectually weak and even irresponsible (charges of charlatanism are not uncommon), depending more on sleight-of-hand than reasoned canons of argument to make its often far-fetched points. Postmodernism is also accused of fostering irrationalism, and thus misleading the young and impressionable. These are charges we will find repeatedly throughout the literature, along with the claim that reports of modernity's death have been greatly exaggerated. Modernity and the Enlightenment project do not just live on for such critics, but fully deserve to live on and command our enthusiastic support. This latter group contains many feminist theorists, for whom Enlightenment and modernity for all their faults (their generally masculinist bias, for example) are nevertheless rooted in liberationist ideals that they are loath to lose. Marxist theorists, too, especially those of the classical variety, are still more than willing to defend modernity – again, despite its many perceived faults. Without modernity, they argue, we are in danger of falling back into a dark age in which humanity's best qualities will be denied expression.

In terms of the arts, postmodernism is criticised for encouraging an essentially lazy approach to artistic creation, in which older forms, themes, styles and methods are endlessly, and boringly, recycled. For many of its critics, postmodernism communicates a sense of creative exhaustion, of there being nothing left to say – hence its constant raids on the creative legacy of the past to disguise its own emptiness. The ironic attitude adopted towards the repackaging of the past can also register as an irritating glibness, suggesting superficiality and trivialisation rather than cultural breadth and cleverness. Such repackaging, particularly noticeable in the practice of architecture, is taken to reveal a failure of imagination on the part of the postmodern artistic community – a failure, some critics consider, that amounts almost to a moral weakness. What Charles Jencks celebrates as a liberating 'radical eclecticism', in which old and new styles are mixed together in a manner that captures the positive aesthetic qualities of both (double coding in action), is, from the point of view of the detractors, little better than building by numbers in which the creative element is all but excised from the practice of architecture.[2]

When it comes to postmodern science, too, there is deep scepticism about the claims made for the discipline by major theorists of the postmodern, with many commentators declaring these to be intellectually dishonest. At best, such sceptics insist, postmodernists misunderstand the new physics (quantum mechanics, catastrophe theory, chaos theory, complexity theory and so on); at worst, they distort it to fit their own world picture. Whether postmodern science actually exists at all becomes an issue in its own right for many contributors to the debate, as does the issue of whether science is an essentially modernist enterprise, thus at variance with the postmodern ethos. Technological progress, the very backbone of modernity, is not always regarded as an unproblematical good by theorists of the postmodern. Some others, though (most notably the feminist theorists Donna Haraway and Sadie Plant), are able to detach it from its modernist heritage and adapt it to the cause of the postmodern. Nor is this an esoteric debate: it has critical implications for the practice of a discipline like medicine, for example, in which case it affects all our lives in some way or other.

We move on now to consider how that spectrum of response is communicated across the range of discourses and intellectual disciplines we have identified – in other words, to postmodernism, the case for and against. We will find ourselves having to consider the merits of not only incredulity towards modernism, therefore, but also incredulity towards postmodernism. Irony and crisis, we will see, can be interpreted in a wide variety of ways for a wide variety of uses.

CHAPTER ONE

The Emergence of the Postmodern

When did we first become postmodern? Use of the term can be noted as far back as the 1870s, when the English painter John Watkins Chapman described art that was more avant-garde than French impressionism as 'postmodern painting'.[1] 'Post-modern' appears in a work published in German in 1917.[2] Then the theologian Bernard Iddings Bell writes two books in the 1920s and 30s entitled *Postmodernism and Other Essays* and *Religion for Living: A Book for Postmodernists*.[3] To Bell, a postmodernist is someone who has rejected all the political systems of the modern world (liberalism, communism and fascism), in favour of religion: 'Such a man is the Postmodernist – intellectually humble and spiritually hungry. He who writes this book is one of the breed, who thanks God for the finding of that treasure which his soul desired.'[4] None of these uses leaves any great mark on cultural theory, however, and the idea of the postmodern gradually emerges over the course of the twentieth century until it comes to take on the meaning of 'incredulity toward metanarratives' – whatever area of human endeavour those metanarratives happen to apply in. It will be between the 1940s and the 1970s that this meaning is hammered out.

Initially, 'postmodern' is a far less politically loaded term, although it has always carried the sense of significant cultural change, as it does in its appearance in an abridged version of volumes 1–6 of Arnold Toynbee's *A Study of History*, published just after the Second World War. There we are informed that,

> there is ample reason for supposing that we have recently passed into a new chapter whose beginnings may be placed round about 1875. So we have:
>
> Western I ('Dark Ages'), 675–1075.
> Western II ('Middle Ages'), 1075–1475.
> Western III ('Modern'), 1475–1875.

> Western IV ('Post-Modern'?), 1875–?.
>
> (Arnold Toynbee, *A Study of History*, vols. I–VI, abridged by D.C. Somervell, New York and London: Oxford University Press, 1947, p. 39.)

In later volumes of the series, Toynbee is much more explicit about the nature of this new chapter in humankind's development:

> A post-Modern Age of Western history which had opened in the seventh and eighth decades of the nineteenth century had seen the rhythm of a Modern Western war-and-peace cycle broken, in the course of its fourth beat, by the portent of one general war following hard at the heels of another, with an interval of only twenty-five years between the outbreaks in A.D. 1939 and in A.D. 1914, instead of the interval of 120 years or more which had separated A.D. 1914 from A.D. 1792 and A.D. 1792 from A.D. 1672. ... At a moment in the post-Modern chapter of Western history at which the denouement of the double Germano–Western War of A.D. 1914–18 and A.D. 1939–45 was not yet an accomplished fact, the approaching overturn of a Balance of Power which had maintained its precarious existence since its inauguration in the last decade of the fifteenth century had already been announced by a rise in the death-rate of Western or Westernizing Great Powers that had been as steep as it had been sudden; and this carnage was ominous, considering that the first law of every balance, political and physical alike, is that the instability of the equilibrium varies in inverse ratio to the number of its *points d'appui*. (Arnold Toynbee, *A Study of History*, vol. IX, London: Oxford University Press, 1954, p. 235.)

There is a clear sense here of general cultural decline, and the tone is deeply pessimistic as to humankind's prospects. Toynbee's 'post-Modern Age' is a troubled period in which the relative stability of the previous modern era crumbles away with worrying consequences for us all. Post-1875 is to be considered a condition of crisis. This is a recurrent theme of commentators on the postmodern, and Toynbee's fears come to be voiced by many of them. Equally, many others will regard the shift from the modern to the postmodern as a liberating rather than disorienting prospect for humankind – our opportunity to escape from the excesses of the previous ideological regime. From the beginning, however, 'post-modern' carries the sense of an unmistakable paradigm shift in which the values of the modern age are eroded – particularly the commitment of that age to rationality. Already in Toynbee we have a vision of post-modernity as a journey into unknown territory where the old cultural constants no longer apply, and our collective security is potentially compromised. The postmodern spells risk: as one cultural historian put it in 1957, 'the postmodern world offers man everything or nothing'.[5]

By the 1950s the notion of the postmodern is beginning to be more widely established. Thus the management theorist Peter F. Drucker can speak of us having 'imperceptibly moved out of the "Modern Age" and into a new, as yet nameless, era' that merits the appellation 'post-modern'.[6] Similarly, we note the sociologist C. Wright Mills claiming that we are on the threshold of a new cultural paradigm that will shake the foundations of all our social structures:

> Nowadays men everywhere seek to know where they stand, where they may be going, and what – if anything – they can do about the present as history and the future as responsibility. Such questions as these no one can answer once and for all. Every period provides its own answers. But just now, for us, there is a difficulty. We are now at the ending of an epoch, and we have got to work out our own answers. We are at the ending of what is called The Modern Age. Just as Antiquity was followed by several centuries of Oriental ascendancy, which Westerners provincially call The Dark Ages, so now The Modern Age is being succeeded by a post-modern period. Perhaps we may call it: The Fourth Epoch. ... The ideological mark of The Fourth Epoch – that which sets it off from The Modern Age – is that ideas of freedom and of reason have become moot; that increased rationality may not be assumed to make for increased freedom. The role of reason in human affairs and the idea of the free individual as the seat of reason are the most important themes inherited by twentieth-century social scientists from the philosophers of the Enlightenment. If they are to remain the key values in terms of which troubles are specified and issues focused, then the ideals of reason and of freedom must now be re-stated as problems in more precise and solvable ways than have been available to earlier thinkers and investigators. For in our time these two values, reason and freedom, are in obvious yet subtle peril. The underlying trends are well known. Great and rational organizations – in brief – bureaucracies – have indeed increased, but the substantive reason of the individual at large has not. Caught in the limited milieux of their everyday lives, ordinary men often cannot

> reason about the great structures rational and irrational – of which their milieux are subordinate parts. (C. Wright Mills, *The Sociological Imagination*, New York: Oxford University Press, 1959, pp. 165–6, 167–8.)

Effectively, what Wright Mills is describing is the early stirrings of 'incredulity toward metanarratives', as expressed in the increasing alienation of the bulk of the population from the 'great and rational organizations'. As with Toynbee, there is a pessimistic tone to his pronouncements and a sense of regret at what we have lost. There is that characteristic fear of the threat posed to reason by the coming new order, although it is precisely the uncritical commitment to reason that postmodern thinkers will come increasingly to question. The argument of the postmoderns will be that, far from being the solution to our problems, reason is in fact the source of most of them, and that it has led to such tragic events of our time as the Holocaust, the Cold War, and the Vietnam War.

The note of pessimism struck by so many early theorists of the postmodern does raise the question of whether the postmodern describes a set of attitudes or a more deep-rooted cultural change. The point has been well put by Thomas Docherty:

> The word 'postmodern' is thus characterised, from its very inception, by an ambiguity. On the one hand it is seen as a historical period; on the other it is simply a desire, a mood which looks to the future to redeem the present. The word, with this ambivalence, then hovers around the edges of sociological arguments and the 'end of ideology' debates in the 1950s. But it is in the theories of architecture and in the discourses of literary criticism that the peculiar tension in the term begins to articulate itself more pointedly. In both, there is a tension between, on the one hand, thinking of the postmodern as a chiliastic [millenarian] historical period which 'after modernity', we either have entered or are about to enter, while on the other realising that we are condemned to live in a present, and adopting a specific – some have said 'schizophrenic' – mood as a result of acknowledging that the present is characterised by struggle or contradiction and incoherence. In this latter case, the mood in question is in the first instance seemingly determined by a quasi-Nietzschean 'active forgetting' of the past-historical conditioning of the present, in the drive to futurity.
>
> This tension is one which also lays bare the underlying tension

> between an attitude to postmodernism as an aesthetic style and postmodernity as a political and cultural reality; that is, it opens a question which had been debated before, on the proper relation between aesthetics and politics. ('Postmodernism: An Introduction', in Thomas Docherty, *Postmodernism: A Reader*, Hemel Hempstead: Harvester-Wheatsheaf, 1993, pp. 1–31 (pp. 2–3).)

We will frequently return over the course of this volume to both that tension and that 'proper relation'. And we will hear much more, too, about struggle, contradiction and incoherence – although these will not necessarily be thought of as negative characteristics. We will also see thinkers like Gilles Deleuze and Felix Guattari recommending schizophrenia to us as the most appropriate model for behaviour in the face of repressive authority.

In architectural discourse, we can find the term 'postmodern' being used as early as 1945, by Joseph Hudnut (an associate of the Bauhaus School founder Walter Gropius at Harvard University), in reference to post-war prefabricated buildings. Hudnut feels that these structures succeed in capturing a new public mood that is worth responding to and developing:

> I shall not imagine for my future house a romantic owner, nor shall I defend my client's preferences as those foibles and aberrations usually referred to as 'human nature'. No, he shall be a modern owner, a post-modern owner, if such a thing is conceivable. Free from all sentimentality or fantasy or caprice. His vision, his tastes, his habits of thought shall be those most necessary to a collective-industrial scheme of life; the world shall, if it pleases him, appear as a system of casual sequences transformed each day by the cumulative miracles of science. Even so he will claim for himself some inner experiences, free from outward control, unprofaned by the collective conscience. That opportunity, when the universe is socialized, mechanized and standardized, will yet be discoverable in the home. Though his house is the most precise product of modern processes there will be entrenched within it this ancient loyalty invulnerable against the siege of our machines. It will be the architect's task, as it is today, to comprehend that loyalty – to comprehend it more firmly than anyone else – and, undefeated by all the armaments of industry, to bring out its true and beautiful character. (Joseph Hudnut, 'The Post-modern House', *Architectural Record*, 97, 1945, pp. 70–5 (p. 75); later reprinted

> in the same author's *Architecture and the Spirit of Man*, Cambridge, MA: Harvard University Press, 1949, pp. 108–19 (p. 119).)

Hudnut's conception of the postmodern is not quite what we expect from the term nowadays, as Margaret A. Rose has pointed out:

> Hudnut's concept of the post-modern ... is clearly used to describe what could also be denoted in Hudnut's own terms a modern or ultra-modern owner. ... Hudnut's post-modern owner's house is described in his conclusion as the epitome of the results of 'the cumulative miracles of science', which might even be termed the forces of 'modernisation', given that Hudnut had also spoken in his article of a 'collective-industrial scheme of life' which now appears to have looked back to the relations of modern industrial society rather than forward to any new 'post-industrial' scheme of things similar to those spoken of by Jencks in his writings on the post-modern in architecture. For this reason too Hudnut's vision could be said to be 'ultra' rather than 'post'-modern. Only when Hudnut goes on to speak of the architect as providing an antidote to the machine, by providing the way of bringing out the 'true and beautiful character' of the post-modern house, might we in fact find something which looks forward to at least some of the post-modern architectural theory of the 1970s. (Margaret A. Rose, *The Post-Modern and the Post-Industrial: A Critical Analysis*, Cambridge: Cambridge University Press, 1991, pp. 7–8.)

Charles Jencks claims that it was Hudnut who made the architectural profession aware of the notion of the postmodern (lodging it in its 'subconscious' in the first instance),[7] although Rose feels that Jencks overstates the case. Rose's point about Hudnut being a champion of the ultra-modern as opposed to the postmodern – as we now understand the term – is well taken, but there are some interesting signals towards the more mature concept of the postmodern to note in Hudnut nonetheless. There is a sense of the modern as something that we can go beyond, and the reference to 'inner experiences, free from outward control' at least hints at a sceptical attitude towards institutional authority (Mills's 'great and rational organisations'). And perhaps the recognition that we need to protect ourselves against 'the siege of our machines' points towards a consciousness that is small-scale rather than based on grand narrative. For better or worse, however, the 'postmodern' is now on the architectural agenda.

The notion that we had entered a 'post-industrial' age was a further key stage in the emergence of the postmodern as a distinct cultural paradigm. The work of Daniel Bell is particularly noteworthy in this respect, with *The Coming of Post-Industrial Society* describing how modernity was being superseded by new forms of production and wealth-creation. For Bell, the shift from industrial to post-industrial society is largely a matter of a move from a production-based to a service-based economy:

> Industrial societies ... are goods-producing societies. Life is a game against fabricated nature. The world has become technical and rationalized. The machine predominates, and the rhythms of life are mechanically paced: time is chronological, methodical, evenly spaced. ... A post-industrial society is based on services. Hence, it is a game between persons. What counts is not raw muscle power, or energy, but information. The central person is the professional, for he is equipped, by his education and training, to provide the kinds of skill which are increasingly demanded in the post-industrial society. If an industrial society is defined by the quantity of goods as marking a standard of living, the post-industrial society is defined by the quality of life as measured by the services and amenities – health, education, recreation, and the arts – which are now deemed desirable and possible for everyone. The word 'services' disguises different things, and in the transformation of industrial to post-industrial society there are several different stages. First, in the development of industry there is a necessary expansion of transportation and of public utilities as auxiliary services in the movement of goods and the increasing use of energy, and an increase in the non-manufacturing but still blue-collar force. Second, in the mass consumption of goods and the growth of populations there is an increase in distribution (wholesale and retail), and finance, real estate, and insurance, the traditional centers of white-collar employment. Third, as national incomes rise, one finds, as in the theorem of Christian Engel, a German statistician of the latter half of the nineteenth century, that the proportion of money devoted to food at home begins to drop, and the marginal increments are used first for durables (clothing, housing, automobiles) and then for luxury items, recreation, and the like. Thus, a third sector, that of personal services, begins to grow: restaurants, hotels, auto services, travel, entertainment, sports, as people's horizons expand and new wants and tastes develop. But here a new

> consciousness begins to intervene. The claims to the good life which the society has promised become centered on the two areas that are fundamental to that life – health and education. ... So we have here the growth of a new intelligentsia, particularly of teachers. (Daniel Bell, *The Coming of Post-Industrial Society: A Venture in Social Forecasting*, Harmondsworth: Penguin, 1976, pp. 127–8.)

Although not all of Bell's predictions have come true, much of the above looks remarkably prescient when viewed from a quarter of a century later. We have in the interim become used to service industries dominating the economic sector (the Thatcher government actively encouraged this development during the 1980s in Britain), of considerable growth in the professional classes and of the advent of mass higher education in countries such as Britain. We recognise, too, that we live now in an overwhelmingly information-based society. What is also striking about Bell's analysis is the tone of optimism concerning radical social change, far removed from the pessimism of thinkers such as Toynbee and Wright Mills. The post-industrial era is something to be welcomed enthusiastically, offering as it does the enticing prospect of social existence on a more human scale than hitherto.

For Bell, the postmodern is on the cultural agenda, although as yet in a rather undefined way. He quotes Amitai Etzioni to make the point:

> A central characteristic of the modern period has been continued increase in the efficacy of the technology of production which poses a growing challenge to the primacy of the values they are supposed to serve. The post-modern period, the onset of which may be set at 1945, will witness either a greater threat to the status of these values by the surging technologies or a reassertion of their normative priority. Which alternative prevails will determine whether society is to be the servant or the master of the instrument it creates. (Amitai Etzioni, *The Active Society: A Theory of Societal and Political Processes*, London and New York: Free Press, 1968, p. vii.)

That ambivalence about technology will become ever more pronounced as postmodernism develops. Some will treat technology as our potential cultural saviour (for example, Haraway and Plant); others will treat it as a threat to our humanity and possibly our very existence as a species (Lyotard). We will consider the range of response that technology can generate in postmodern circles in Chapter four.

In *The Cultural Contradictions of Capitalism*, Bell is critical of both modernism *and* postmodernism, which might help explain why – much to his displeasure, it should be said – commentators like Habermas (see Chapter two) have described him as a neoconservative at heart:

> Traditional modernism sought to substitute for religion or morality an aesthetic justification of life; to create a work of art, to be a work of art – this alone provided meaning in man's effort to transcend himself. ... In the 1960s a powerful current of post-modernism developed which carried the logic of modernism to its farthest reaches. In the theoretical writings of Norman O. Brown and Michel Foucault, in the novels of William Burroughs, Jean Genet and, up to a point, Norman Mailer, and in the porno-pop culture that is now all about us, one sees a logical culmination of modernist intentions. ...
>
> There are several dimensions to the post-modernist mood. Thus, against the aesthetic justification for life, post-modernism has completely substituted the instinctual. Impulse and pleasure alone are real and life-affirming; all else is neurosis and death. ... Post-modernism overflows the vessels of art. It tears down the boundaries and insists that *acting out*, rather than making distinctions, is the way to gain knowledge. The 'happening' and the 'environment', the 'street' and the 'scene', are the proper arena not for art but for life. ...
>
> The post-modern temper, looked at as a set of loosely associated doctrines, itself goes in two directions. One is philosophical, a kind of negative Hegelianism.[8] Michel Foucault sees man as a short-lived historical incarnation, 'a trace on the sand', to be washed away by the waves. The 'ruined and pest-ridden cities of man called "soul" and "being" will be de-constructed'. It is no longer the decline of the West, but the end of all civilization. Much of this is modish, a play of words pushing a thought to an absurd logicality. Like the angry playfulness of Dada or surrealism, it will probably be remembered, if at all, as a footnote to cultural history.
>
> But the post-modern temper, moving in another direction, does carry a much more significant implication. It provides the psychological spearhead for an onslaught on the values and motivational patterns of 'ordinary' behavior, in the name of liberation, eroticism, freedom of impulse, and the like. It is this, dressed up in more popular form, which is the importance of the post-modernist doctrine. For it means that a crisis of middle-class values is at hand. (Daniel Bell, *The Cultural Contradictions of Capitalism*, London: Heinemann, 1976, pp. 51–2.)

Bell's version of postmodernism is something of a caricature, it has to be said. It misses altogether, for example, the anti-authoritarian imperative of the movement, as well as its political radicalism. Postmodernism comes across instead as an intellectually trivial, and even potentially destructive, phenomenon, which manages to amplify all the very worst traits of modernism. For Bell, the most glaring contradiction in capitalism is between its deferred gratification and pleasure-seeking sides, with the American value system deriving largely from the former and its source in the Protestant work ethic. Postmodernism, in this reading, is on the wrong side of the cultural divide: an advocate of gratification now rather than later. The post-industrial and the postmodern would seem to have little in common: one is a socially positive, the other a socially negative, force. What postmodernism announces for Bell is a weakness in human character. It is a point we will find repeated by critics over a wide range of disciplines for the next few decades. The fact that it *is* repeated over a period of decades, moreover, suggests that postmodernism is much more than a mere 'footnote to cultural history'.

In contrast to Bell, Margaret A. Rose sees the postmodern and the post-industrial as being intimately linked together in socio-historical terms:

> [T]heories of the post-modern and the post-industrial have, despite their many differences ... now come to form a body of literature in which not only the modern, modernism, modernisation or modernity have been defined as phenomena or traditions of the past to be criticised or transformed, but new ideals or goals set for the future. ... If this book can be said to have its own view on the usefulness of the concepts of the post-modern and the post-industrial discussed in it, it is, furthermore, that those concepts have been particularly useful not only when leading us to question ideologies which have been carried forward into this century from the last (rather than adding new and often even more questionable ones which will need to be demythologised in the future), but also, as in the case of Charles Jencks and some others, when returning or restoring the idea lost in some late modern theory of the importance of the subject as someone who is both able to make up their own mind about the ideas and values of the day, and willing and able to communicate these to others. (Rose, *The Post-Modern and the Post-Industrial*, p. 177.)

Rose's main concern in this study is to clarify the various senses that the terms 'postmodern' and 'post-industrial' have taken on over the course of the twentieth century (she can trace meaningful usages of the latter back to 1914, as in Ananda K. Coomaraswamy and Arthur J. Penty, eds, *Essays in Post-Industrialism: A Symposium of Prophecy Concerning the Future of Society*).[9] She gives a cautious welcome to those versions of postmodern thought that directly question received authority (such as the Jencksian) as opposed to those that, in her opinion, merely mystify communication to the extent that received values are not really seriously threatened (that is, deconstruction).

The postmodern emerges, therefore, from a variety of cultural sources – one scholar has spoken of a 'forest of origins'[10] – either calling for, or recording, cultural change. Such change can take the form either of rejection or transcendence – of modernity and the Enlightenment project, for example. It remains a somewhat diffuse term, although it does take on an agreed range of meanings by the later decades of the twentieth century. By the time we reach the pronouncements of Jencks on Pruitt–Igoe, and Lyotard on the 'postmodern condition', its existence is well established and it is firmly on the cultural map. We will now consider how these agreed ranges of meanings have been received, by both supporters and detractors, whether as paradigm shift or footnote, everything or nothing.

CHAPTER TWO

The Philosophy of the Postmodern

Postmodernism has been a crucial part of recent continental philosophy, and many of its most famous exponents – for example, Lyotard, Deleuze and Jacques Derrida – come from that tradition. Its roots, however, lie in much earlier philosophical discourses, going back, some would argue, to Immanuel Kant's 'third' Critique, the *Critique of Judgement* (1790). In that work Kant sought to find a bridge between understanding and reason, the subjects of his two other monumental philosophical treatises, the *Critique of Pure Reason* (1781, 1787) and the *Critique of Practical Reason* (1788).[1]

We might just elaborate briefly on Kant's project in these two works. In the *Critique of Pure Reason*, the objective is to outline the process by which we come to have knowledge of the world. Knowledge comes from both sense experience and the understanding, but the former has to be ordered by the twelve 'categories', or concepts, of the latter before we can make sense of the world around us (space and time being examples of such 'structuring' categories/concepts). The *Critique of Practical Reason*'s brief is to demonstrate how we arrive at moral principles. According to Kant, the method we employed to test such principles was the 'categorical imperative', which enjoined us to act only if our reason for doing so could be turned into a universal law (a more complex version of the Christian doctrine 'Do unto others as you would be done by').

What Kant is concerned to establish over the course of the two critiques is that the process of gaining knowledge is governed by *a priori* principles – that is, 'constitutive' principles that ensure, before the event, that our knowledge will consist of certain truths. Constitutive principles can be contrasted with 'regulative' principles, those in which rules are applied. Regulative principles can always be changed (as, for example, in the case of bye-laws), but constitutive principles have the force of necessity behind them. Given that force, the categories provide a secure base for the acquisition of knowledge, then the categorical imperative guarantees that our moral judgements will be the correct ones to have made in each instance. In the following extract from the *Critique of Judgement*, Kant sums up the objectives of the first two critiques:

> The faculty of knowledge from *a priori* principles may be called *pure reason*, and the general investigation into its possibility and bounds the Critique of pure reason. This is permissible although 'pure reason', as was the case with the same use of terms in our first work [*Critique of Pure Reason*], is only intended to denote reason in its theoretical employment, and although there is no desire to bring under review its faculty as practical reason and its special principles as such. That Critique is, then, an investigation addressed simply to our faculty of knowing things *a priori*. Hence it makes our *cognitive faculties* its sole concern, to the exclusion of the feeling of pleasure or displeasure and the faculty of desire; and among the cognitive faculties it confines its attention to *understanding* and its *a priori* principles, to the exclusion of *judgement* and *reason*, (faculties that also belong to theoretical cognition,) because it turns out in the sequel that there is no cognitive faculty other than understanding capable of affording constitutive *a priori* principles of knowledge. Accordingly the Critique which sifts these faculties one and all, so as to try the possible claims of each of the other faculties to a share in the clear possession of knowledge from roots of its own, retains nothing but what *understanding* prescribes *a priori* as a law for nature as the complex of phenomena – the form of these being similarly furnished *a priori*. All other pure concepts it relegates to the rank of ideas, which for our faculty of theoretical cognition are transcendent: though they are not without their use nor redundant, but discharge certain functions as regulative principles. For these concepts serve partly to restrain the officious pretensions of understanding, which, presuming on its ability to supply *a priori* the conditions of the possibility of all things which it is capable of knowing, behaves as if it had thus determined these bounds as those of the possibility of all things generally, and partly also to lead understanding, in its study of nature, according to a principle of completeness, unattainable as this remains for it, and so to promote the ultimate aim of all knowledge.
>
> Properly, therefore, it was *understanding* – which, so far as it contains constitutive *a priori* cognitive principles, has its special realm, and one, moreover, in our *faculty of knowledge* – that the Critique, called in a general way that of Pure Reason, was intended to establish

> in secure but particular possession against all other competitors. In the same way *reason*, which contains constitutive *a priori* principles solely in respect of the *faculty of desire*, gets its holding assigned to it by the Critique of Practical Reason. (Immanuel Kant, *The Critique of Judgement*, trans. James Creed Meredith, Oxford: Clarendon Press, 1952, pp. 3–4.)

Understanding and reason are therefore governed by *a priori* constitutive principles that yield certain truths. The business of the third critique is to discover whether constitutive *a priori* principles also apply in the aesthetic realm – that is, whether there is a categorical imperative lying behind judgements of taste (feelings of 'pleasure and displeasure', as Kant puts it) as well as behind moral judgements, as opposed to mere regulative principles:

> But now comes *judgement*, which in the order of our cognitive faculties forms a middle term between understanding and reason. Has *it* also got independent *a priori* principles? If so, are they constitutive, or are they merely regulative, thus indicating no special realm? And do they give a rule *a priori* to the feeling of pleasure and displeasure, as the middle term between the faculties of cognition and desire, just as understanding prescribes laws *a priori* for the former and reason for the latter? This is the topic to which the present Critique is devoted. ...
>
> We may readily gather, however, from the nature of the faculty of judgement (whose correct employment is so necessary and universally requisite that it is just this faculty that is intended when we speak of sound understanding) that the discovery of a peculiar principle belonging to it – and some such it must contain in itself *a priori*, for otherwise it would not be a cognitive faculty the distinctive character of which is obvious to the most commonplace criticism – must be a task involving considerable difficulties. For this principle is one which must not be derived from *a priori* concepts, seeing that these are the property of understanding, and judgement is only directed to their application. It has, therefore, itself to furnish a concept, and one from which, properly, we get no cognition of a thing, but which it can itself employ as a rule only – but not as an objective rule to which it can adapt its judgement, because, for that, another faculty of judgement would again be required to enable us to decide whether the case was one for the application of the rule or not.
>
> It is chiefly in those estimates that are called aesthetic, and which

> relate to the beautiful and sublime, whether of nature or of art, that one meets with the above difficulty about a principle (be it subjective or objective). (Kant, *The Critique of Judgement*, pp. 4, 5.)

It is when Kant turns to the sublime that he runs into the greatest difficulty in identifying principles that would operate with the force and authority of the categorical imperative, since there concepts are confronted by the inconceivable (infinity and the absolute being notable examples). Size is a way of comparing objects, and we can speak of them being relatively larger or smaller than each other; but the sublime involves the quality of *absolute* greatness, and that notion transcends our rational faculty:

> *Sublime* is the name given to what is *absolutely great.* But to be great and to be a magnitude are entirely different concepts (*magnitudo* and *quantitas*). In the same way to *assert without qualification* (*simpliciter*) that something is great, is quite a different thing from saying that it is *absolutely great* (*absolute, non comparative magnum*). The latter is *what is beyond all comparison great.* – What, then, is the meaning of the assertion that anything is great, or small, or of medium size? What is indicated is not a pure concept of understanding, still less an intuition of sense; and just as little is it a concept of reason, for it does not import any principle of cognition. It must, therefore, be a concept of judgement, or have its source in one, and must introduce as basis of the judgement a subjective finality of the representation with reference to the power of judgement. ... [T]he estimate of things as great or small extends to everything, even to all their qualities. Thus we call even their beauty great or small. The reason of this is to be found in the fact that we have only got to present a thing in intuition, as the precept of judgement directs, (consequently to represent it aesthetically,) for it to be in its entirety a phenomenon, and hence a quantum.
>
> If, however, we call anything not alone great, but, without qualification, absolutely, and in every respect (beyond all comparison) great, that is to say, sublime, we soon perceive that for this it is not permissible to seek an appropriate standard outside itself, but merely in itself. It is a greatness comparable to itself alone. Hence it comes that the sublime is not to be looked for in the things of nature, but only in our own ideas. ... *The sublime is that, the mere capacity of thinking which evidences a faculty of mind transcending every standard of sense.* (Kant, *The Critique of Judgement*, pp. 94–5, 96–7, 98.)

The general consensus among the philosophical community is that Kant fails to find the desired bridge between reason and understanding, and that the sublime represents a highly significant gap in his epistemological project – the point at which both reason and understanding prove inadequate to the task of making the world and our concepts conform to each other (that being what constitutes the basis of knowledge in Kant). No concept can constitute the sublime, which, in fact, lies beyond the possibility of constitution – that is, beyond the *a priori* principles that apply in the case of both understanding and reason.

The implications of the third critique have not been lost on post-structuralists and postmodernists, who have proceeded to exploit the unresolved problems left by the Kantian sublime to their own advantage. What it means for someone like Lyotard is that any totalising project is doomed to fail – that the sublime will always constitute a barrier to any such attempts, and that not even the invocation of the imagination by Kant can bridge the gap opened up by the sublime:

> The hypothesis is as follows: in the excess of its productive play with forms or aesthetic Ideas, the imagination can go so far as to prevent the recognition by concept, to dis-concert the 'consciousness' that is dependent upon understanding, the faculty of consciousness. This fury evokes the 'excesses' of the baroque, of mannerism or of surrealism, but is also always a potential disturbance in the 'calm' contemplation of the beautiful. The *Geist*, the life vein of 'animation', can always exceed the 'letter', force it to give in, to resign, and the 'happiness' of writing can thus turn into a delirium through an overabundance of 'images'. ... However, sublime feeling can be thought of as an extreme case of the beautiful. Thus it is through the faculty of concepts that the aesthetic feeling becomes unbound. One can imagine, in effect, that by dint of opposing the power of forms with concepts that are more and more 'extreme' in order to put this power – the imagination – in difficulty, the power of concepts determinable by intuition, understanding, passes its 'hand' (in this play) to the power of concepts of reason's unpresentable objects ... The faculty of concepts no longer requires the imagination to give a rich and pleasant presentation to the concept of domination, in the traits of the master of Olympus, for example, to which it can add a thousand other 'aesthetic attributes', but to the Idea of the all-powerful itself. But the object of this Idea is not presentable in intuition. The imagination cannot 'create' a form that would be adapted for it, for all form

> is circumscription ... and the all-powerful is conceived of as an absolute that excludes all limitation.
>
> The proliferation of forms by an imagination gone wild makes up for this powerlessness of principle, but then creativity is no longer in free play, pleasant, even fortuitous; it falls prey to a regime of anguish. This is what must be understood in the *Ernst*, the 'seriousness', with which Kant qualifies the activity of the imagination in the sublime. It is the seriousness of melancholy, the suffering of an irreparable lack, an absolute nostalgia for form's only always being form, that is limitation, *Begrenzung* ... The concept places itself out of the reach of all presentation: the imagination founders, inanimate. All of its forms are inane before the absolute. (Jean-François Lyotard, *Lessons on the Analytic of the Sublime*, trans. Elizabeth Rottenberg, Stanford, CA: Stanford University Press, 1994, pp. 74–5, 76.)

Postmodernism is a philosophy that, on principle, resists the totalising impulse, being concerned instead to emphasise the factor of difference as the crucial element in human affairs. In the postmodernist reading of Kant it is the sublime, with, as Lyotard puts it above, its ability to instil in us a sense of an 'irreparable lack' within reason and understanding, which provides that impetus. Given that Kant's is the most ambitious epistemological project in modern philosophy, his failure to bridge the gap between reason and understanding takes on immense symbolic importance for the postmodernist movement. Unwittingly, Kant has revealed the impossibility of the totalising imperative in general. From within the very heart of modernity comes a tacit admission of its limitations. In philosophical terms of reference, the Kantian sublime is modernity's weakest link, and postmodernists will not let their opponents forget this.

Another philosopher to be taken to heart by the postmodernist movement is Friedrich Nietzsche, whose call for a 'radical transvaluation' of all values strikes a chord with all those who are sceptical of authority. Nietzsche's approach to cultural values is unashamedly iconoclastic in tone:

> This problem of the *value* of compassion and of the morality of compassion (– I am an opponent of the shameful modern weakening of sensibility –) seems at first merely an isolated issue, a free-standing question-mark. But whoever pauses here, whoever *learns* to ask questions here, will undergo the same experience as I – that of a huge new

> prospect opening up, a vertiginous possibility, as every kind of mistrust, suspicion, and fear leaps forward, and the belief in morality, all morality, falters. Finally, a new demand finds expression. Let us articulate this *new demand*: We stand in need of a *critique* of moral values, *the value of these values itself should first of all be called into question*. This requires a knowledge of the conditions and circumstances of their growth, development, and displacement (morality as consequence, symptom, mask, Tartufferie, illness, misunderstanding; but also as cause, cure, stimulant, inhibition, poison); knowledge the like of which has never before existed nor even been desired. The *value* of these 'values' was accepted as given, as fact, as beyond all question. Previously, no one had expressed even the remotest doubt or shown the slightest hesitation in assuming the 'good man' to be of greater worth than the 'evil man', of greater worth in the sense of his usefulness in promoting the progress of human *existence* (including the future of man). What? And if the opposite were the case? What? What if there existed a symptom of regression in the 'good man', likewise a danger, a temptation, a poison, a narcotic, by means of which the present were living *at the expense of the future*? Perhaps more comfortably and less dangerously, but also in less grand style, in a humbler manner? ... So that none other than morality itself would be the culprit, if the *highest power and splendour* of the human type, in itself a possibility, were never to be reached? So that morality would constitute the danger of dangers? (Friedrich Nietzsche, *On the Genealogy of Morals: A Polemic* (1887), trans. Douglas Smith, Oxford and New York: Oxford University Press, 1996, pp. 19, 7–8.)

Nietzsche's point is that value judgements are essentially conventional, and are derived in the first instance from the power structures of a given society. Those in power impose their own values on the rest of the populace, a thesis that will be developed further by various postmodernist thinkers – most notably, perhaps, by Michel Foucault, for whom all cultural discourses are expressions of underlying power relations. Following Nietzsche's lead, the 'value of values' will consistently be called into question by postmodernist thinkers, with no value being considered as sacrosanct. Indeed, in the more extreme versions of postmodern philosophy, forming a value *at all* can seem an impossible task.

Nietzsche also has some particularly radical things to say about the concept of truth, which he takes to be no less conventional in nature:

What, then, is truth? A mobile army of metaphors, metonymies, anthropomorphisms, in short a sum of human relations which have been subjected to poetic and rhetorical intensification, translation, and decoration, and which, after they have been in use for a long time, strike a people as firmly established, canonical, and binding; truths are illusions of which we have forgotten that they are illusions, metaphors which have become worn by frequent use and have lost all sensuous vigour, coins which, having lost their stamp, are now regarded as metal and no longer as coins. Yet we still do not know where the drive to truth comes from, for so far we have only heard about the obligation to be truthful which society imposes in order to exist, i.e. the obligation to use the customary metaphors, or, to put it in moral terms, the obligation to lie in accordance with firmly established convention, to lie *en masse* and in a style that is binding for all. Now, it is true that human beings forget that this is how things are; thus they lie unconsciously in the way we have described, and in accordance with centuries-old habits – and precisely *because of this unconsciousness*, precisely because of this forgetting, they arrive at the feeling of truth. The feeling that one is obliged to describe one thing as red, another as cold, and a third as dumb, prompts a moral impulse which pertains to truth; from its opposite, the liar whom no one trusts and all exclude, human beings demonstrate to themselves just how honourable, confidence-inspiring and useful truth is. As creatures of *reason*, human beings now make their actions subject to the rule of abstractions; they no longer tolerate being swept away by sudden impressions and sensuous perceptions; they now generalize all these impressions first, turning them into cooler, less colourful concepts in order to harness the vehicle of their lives and actions to them. Everything which distinguishes human beings from animals depends on this ability to sublimate sensuous metaphors into a schema, in other words, to dissolve an image into a concept. This is because something becomes possible in the realm of these schemata which could never be achieved in the realm of those sensuous first impressions, namely the construction of a pyramidal order based on castes and degrees, the creation of a new world of laws, privileges, subordinations, definitions of borders, which now confronts the other, sensuously perceived world as something firmer, more general, more familiar, more human, and hence as something regulatory and imperative. Whereas every metaphor standing for a sensuous perception is individual and unique and is therefore always able to escape classifi-

> cation, the great edifice of concepts exhibits the rigid regularity of a Roman *columbarium*, while logic breathes out that air of severity and coolness which is peculiar to mathematics. Anyone who has been touched by that cool breath will scarcely believe that concepts too, which are as bony and eight-cornered as a dice and just as capable of being shifted around, are only the left-over *residue of a metaphor*, and that the illusion produced by the artistic translation of a nervous stimulus into images is, if not the mother, then at least the grandmother of each and every concept. Within this conceptual game of dice, however, 'truth' means using each die in accordance with its designation, counting its spots precisely, forming correct classifications, and never offending against the order of castes nor against the sequence of classes of rank. (Friedrich Nietzsche, 'On Truth and Lying in a Non-Moral Sense', in *The Birth of Tragedy and Other Writings* (1873), trans. Ronald Spiers, eds, Raymond Geuss and Ronald Spiers, Cambridge: Cambridge University Press, 1999, pp. 139–53 (pp. 146–7).)

It is what one commentator has dubbed Nietzsche's 'impatience with all system and ideology' – well represented in the extract above – that recommends him most to the postmodernist camp.[2] With his dismissive references to convention, the rule of abstractions, schemas and pyramidal orders, Nietzsche clearly demonstrates his anti-grand narrative credentials. If we put together the 'irreparable lack' of the Kantian sublime and the Nietzschean impatience with system, then we are well on the way to the 'postmodern condition'.

Nietzsche's mark can be found throughout postmodern philosophy, including such notable forerunners of the poststructuralist movement as Theodor W. Adorno – one of the few Marxist thinkers to draw freely on Nietzsche for inspiration. Adorno's 'negative dialectics' have a Nietzschean quality to them in that they prevent the formation of absolute truths (they prefigure Derrida's work quite strikingly in that respect). What Adorno is concerned to encourage instead is what he calls 'nonidentity thinking', which reveals 'the untruth of identity, the fact that the concept does not exhaust the thing conceived', going on to argue that such thinking undermines any attempt at constructing a totalising philosophy (in postmodern terms, a metanarrative):

> The name of dialectics says no more, to begin with, than that objects

> do not go into their concepts without leaving a remainder, that they come to contradict the traditional norm of adequacy. Contradiction is not what Hegel's absolute idealism was bound to transfigure it into: it is not of the essence in a Heraclitean sense. It indicates the untruth of identity, the fact that the concept does not exhaust the thing conceived. … The thoughts of transcendental apperception or of Being could satisfy philosophers so long as they found those concepts identical with their own thoughts.[3] Once we dismiss such identity in principle, the peace of the concept as an Ultimate will be engulfed in the fall of identity. Since the basic character of every general concept dissolves in the face of distinct entity, a total philosophy is no longer to be hoped for …
>
> Totality is to be opposed by convicting it of nonidentity with itself – of the nonidentity it denies, according to its own concept. Negative dialectics is thus tied to the supreme categories of identitarian philosophy as its point of departure. Thus, too, it remains false according to identitarian logic: it remains the thing against which it is conceived. It must correct itself in its critical course – a course affecting concepts which in negative dialectics are formally treated as if they came 'first' for it, too. It is one thing for our thought to close itself under compulsion of the form which nothing can escape from, to comply in principle, so as immanently to deny the conclusive structure claimed by traditional philosophy; and it is quite another thing for thought to urge that conclusive form on its own, with the intent of making itself 'the first'. …
>
> Identity is the primal form of ideology. We relish it as adequacy to the thing it suppresses; adequacy has always been subjection to dominant purposes and, in that sense, its own contradiction. After the unspeakable effort it must have cost our species to produce the primacy of identity even against itself, man rejoices and basks in his conquest by turning it into the definition of the conquered thing: what has happened to it must be presented, by the thing, as its 'in-itself.' Ideology's power of resistance to enlightenment is owed to its complicity with identifying thought, or indeed with thought at large. (Theodor W. Adorno, *Negative Dialectics*, trans. E. B. Ashton, London: Routledge and Kegan Paul, 1973, pp. 5, 136, 147, 148.)

Whereas in Hegelian dialectics the contradiction that results when a thesis generates its antithesis is held to be 'resolved' in the creation of a new thesis, for Adorno it is instead a case of the endless creation of new contradictions undermining any notion of resolution. The process simply rolls on, overtaking each apparent resolution in turn. Adorno regards the insistence on the primacy of resolution in dialectical processes as the first step on the road to ideological control of our thought. If one emphasises contradiction, a very different picture of our world emerges.

The 'total philosophy' that Adorno is seeking most of all to undermine by nonidentity thinking is classical Marxism, the form that lies behind the foundation of the Soviet bloc. In challenging one of the most powerful metanarratives of his lifetime, and the interpretation of the theory on which that metanarrative has been constructed, Adorno is pointing the way forward to postmodernism. As we have noted before, postmodern philosophy takes it as its brief to resist the totalising imperative in general, and Adorno's problematisation of classical Marxism, and its dialectical heritage in Hegel's philosophy, can be considered a significant part of its pre-history.

Adorno's other major philosophical works reveal him to be an explicit opponent of the Enlightenment project as well. His collaborative study with his Frankfurt School colleague Max Horkheimer, *Dialectic of Enlightenment*, is a case in point. The book's uncompromising opening statement almost sounds like a battle-cry for the postmodern movement: 'In the most general sense of progressive thought, the Enlightenment has always aimed at liberating men from fear and establishing their sovereignty. Yet the fully enlightened earth radiates disaster triumphant.' (Theodor W. Adorno and Max Horkheimer, *Dialectic of Enlightenment* (1944), trans. John Cumming, London and New York: Verso, 1979, p. 3.) The study goes on to contend that the Enlightenment ideal of exerting control over one's environment has led to both the West and the Soviet bloc becoming bureaucratic, 'administered' societies in which individual freedom has been severely curbed:

> Any decision-taking functions which still appear to be left to individuals are in fact taken care of in advance. The irreconcilable nature of ideologies as thundered out from the political platforms is simply an ideology of the blind constellation of power. The ticket thinking which is a product of industrialization and its advertising machine, extends to international relations. The choice by an individual citizen of the Communist or Fascist ticket is determined by the influence which the Red Army or the laboratories of the West have on him. The objectification by which the power structure (which is made possible only by the passivity of the masses) appears as an iron reality, has

> become so dense that any spontaneity or even a mere intimation of the true state of affairs becomes an unacceptable utopia, or deviant sectarianism. The illusion has become so concentrated that a mere attempt to penetrate it objectively itself appears as an illusion. On the other hand, support for a political ticket means support for the illusion-reality, which is thus prolonged indefinitely. The person who has doubts is already outlawed as a deserter. (Adorno and Horkheimer, *Dialectic of Enlightenment*, p. 205.)

The power and reach of metanarratives have rarely been put better than this. Enlightenment is pictured as a repressive force that demands extreme conformity from individuals. This interpretation of the development of Western culture constitutes a significant step on the road to the postmodern ethos. Adorno's anti-Enlightenment, post-Marxist stance is one that commends him to French postmodernist thinkers in particular. That 'person who has doubts' might well be regarded as the postmodernist in germ.

Philosophically speaking, we are on the cusp of the postmodern at this point – although it would have to be admitted that Adorno himself would have been out of sympathy with certain aspects of postmodern thought (such as its anti-rationalist bias).

Martin Heidegger's work also helps to usher in the poststructuralist/postmodernist era in continental philosophy. Most of the major thinkers in French philosophy from Jean-Paul Sartre onwards are heavily influenced by Heidegger, with his short post-war work, the 'Letter on Humanism', being one of the acknowledged starting points for the development of French poststructuralism. In the 'Letter' Heidegger develops the notion of there being a 'turn' (*Kehre*) in his philosophy, which differentiates it not just from his own earlier writings, but from the main tradition of Western metaphysics dating back to Greek classical times. Part of that turn is an opposition to humanism, or what humanism has come to mean in the modern world – for Heidegger a rather empty term (even Jean-Paul Sartre was claiming to be a humanist at that point).[4] He speaks of wanting to devise 'a "humanism" that contradicts all previous humanism', and, invoking Nietzsche, of that new 'humanism' involving a radical rethinking of the values of our society – including our philosophical heritage:

> It is time to break the habit of overestimating philosophy and of thereby asking too much of it. What is needed in the present world

> crisis is less philosophy, but more attentiveness in thinking; less literature, but more cultivation of the letter.
>
> The thinking that is to come is no longer philosophy, because it thinks more originally than metaphysics – a name identical to philosophy. However, the thinking that is to come can no longer, as Hegel demanded, set aside the name 'love of wisdom' and become wisdom itself in the form of absolute knowledge. Thinking is on the descent to the poverty of its provisional essence. Thinking gathers language into simple saying. In this way language is the language of Being, as clouds are the clouds of the sky. With its saying, thinking lays inconspicuous furrows in the language. They are still more inconspicuous than the furrows that the farmer, slow of step, draws through the field. (Martin Heidegger, 'Letter on Humanism' (1947), in David Farell Krell, ed., *Basic Writings: Martin Heidegger*, 2nd edn, London: Routledge, 1993, pp. 214–65 (pp. 248, 265).)

The notion that Western metaphysics has come to an end, and that a new attitude towards that tradition of thought is necessary – in Heidegger's terms, a need to 'think against "values"' (Ibid., p. 251) – underpins poststructuralist thought. Poststructuralists, too, will call the assumptions of Western metaphysics such as the possibility of 'absolute knowledge' openly into question, arguing the case for that paradigm having lost its cultural authority. Given that philosophy traditionally emphasises the importance of reason, and that the Enlightenment is based on reason being the key to resolving all human problems, Heidegger's rejection of Western metaphysics takes on a critical cultural resonance. The *Kehre* comes to be treated as an early version of 'incredulity toward metanarratives', and continental philosophy from Heidegger onwards will be an activity with a deep sense of suspicion about its own history, methods and conclusions.

I have argued myself that the defining characteristic of contemporary continental philosophy, subsuming the poststructural and the postmodern within that, is that it is an updated form of scepticism – a 'superscepticism' designed to deflect all critique of its enquiries by the analytical tradition (the mainstay of Anglo-American institutional philosophy over the course of the twentieth century, and heir of the Western metaphysical tradition rejected by Heidegger):

> Continental philosophy is a widely-used term but in many ways a

highly problematical one, and its exact frame of reference is not always as clear as it might be. For many in the English-speaking academic world it tends in practice to mean *French* philosophy of the last few decades: more specifically, French philosophy influenced by linguistics, phenomenology, psychoanalysis, and Marxism – which inevitably leads one some way into the German tradition, where the last three discourses have their origins. As Tom Rockmore has pointed out, 'there is a measure of truth to Heidegger's boast that when the French begin to think, they think in German'. In the English-speaking academic world, however, the problem is not so much one of origins as whether the post-Heideggerean French still think *philosophically* – at least in any of the former discourse's recognized senses of that activity. Contemporary continental philosophy, particularly in its more recent French manifestation, continues to arouse considerable controversy, create bitter divisions in the academic community ... and generally suggest that something more fundamental is at stake than just an issue of approach to the subject, or of methodological origins. In short, the real question to many non-continentals is whether we are in the presence of a philosophy *at all*. The frequent accusations of charlatanism levelled against poststructuralist and postmodernist thinkers argue that the answer is more often than not in the negative.

Much of the work in the recent continental tradition, particularly the French, can be fitted into a longer-running philosophical tradition of scepticism – if of a far less extreme kind. Scepticism has always had that power to provoke and unsettle the philosophical establishment; as C. H. Whiteley has pointedly remarked, scepticism, 'being an uncomfortable position ... is tolerable only if it can be employed to make self-important people still more uncomfortable'. While the factor of difference needs to be, and will be, emphasised in this study, thinkers such as Derrida and Jean-François Lyotard are in many ways to be regarded as carrying on the tradition of such thoroughgoing sceptics, and generators of intellectual discomfort, as David Hume. On the one hand, therefore, contemporary continental philosophy is often the philosophy of a world far stranger than you had ever thought possible (*super*-scepticism); on the other, of a world far more familiar (scepticism, all the same). (Stuart Sim, *Contemporary Continental Philosophy: The New Scepticism*, Aldershot and Burlington, VT: Ashgate, 2000, pp. 1–2.)

For others, postmodern scepticism is so extreme in character that it all but disqualifies itself from remaining part of the philosophical family. David West is one such sceptic of the philosophical claims made on behalf of super-scepticism:

> With postmodernism it is as if we pass through the looking-glass of western reason. As we do so, apparently reliable conceptual distinctions are inverted or abolished altogether, and what was previously most solid 'melts into air'. Postmodernism attempts a radical break with all of the major strands of post-Enlightenment thought. For postmodernists both the orthodox Enlightenment 'meta-narrative' of progress and emancipation and the 'speculative' narrative of Hegelianism and Marxism have lost their spell. Phenomenology and existentialism are condemned as varieties of humanism or nostalgic philosophies of the subject. Even Derrida's acrobatic manoeuvres on the margins of metaphysics fail to convince. Perhaps not surprisingly, then, it is impossible to provide a straightforward definition of postmodernism. Not only are there conflicting views about what postmodernism is, but postmodernist positions are also adopted within a variety of disciplinary settings. There is a wide range of contexts for what are nevertheless related discourses of modernity and postmodernity. These include history and sociology, philosophy, art and art theory as well as literature and literary criticism. As a result, too, 'postmodern', 'postmodernity' and 'postmodernism' are not always straightforwardly cognate terms either. They have different connotations, depending whether a historical period, a form of society, a philosophical stance or an artistic movement is in question. In other words, postmodernism cannot be regarded as a purely philosophical development. It is just as much a response to the calamitous history of the West. …
>
> In the further development of postmodernism … two separate regions must be distinguished … In the first place, there is a radically sceptical, philosophical critique of the intellectual universe of modernism. This tendency targets both the Enlightenment project and some of its most influential continental critics. Postmodernism in this guise rejects all philosophies of history and provides a radical challenge to the most basic categories of western philosophy and metaphysics. But secondly, and of course not unrelatedly, a number of theorists make a connection between postmodern tendencies in art and culture and the state of contemporary, sometimes 'postindustrial',

> sometimes 'late' or 'advanced capitalist', sometimes 'postmodern' societies. This is primarily a postmodernism of social and cultural theory, identifying postmodernity as a stage in western society. Evidently there are significant tensions between the two approaches. Philosophical postmodernism seems to deny what postmodern social and cultural thought seems to require – a philosophy or, at least, an overall account of history. (David West, *An Introduction to Continental Philosophy*, Cambridge and Oxford: Polity Press and Blackwell, 1996, pp. 189–90, 196–7.)

At best, therefore, postmodernism is a philosophically confused project; although one could argue that West misses the historical consciousness involved in rejecting a previous tradition of thought for its perceived failings, as postmodernists do with modernity. The break with the Enlightenment metanarrative is made to sound wilful in this account rather than in any way principled, as if the reaction against authority were a mere whim on the part of a few iconoclastically-minded individuals. Iconoclasm remains a handy stick with which to beat postmodernist thinkers.

Poststructuralism is a critical part of the postmodernist movement, and there is certainly a concerted critique of received wisdom in the work of arguably its major voice, Jacques Derrida. Derrida's work has engendered a storm of controversy, with both the critical and philosophical establishment in the English-speaking world condemning what they see as his cavalier attitude to accepted canons of intellectual enquiry. The American philosopher John Searle is a case in point, and his exchanges with Derrida on the issues of meaning and intention take on a highly symbolic character. Against what he takes to be Derrida's opaque pronouncements on the relationship between meaning and intention in language, both spoken and written, Searle's argument is that

> there is no way of getting away from intentionality, because a *meaningful sentence is just a standing possibility of the corresponding* (*intentional*) *speech act*. To understand it, it is necessary to know that anyone who said it and meant it would be performing that speech act determined by the rules of languages that give the sentence its meaning in the first place.
>
> There are two obstacles to understanding this rather obvious point, one implicit in Derrida, the other explicit. The first is the illu-

sion that somehow illocutionary intentions if they ever really existed or mattered would have to be something that *lay behind* the utterances, some inner pictures animating the visible signs. But of course in serious literal speech the sentences are precisely the realizations of the intentions: there need be no *gulf* at all between the illocutionary intention and its expression. The sentences are, so to speak, fungible intentions. Often, especially in writing, one forms one's intentions (or meanings) in the process of forming the sentences: there need not be two separate processes. This illusion is related to the second, which is that intentions must all be conscious. But in fact rather few of one's intentions are ever brought to consciousness as intentions. Speaking and writing are indeed conscious intentional activities, but the intentional aspect of illocutionary acts does not imply that there is a separate set of conscious states apart from simply writing and speaking.

To the extent that the author says what he means the text is the expression of his intentions. It is always possible that he may not have said what he meant or that the text may have become corrupt in some way; but exactly parallel considerations apply to spoken discourse. The situation as regards intentionality is exactly the same for the written word as it is for the spoken: understanding the utterance consists in recognizing the illocutionary intentions of the author and these intentions may be more or less perfectly realized by the words uttered, whether written or spoken. And understanding the sentence apart from any utterance is knowing what linguistic act its utterance would be the performance of. (John R. Searle, 'Reiterating the Differences: A Reply to Derrida', *Glyph*, 1, 1977, pp. 198–208 (p. 202).)

Derrida stands accused of trying to mystify what is for Searle a relatively transparent process in which words communicate meanings that are present in the writer's or speaker's mind on to the reader or listener. This is what Derrida has dubbed 'logocentricity' – in his view as problematical an entity as truth is for Nietzsche. Belief in logocentricity is what he calls the 'metaphysics of presence', against which deconstruction directs itself. For Derrida, words are always contaminated by other meanings, words and contexts (that is, by 'intertextuality'), and can never be pinned down in the way that someone like Searle believes. Meaning never has the purity that Searle and his fellow logocentrists simply take for granted.

Derrida's reply to Searle's essay constitutes for many an example of deconstruction at its most irritating and intellectually irresponsible. There is no pretence at academic debate in its standardly understood form, with Derrida in the first instance launching a bizarre attack on Searle's use of a copyright symbol on the essay's title page:

> What is the infelicity of this – I mean, of Searle's seal? It resides in the fact that if Searle speaks the truth when he claims to be speaking the truth, the obviously true, then the copyright is irrelevant and devoid of interest: everyone will be able, will in advance *have been able*, to reproduce what he says. Searle's seal is stolen in advance. Hence, the anxiety and compulsion to stamp and to seal the truth. On the other hand, however, if Searle had the vague feeling that what he was saying was not obviously true, and that it was not obvious to everyone, then he would attempt passionately, but no less superfluously, to preserve this originality, to the point of provoking the suspicion, by virtue of his repeated and thus divided seal, that his confidence in the truth he claims to possess is a poor front for considerable uneasiness. … And, of course, how can I be absolutely sure that John R. Searle himself (who is it?) is in fact the author? Perhaps it is a member of his family, his secretary, his lawyer, his financial advisor, the 'managing editor' of the journal, a joker or a namesake?
>
> Or even D. Searle (who is it?), to whom John R. Searle acknowledges his indebtedness: 'I am indebted to H. Dreyfus and D. Searle for discussion of these matters'. This is the first note of the Reply. Its acknowledgement of indebtedness does not simply fit into the series of four footnotes since its appeal is located not in the text but in the title, on the boundary, and is directed, curiously enough, at my name – '*Reply to Derrida*' –
>
> If John R. Searle owes a debt to D. Searle concerning this discussion, then the 'true' copyright ought to belong (as is indeed suggested along the frame of this *tableau vivant*) to a Searle who is divided, multiplied, conjugated, shared. What a complicated signature! And one that becomes even more complex when the debt includes my old friend, H. Dreyfus, with whom I myself have worked, discussed, exchanged ideas, so that if it is indeed through him that the Searles have 'read' me, 'understood' me, and 'replied' to me, then I, too, can claim a stake in the 'action' or 'obligation', the stocks and bonds, of this holding company, the Copyright Trust. And it is true that I have occasionally had the feeling … of having almost '*dictated*' this reply. 'I' therefore feel obliged to claim my share of the copyright of this

> *Reply*. ... [F]aced with a *Reply* so serenely dogmatic in regard to the intention and the origin of an utterance or of a signature, I wanted before all 'serious' argument to suggest that the terrain is slippery and shifting, mined and undermined. And that this ground is, by essence, an underground. (Jacques Derrida, *Limited Inc*, trans. Samuel Weber and J. Mehlman, Evanston, IL: Northwestern University Press, 1988, pp. 30–1, 34.)

Derrida is soon playing games with Searle's name, eventually referring to him as 'Sarl', after the French phrase 'Société à responsabilité limitée' ('Society with Limited Liability'), indicating what Derrida takes to be the collective nature of Searle's response. However, behind Derrida's knockabout approach to Searle's arguments is a serious point about intellectual copyright. Thought is to be considered a collective endeavour in which we all participate, but without any one of us being able to claim ownership of particular ideas ('Sarl' rather than 'Searle' being the norm). For Derrida, Searle is claiming such ownership, which is no less an illusion than the illusion of truth that Nietzsche castigates us for assuming. In effect, Derrida is criticising an entire cultural ethos based on the notion that truth is a realisable ideal, and there are definite echoes of Nietzsche's 'impatience with system' to be noted in the deconstructive project, which has no time for the claims to authority made by grand narratives. Derridean deconstruction pictures itself as an essentially subversive operation from within culture:

> I do not believe in decisive ruptures, in an unequivocal 'epistemological break', as it is called today. Breaks are always, and fatally, reinscribed in an old cloth that must continually, interminably be undone. This interminability is not an accident or contingency; it is essential, systematic, and theoretical. And this in no way minimizes the necessity and relative importance of certain breaks, of the appearances of new structures. (Jacques Derrida, *Positions*, trans. Alan Bass, London: Athlone Press, 1981, p. 24.)

That sense of frustrating the actions both of those seeking to maintain existing grand narratives and of those seeking to replace them with equally oppressive new grand narratives brings out the intrinsically sceptical nature of the deconstructive enterprise – a scepticism it shares with the postmodern movement in general.

Deconstruction, in common with most strains of postmodern thought, has been at pains to prevent itself from turning into a grand narrative in its own right, although that has not prevented its more vociferous critics from accusing it of falling into just that trap. One such critic has been Denis Donoghue, who has hit out at the entire cultural theory enterprise, of which deconstruction has been such an important part in recent decades, in fairly venomous fashion:

> If the word 'theory' denotes a loose federation among scholars of diverse interests, and if many of these share nothing but a prejudice that they have certain enemies in common, then it is strange that the play supposedly of notions and hypotheses, by definition severed from the ultimate questions, is conducted in remarkably insistent terms. Reading essays in critical theory, I often find myself wondering about the authors: where have they found such conviction, in the declared absence of any ground of ultimacy? They tell me that nothing can be established, but they show no misgiving in producing a tone of certitude in the admonition. Having rid themselves and us of certainty, they seem unwilling to act upon the diminished thing or to learn a tentative style from a despair. It begins to appear that theory denotes not an affiliation of theorists in search of tenable theories to establish whatever it is that exerts a claim upon them; but, on the contrary, a concatenation of largely independent ideologies as blatant as the certitudes they begin by undermining. (Denis Donoghue, *The Pure Good of Theory*, Oxford and Cambridge, MA: Blackwell, 1992, pp. 36–7.)

Donoghue goes on to concede that some accommodation with deconstruction may be possible, although it is clear that he still finds its lack of an explicit moral dimension worrying, as the following reply to an interviewer's probing question reveals:

> My relation to deconstruction for a time was indeed hostile, but has in fact become much less so. What I've written about Derrida, Paul de Man, and others in the last few years is much more appreciative than earlier stuff I published. … But I would suggest a difference in our various modes of deferment and postponement. The reason I want to postpone a critical judgement is that I think the moral consideration is humiliated by any premature application. I would feel justified in proposing a moral judgement on a work of art, but only after I had given it considerable latitude in its own terms, whatever they are. The situation has changed from the time when Eliot said

> that the function of criticism is the elucidation of works of art and the correction of taste. It is still feasible to say that criticism is the elucidation of works of art, but how would you even go about correcting taste? What is the taste to be corrected? How could we appeal to it? If I wanted to separate myself from the deconstructionists, I would say that there is a kind of shadow, a dark consideration which is moral, indeed ethical, and which demands to be acknowledged; but I would always be saying yes, but not just yet. There will be time. (Donoghue, *The Pure Good of Theory*, pp. 92–3.)

The lack of explicit moral content noted by Donoghue has even led some commentators to define the poststructuralist movement in general as anti-modernist in intention. Thus we have Jürgen Habermas complaining of the recent French intellectual tradition that,

> They claim as their own the revelations of a decentered subjectivity, emancipated from the imperatives of work and usefulness, and with this experience they step outside the modern world. On the basis of modernistic attitudes, they justify an irreconcilable anti-modernism. They remove into the sphere of the far away and the archaic the spontaneous powers of imagination, of self-experience and of emotionality. To instrumental reason, they juxtapose in manichean fashion a principle only accessible through evocation, be it the will to power or sovereignty, Being or the dionysiac force of the poetical. In France this line leads from Bataille via Foucault to Derrida. … I fear that the ideas of anti-modernity, together with an additional touch of pre-modernity, are becoming popular in the circles of alternative culture. When one observes the transformations of consciousness within political parties in Germany, a new ideological shift (*Tendenzwende*) becomes visible. And this is the alliance of postmodernists with pre-modernists. (Jürgen Habermas, 'Modernity versus Postmodernity', *New German Critique*, 22, 1981, pp. 3–14, (pp. 13, 14).)

Habermas's countryman Manfred Frank has also expressed disquiet about the impact of anti-Enlightenment thought on the impressionable minds of the new generation:

> The new French theories are taken up by many of our students like an evangel. … It seems to me that young Germans are here eagerly sucking back in, under the pretense of opening up to what is French

> and international, their own irrationalist tradition, which had been broken off after the Third Reich. (Quoted in Jürgen Habermas, 'Work and Weltanschauung: The Heidegger Controversy from a German Perspective', trans. John McCumber, *Critical Inquiry*, 15, 1989, pp. 431–56 (p. 436).)

In this perspective, deconstruction is aligned with an irrational strain in Western culture that is felt to have lost sight of the very real benefits that have flowed from Enlightenment thought – particularly the general liberalisation of social and political life that is such a highly prized feature of modern existence in the West. Frank, like Toynbee before him, fears for the future if such anti-modernist ideas take root. Seeking to be 'liberated' from a project itself dedicated to liberalisation simply makes no sense to such commentators, who again detect iconoclasm being pursued for its own sake.

The success of anti-modernism to date gives Habermas pause for thought as to how a defender of modernity and Enlightenment should proceed against such intrinsically slippery opponents:

> The project of modernity formulated in the 18th century by the philosophers of the Enlightenment consisted in their efforts to develop objective science, universal morality and law, and autonomous art, according to their inner logic. At the same time, this project intended to release the cognitive potentials of each of these domains to set them free from their esoteric forms. The Enlightenment philosophers wanted to utilize this accumulation of specialized culture for the enrichment of everyday life, that is to say, for the rational organization of everyday social life.
>
> Enlightenment thinkers of the cast of mind of Condorcet still had the extravagant expectation that the arts and sciences would promote not only the control of natural forces, but would also further understanding of the world and of the self, would promote moral progress, the justice of institutions, and even the happiness of human beings. The 20th century has shattered this optimism. The differentiation of science, morality, and art has come to mean the autonomy of the segments treated by the specialist and at the same time letting them split off from the hermeneutics of everyday communication. This splitting off is the problem that has given rise to those efforts to 'negate' the culture of expertise. But the problem won't go away: should we try to hold on to the *intentions* of the Enlightenment, feeble as they may be,

> or should we declare the entire project of modernity a lost cause? (Habermas, 'Modernity versus Postmodernity', p. 9.)

Habermas for one is not yet ready to consign modernity to the domain of lost causes, and he is adamant that anti-modernism should be resisted. Postmodernism is seen in almost entirely negative terms, with Habermas being unwilling to countenance the dissolution of ideological boundaries that postmodern thought tends to encourage. When the forces of political radicalism and conservatism start to find common ground then the spectre of cultural decline looms for Habermas, who scents a conspiracy behind the search for new alliances. The gulf between the two sides in the dispute becomes very apparent at such points, given that postmodernist thinkers are themselves only too prone to see a conspiracy on behalf of reason lurking within the Enlightenment project and its various cultural offshoots. To paraphrase Nietzsche, reason is seen by postmodernists as the 'danger of dangers'. Suspicion seems to be the dominant response on either side of this intellectual divide.

Habermas has gone so far as to accuse Derrida of lapsing into a mysticism that not only pre-dates the Enlightenment, but also serves further to demonstrate the virtues of the latter:

> Derrida, all denials notwithstanding, remains close to Jewish mysticism. He is not interested in going back, in the fashion of the New Paganism, beyond the beginnings of monotheism, beyond the concept of a tradition that sticks to the traces of the lost divine scripture and keeps itself going through heretical exegesis of the scriptures. ...
>
> Derrida's grammatologically circumscribed concept of an archewriting whose traces call forth all the more interpretations the more unfamiliar they become, renews the mystical concept of tradition as an ever *delayed* event of revelation. Religious authority only maintains its force as long as it conceals its true face and thereby incites the frenzy of deciphering interpreters. Earnestly pursued deconstruction is the paradoxical labor of continuing a tradition in which the saving energy is only renewed by expenditure: The labor of deconstruction lets the refuse heap of interpretations, which it wants to clear away in order to get at the buried foundations, mount ever higher.
>
> Derrida means to go beyond Heidegger; fortunately, he goes back behind him. Mystical experiences were able to unfold their explosive force, their power of liquefying institutions and dogmas, in Jewish

> and Christian traditions because they remained related in these contexts to a hidden, world-transcendent God. Illuminations cut off from this concentrated font of light become peculiarly diffuse. The path of their consistent secularization points into the domain of radical experiences that avant-garde art has opened up. Nietzsche had taken his orientations from the purely aesthetic rapture of ecstatic subjectivity, gone out from itself. Heidegger took his stand halfway down this path; he wanted to retain the force of an *illumination without direction* and yet not pay the price of its secularization. So he toyed with an aura that the sacred had lost. Within a mysticism of Being, illuminations retrogress back into the magical. In the mysticism of the New Paganism, the unbounded charisma of what is outside the everyday does not issue in something liberating, as it does with the aesthetic; nor in something renewing, as with the religious – it has at most the stimulus of charlatanry. Derrida purifies the mysticism of Being of this stimulus, taking it back into the context of the monotheistic tradition.
>
> If this suspicion is not utterly false, Derrida returns to the historical locale where mysticism once turned into enlightenment. (Jürgen Habermas, *The Philosophical Discourse of Modernity: Twelve Lectures*, trans. Frederick Lawrence, Cambridge and Oxford: Polity Press and Blackwell, 1987, pp. 182, 183–4.)

Others have tried to defend Derrida from the charge of irrationalism by pointing out the difficulties he faces in setting out to challenge the received assumptions of Western discourse from within:

> Deconstruction stresses the irreducibility of metaphor, the difference at play within the very constitution of literal meaning. It should be remembered that deconstruction is not simply a strategic reversal of categories which otherwise remain distinct and unaffected. It is an activity of reading in which texts must be read in a radically new way. There must be an awareness of ambivalence, of the discrepancy between meaning and the author's assertion. Derrida discovers a set of paradoxical themes at odds with their manifest argument. His method consists of showing how the privileged term is held in place by the force of a dominant metaphor and not, as it might seem, by any conclusive logic. Metaphors often disrupt the logic of an argument.
>
> Derrida writes that we have a metaphysical desire to make the end coincide with the means, create an enclosure, make the definition

> coincide with the defined, the 'father' with the 'son'; within the logic of identity to balance the equation, close the circle. In short, he is asking us to change certain habits of mind; he is telling us that the authority of the text is provisional, the origin is a trace. Contradicting logic, we must learn to use and erase our language at the same time. Derrida wants us to 'erase' all oppositions, undoing yet preserving them.
>
> Deconstructionists tend to say that if a text seems to refer beyond itself, that reference can only be to another text. Just as signs refer only to other signs, texts can refer only to other texts, generating an intersecting and indefinitely expandable web called *intertextuality*. There is a proliferation of interpretations, and no interpretation can claim to be the final one. Now, Derrida is sometimes taken to be denying the possibility of truth. This is not so. It is more plausible to think of him as trying to avoid assertions about the nature of truth.
>
> The usual superficial criticism of Derrida is that he questions the value of 'truth' and 'logic' and yet uses logic to demonstrate the truth of his own arguments. The point is that the overt concern of Derrida's writing is the predicament of having to use the resources of the heritage that he questions. (Madan Sarup, *An Introductory Guide to Post-structuralism and Postmodernism*, Hemel Hempstead: Harvester Wheatsheaf, 1988, pp. 57–8.)

Derrida himself tends to bridle at the notion that he has a method, especially one that can be easily appropriated by others (see below on 'American deconstruction'), but for a commentator like Sarup there is a world of difference between irrationalism and 'contradicting logic' in the service of an anti-authoritarian scepticism. All sceptics are caught within the vicious circle described by Sarup, but that does not invalidate their critique of received assumptions. Intertextuality can be a powerful argument against traditional notions of truth, intellectual copyright and so on. No one can really say where an idea originates or, as Searle had done in his exchange with Derrida, claim copyright on it. To critics of deconstruction, however, this is not enough to justify avoidance of assertions about the nature of truth; that is carrying iconoclasm to the point of intellectual dishonesty.

Barry Smart has also tried to clear postmodern thinkers in general of the charges of irrationalism and neoconservatism, by arguing that postmodernism is a critique of, rather than a swerve away from, reason:

> It is how the postmodern condition is conceived that determines its appropriateness or relevance for an analysis of the present. Without doubt, major differences over the conceptualisation of the postmodern, and the associated question of its relationship to the project of modernity, are behind the contrasting judgments made of its political import. Setting postmodernism up as 'anti-rational' and '(neo)conservative' makes it a relatively simple target for criticism. But postmodernism cannot be disposed of so readily. The opposition to 'reason' frequently attributed to 'postmodern' analyses is, to be more precise, an opposition to a totalising idea of reason, hence the association of reason and terror. There is no 'postmodern' opposition to rationality *per se*. Rather it is the existence of a plurality of 'rationalities which are, at the least, respectively theoretical, practical, aesthetic' (Lyotard, 1988 ['An Interview with Jean-François Lyotard', *Theory, Culture and Society*, 5], p. 279) that constitutes the necessary focus for 'postmodern' critical theorising and analyses. It is in this respect that the postmodern condition constitutes a contemporary diagnosis of the near century-long 'crisis' to which scientific forms of rationality have been subject. In other words, the postmodern condition does not signify an abandonment of rationality, but rather a 'critical interrogation of reason' or, to be more specific, a critical reflection on the project of modernity and its rationalities. It is worth emphasising that it is equally problematic simply to dismiss postmodernism as conservative or reactionary, for there are a number of different strands of postmodern thought, some of which ... have been interwoven with Marxism. (Barry Smart, *Modern Conditions, Postmodern Controversies*, London and New York: Routledge, 1992, pp. 180–1.)

As in Sarup's comment about Derrida, the predicament the postmodern theorist finds herself in is that she is trying to offer a critique of a system of thought from the inside – in this case, demonstrating reason's abuses to a culture that treats reason in general as an ideal to which we should all be aspiring. Smart's point about the existence of 'rationalities', and the differences between them, is well taken. However, that is unlikely to placate the critics of the postmodern, who see the movement as being more than just an attack on sporadic abuses of reason. The distinction between 'opposition to reason' and a 'critical interrogation of reason' will be lost on such critics – especially when it comes to consideration of the work of the more extreme postmodernists, such as Jean Baudrillard and the team of Deleuze and Guattari. Calling on Marxism to reinforce postmodernism's political radicalism, as Smart does here, might prove a mixed blessing as well, since Marxism is for many postmodernists an example of an Enlightenment metanarrative that has become conservative and reactionary in its turn. (The reaction to Marxism in the post-modernist camp is considered on pages 72–87.)

American deconstruction, as practised by such luminaries as the 'Yale Critics' (Harold Bloom, Paul de Man, Geoffrey Hartman and J. Hillis Miller) has also been a target for criticism.[5] For one of Derrida's American disciples, Rodolphe Gasché, for example, American deconstruction is more like New Criticism than French deconstruction.[6] Further, it largely misses the point of deconstruction, failing to recognise just how radical its philosophical approach is:

> My contention is that Derrida's marked interest in literature, an interest that began with his questioning the particular ideality of literature, has in his thinking never led to anything remotely resembling literary criticism or to a valorization of what literary critics agree to call literature. Paradoxically, Derrida's initial inquiry into the ideality of the literary object had the effect of situating his work at the margins not only of philosophy but of literature as well.
>
> Such an observation does not mean, however, that Derrida's philosophy is without relevance to literary criticism. Rather it implies that the importance of Derrida's thinking for the discipline of literary criticism is not immediately evident, and that any statement of its relevance to that discipline requires certain mediating steps beforehand. So-called deconstructive criticism, which, however important, is but an offspring of New Criticism, has not, to my knowledge, undertaken these preparatory steps and has done little more than apply what it takes to be a method for reading literary texts to the unproblematized horizon of its discipline. As a result, the genuine impact that Derrida's philosophy could have on literary criticism has not been, or at best has hardly been, noticed. ... Yielding from the outset to the constraints of its philosophical conceptualization, literature, like philosophy, includes 'the project of effacing itself in the face of the signified content which it transports and in general teaches' (Derrida, *Of Grammatology* [trans. Gayatri Chakravorty Spivak, Baltimore, MD and London: Johns Hopkins University Press, 1976], p. 160). The specificity of philosophy and literature alike rests on this systematic

> curtailment of the signifier. Consequently, reading is in essence always a transcendental reading in search of the signified. ...
>
> What is more, this philosophical inauguration has not only governed the reading of literature but has determined the mode of its writing as well. With the exception of certain rare examples, literary writing has subjugated itself to the constraints of the concept and to the ethos of philosophy. Literature, then, speaks the voice of philosophy. It is a mere proxy, stillborn. There has hardly ever been any literature, if literature is supposed to mean something other than philosophy. The contemporary trend – a trend that begins with early Romanticism – of minimizing the difference between literature and philosophy is at least to some extent an involuntary recognition of this state of affairs. It remains within the tradition of literary secondariness. (Rodolphe Gasché, *The Tain of the Mirror: Derrida and the Philosophy of Reflection*, Cambridge, MA and London: Harvard University Press, 1986, pp. 255–7.)

Paul Bové rejects the charge that deconstruction is merely an updated form of New Criticism, although he concedes that it runs the risk of turning into a new critical orthodoxy in the American academic system, and losing much of its initial subversive power in the process:

> For there can be no denying that the representation of 'crisis' in criticism in the late 1960s is the work of deconstruction and those it influenced. Nor can it be denied that the polemical conflicts which resulted both from this declaration of crisis – to which deconstruction is the rigorously appropriate response – and the rising prominence of deconstructive techniques sustained the seeming vitality of the institution through the 1970s into the 1980s. Careers have been made, books published, journals begun, programs, schools, and institutes founded, courses offered, reviews written, and conferences held. The point is simple: no matter which 'side' one takes in the battle, the fact is that deconstruction effectively displaced other intellectual programs in the minds and much of the work of the literary avant garde ...
>
> No legitimate argument can be made denying the importance of ethical, political, epistemological, or pedagogical critiques of de Man, Derrida, and the other deconstructors. But political critiques of deconstruction must take into account the subversive effects it has had on an academy still largely unwilling either to accept the rigor of its analyses and the intelligence of its speculations or to employ its

> students. Similarly, a complete genealogical analysis … would have to describe deconstruction's specific turns upon the shape of the academy in order to avoid merging deconstruction back into the relief of institutional criticism out of which it has raised itself. A criticism which sees no difference between deconstruction and its predecessors is naive and does a disservice to our self-understanding. Yet such an understanding requires an awareness that deconstruction, in a seemingly paradigmatic way, redeployed critical power and sustained much of the institution. The curious can only ask if the increasing number of intelligent and distorting attacks on deconstruction, from both right and left, as well as a sense in some quarters that it is 'finished', mark the beginning of another local variation in the forms of the institution. Has the energy of deconstruction begun to flag, and is all the current critical dance around it a ritual feast of renewal? Is a new transformation of the New Critical-deconstruction 'line' to appear? If so, then we might ask, what dark shape marches forward threatening to be born? (Paul A. Bové, 'Variations on Authority: Some Deconstructive Transformations of the New Criticism', in Jonathan Arac, Wlad Godzich and Wallace Martin, eds, *The Yale Critics: Deconstruction in America*, Minneapolis, MN: University of Minnesota Press, 1983, pp. 3–19 (pp. 6, 18).)

Again, we have an argument for a paradigm shift. Deconstruction is pictured as an attack on the academy, which has begun to regroup in order to reassert its authority. It is a typically postmodern scenario that we are presented with: an outdated metanarrative confronted by a liberating radical critique. Battle lines are quickly drawn, and compromise seems out of the question. Neither side can really accept the terms of reference of the other.

Even Derrida himself can be doubtful about the uses to which his work has been put, particularly in an American intellectual context. Thus we have him responding to a questioner at an academic conference in the following, somewhat exasperated, manner:

> [H]ere you are referring to a diagram of deconstruction which would be that of a technical operation used to dismantle systems. Personally, I don't subscribe to this model of deconstruction. … [W]hat has been called the deconstructive gesture (in a moment I will try to say a little more about this) is accompanied, or can be accompanied (in any case, I would hope to accompany it), by an affirmation. It is not

> negative, it is not destructive. This is why the word 'deconstruction' has always bothered me. Yesterday, during a session at McGill University, someone asked me a question about the word 'deconstruction'. I said that when I made use of this word (rarely, very rarely in the beginning – once or twice – so you can see that the paradox of the message transformed by the addressees is fully in play here), I had the impression that it was a word among many others, a secondary word in the text which would fade or which would assume a non-dominant place in a system. For me, it was a word in a chain with many other words – such as trace or differance – as well as with a whole elaboration which is not limited only to a lexicon, if you will. It so happens – and this is worth analyzing – that this word which I had written only once or twice (I don't even remember where exactly) all of a sudden jumped out of the text and was seized by others who have since determined its fate in the manner you well know. Faced with this, I myself then had to justify myself, to explain, to try to get some leverage. But precisely because of the technical and – how shall I put it? – negative connotations that it could have in certain contexts, the word by itself bothered me. I do think it is also necessary to dismantle systems, to analyze structures in order to see what's going on, both when things work and when they don't, why structures don't manage to close themselves off, and so forth. But for me 'deconstruction' was not at all the first or the last word, and certainly not a password or slogan for everything that was to follow. (Christie McDonald, ed., *Texts and Discussions with Jacques Derrida: The Ear of the Other. Otobiography, Transference, Translation*, trans. Peggy Kamuf, Lincoln, NA and London: University of Nebraska Press, 1985, pp. 85–6.)

Whether this squares with Derrida's criticism of Searle's assumption of a copyright on intellectual ideas is an interesting question. Derrida seems to be implying that his American disciples in particular have misread his intentions, which is an odd situation for this thinker to end up in, to say the least. Maybe the word was 'seized by others' because it caught a particular mood and demonstrated a capacity for development that Derrida himself had not fully recognised. 'Deconstruction' becomes what the postmodern movement wants it to become, in order to facilitate its critique of institutional authority.

What is striking about the debate surrounding deconstruction, in its many forms, is the lack of agreement concerning its political implications. Its practitioners invariably claim it as radical, hinting at a left-wing bias, whereas for its detractors it is apolitical or even ideologically conservative. Deconstruction forms something of a microcosm of postmodern philosophy in this respect, as it does of the debate over whether it is intellectually rigorous (as defenders like Bové, see pages 54–5, insist) or intellectually irresponsible and self-deluding. Strong emotions are aroused on either side of the divide and, as we have noted, compromise rarely seems to be on the agenda.

Doubts about the political utility of postmodernism continue to surface among its critics – and even among its defenders. As a case in point, John McGowan, despite a generally optimistic attitude towards the postmodern turn to discourse, offers the following distinctly downbeat assessment of what it stands for:

> *Postmodernism* refers to a distinct shift in the way that humanistic intellectuals (Alvin Gouldner's useful, if inelegant, phrase) view the relation of their work to society at large. The various themes, postures, and stylistic hallmarks of postmodernism can, I believe, be traced to a heightened anxiety about what impact intellectuals have on a world that appears increasingly inimical to the values promoted in the arts and intellectual work. Of course, humanistic intellectuals since the time of the romantics have thought of themselves as distanced from and in opposition to the prevailing mores of commercial society, and have envisioned various schemes for that society's transformation. Postmodernism marks a particular despair about the possible success of these schemes along with a far-reaching search for new strategies of intervention in the dominant order. I believe that postmodernism can best be defined as a particular, if admittedly diminished, version of romantic dreams of transformation – hardly the middle age that poets in their youth would have chosen, but a despondency that is fitting all the same. (John McGowan, *Postmodernism and its Critics*, Ithaca, NY and London: Cornell University Press, 1991, p. 1.)

The transformation that is being sought is philosophical in nature, McGowan describing postmodernism as 'resolutely antifoundational' in its objectives, but it sounds more like a hold-over from the past than a new direction for culture (Ibid., p. ix). Intellectual, rather than cultural, failure lies behind the development of postmodernism, and it will only be when the intellectuals in question face up to their failings that the political potential of their antifoundationalist critique will be realised:

> The legitimation crisis of the intellectuals, their current inability to articulate the way their work could serve the achievement of their stated goals, will end, I suggest, when intellectuals accept that not only do their own activities need to be legitimated, but so do those of all social actors. Postmodern theory has precipitated the legitimation crisis by (in Foucault's case) denying that any legitimation is possible, since all justifying principles are equally suspect; or by (in Rorty's case) insisting that mundane practice feels no need to legitimate itself according to the necessary conditions of social existence or to the norms of the social group in which the practice is undertaken; or by (in Derrida's case) suggesting that all action only 'plays' (or oscillates) within a very limited set of already established possibilities. Intellectuals have been left to consider their legitimating discourse either as just one more example of the tragically inevitable alternations of domination or as a passé obsession with foundational principles. ... In the absence of foundations, principles of legitimation are going to have to come from within the social whole, not from some magical exterior. Furthermore, they will be articulated, ratified, and put into practice through political processes that involve social actors engaged in specific political negotiations. (McGowan, *Postmodernism and its Critics*, pp. 279–80.)

Postmodern philosophy is guilty, therefore, of self-absorption, of treating its own internal crisis as an external social one. Only when it works through that self-absorption (with all the negativity it involves) will it start to realise its undoubted political potential. The one-sided, anti-dialogue nature of postmodernism registers strongly in this assessment (its 'super-scepticism'). Postmodernism may be asking the right questions of modernity, but it is not doing so in a politically astute way: in effect, the philosophical concerns are swamping the political. Too much concern with legitimation inhibits the political action that is needed to bring about fundamental change in society.

Correspondences between Foucault and Nietzsche have already been noted, and the former's work certainly feeds into the postmodern in its critique of institutional authority, as in Foucault's description of what he calls 'the Great Confinement':

> By a strange act of force, the classical age was to reduce to silence the madness whose voices the Renaissance had just liberated, but whose violence it had already tamed.

> It is common knowledge that the seventeenth century created enormous houses of confinement; it is less commonly known that more than one out of every hundred inhabitants of the city of Paris found themselves confined there, within several months. It is common knowledge that absolute power made use of *lettres de cachet* and arbitrary measures of imprisonment; what is less familiar is the judicial conscience that could inspire such practices. Since Pinel, Tuke, Wagnitz, we know that madmen were subjected to the regime of confinement for a century and a half, and that they would one day be discovered in the wards of the Hôpital Général, in the cells of prisons; they would be found mingled with the population of the workhouses or *Zuchthausern* [convict prisons]. But it has rarely been made clear what their status was there, what the meaning was of this proximity which seemed to assign the same homeland to the poor, to the unemployed, to prisoners, and to the insane. It is within the walls of confinement that Pinel and nineteenth-century psychiatry would come upon madmen; it is there – let us remember – that they would leave them, not without boasting of having 'delivered' them. From the middle of the seventeenth century, madness was linked with this country of confinement, and with the act which designated confinement as its natural abode. (Michel Foucault, *Madness and Civilization: A History of Insanity in the Age of Reason*, trans. Richard Howard, London: Tavistock, 1967, pp. 38–9.)

The 'Great Confinement' becomes for Foucault a potent symbol of the modern age, whereby anything that threatens the rule of reason, and the institutional authority developed to implement this, is first of all marginalised and then strictly policed. Control becomes the watchword of modern society, and conformity the social norm. It is a pattern that Foucault will detect being repeated in other areas of social life, such as in the development of the modern prison and medical services.

Foucault's somewhat cavalier attitude to history in his various 'archaeologies', particularly his highly selective use of sources, has drawn criticism, the implication being that this leaves his conclusions open to question. Those conclusions certainly have been provocative, with Foucault regarding modern European culture (that is, from roughly the seventeenth century onwards) as a series of repressive measures taken against vulnerable minority groups, and, indeed, anyone who could be held culpable of 'deviant' behaviour. Deviant in this case comes to mean all those who do not conform to a model of behaviour proposed by the ruling élite – such as the mentally ill and homosexuals.

Foucault's three-volume *History of Sexuality* traces how a heterosexual model came to dominate sexual relations in Western culture; a discourse that not just excluded but actively discriminated against homosexuals. Volume 2 paints a somewhat idealised picture of classical Greek society, where, in Foucault's reading, there was no 'grand narrative' of sexuality, with homosexual and heterosexual relations existing quite happily side by side. This 'golden age' of sexual expression did not survive the early Christian era, but in classical Greece there was certainly no stigma attached to homosexual practices. What concerned the Greeks far more was the ethical attitude that lay behind the sexual act itself, whether homosexual or heterosexual in form. Foucault describes a social morality in ancient Greece that

> did not try to define a field of conduct and a domain of valid rules – subject to the necessary modifications – for the two sexes in common; it was an elaboration of masculine conduct carried out from the viewpoint of men in order to give form to *their* behaviour.
>
> Better still: it did not speak to men concerning behaviors presumably owing to a few interdictions that were universally recognized and solemnly recalled in codes, customs, and religious prescriptions. It spoke to them concerning precisely those conducts in which they were called upon to exercise their rights, their power, their authority, and their liberty: in the practice of pleasures that were not frowned upon, in a marital life where no rule or custom prevented the husband from having extramarital relations, in relationships with boys, which – at least within certain limits – were accepted, commonly maintained, and even prized. These themes of sexual austerity should be understood, not as an expression of, or commentary on, deep and essential prohibitions, but as the elaboration and stylization of an activity in the exercise of its power and the practice of its liberty.
>
> Which does not mean that the thematics of sexual austerity represents nothing more than an inconsequential refinement and a speculation unconnected with any specific concern. On the contrary, it is easy to see that each of these great figures of sexual austerity is tied to an axis of experience and to a cluster of concrete relationships: relations to the body, with the question of health, and behind it the whole game of life and death; the relation to the other sex, with the question of the spouse as a privileged partner, in the game of the family institution and the ties it creates; the relations to one's own sex,

> with the question of partners that one can choose within it, and the problem of the adjustment between social roles and sexual roles; and finally, the relation to truth, where the question is raised of the spiritual conditions that enable one to gain access to wisdom. (Michel Foucault, *The History of Sexuality: Volume 2. The Use of Pleasure*, trans. Robert Hurley, Harmondsworth: Penguin, 1987, pp. 22–3.)

The situation in ancient Greece contrasts dramatically with that of the modern world, in which homosexuality has long since come to be classified as sexually deviant behaviour. While that attitude does change over the course of Foucault's lifetime (in the West at least), the metanarrative of sexuality is still a factor to be contended with in a postmodern world, the power relations of which are founded in a notion of male heterosexual superiority. What Foucault is concerned to do is to demonstrate that this metanarrative (or 'discourse', in his terms of reference) is in no sense natural, that it is socially constructed and that it could be constructed quite differently – as he finds it was in ancient Greece. Postmodern culture ought to be a sexually open and non-judgemental culture, and, at least for men, ancient Greece offers us a model to follow. Foucault's followers will proceed to draw our attention to the non-natural status of a whole range of discourses. Among the most famous of such analyses is Edward W. Said's on the topic of 'orientalism', the West's conception of the Middle East (see the section entitled 'Political Theory' in Chapter three).

Deleuze and Guattari represent yet another poststructuralist critique of received authority, most particularly the authority assumed to be embedded in the psychoanalytical theories of Sigmund Freud, the father of psychoanalysis. *Anti-Oedipus* represents their most sustained attack on this body of thought, for which 'Oedipus' symbolises all the repressive measures that societies like our own bring to bear on individuals to force them to conform. Behind the drive to conform lies a series of narratives that suggest a particular imperative to history (the Enlightenment project, for example, or Marxism's class struggle). Deleuze and Guattari reject such deterministic notions, observing no pattern to history or human behaviour:

> [U]niversal history is the history of contingencies, and not the history of necessity. Ruptures and limits, and not continuity. For great accidents were necessary, an amazing encounter that could have happened

> elsewhere, or before, or might never have happened, in order for the flows to escape coding and, escaping, to nonetheless fashion a new machine bearing the determinations of the capitalist locus. Thus the encounter between private property and commodity production, which presents itself, however, as two quite distinct forms of decoding, by privatization and by abstraction. Or, from the viewpoint of private property itself, the encounter between flows of convertible wealth owned by capitalists and a flow of workers possessing nothing more than their labor capacity ... In a sense, capitalism has haunted all forms of society, but it haunts them as their terrifying nightmare, it is the dread they feel of a flow that would elude their codes. Then again, if we say that capitalism determines the conditions and the possibility of a universal history, this is true only insofar as capitalism has to deal essentially with its own limit, its own destruction – as Marx says, insofar as it is capable of self-criticism (at least to a certain point: the point where the limit appears, in the very movement that counteracts the tendency). In a word, universal history is not only retrospective, it is also contingent, singular, ironic, and critical. (Gilles Deleuze and Felix Guattari, *Anti-Oedipus: Capitalism and Schizophrenia*, trans. Robert Hurley, Mark Seem, and Helen R. Lane, London: Athlone Press, 1984, p. 140.)

Despite the apparently approving nods to Marx, the rejection of universal history constitutes a rejection of classical Marxism, which had laid down a scheme for world history: a determinable progression through class struggle to the current conflict between capitalism and the proletariat, which would finally end in a victory for the latter and the advent of its 'dictatorship'. To reduce history to contingency and accident is to claim that it is not open to manipulation by interested parties (such as ruling classes), and therefore to cast doubt on all metanarrative projects.

In their follow-up study to *Anti-Oedipus* (entitled *A Thousand Plateaus*), Deleuze and Guattari put forward the rhizome as the ideal basis for constructing systems:

> The multiple *must be made*, not by always adding a higher dimension, but rather in the simplest of ways, by dint of sobriety, with the number of dimensions one already has available – always *n*–1 (the only way the one belongs to the multiple: always subtracted). Subtract the unique from the multiplicity to be constituted; write at *n*–1 dimensions. A

> system of this kind could be called a rhizome. A rhizome as subterranean stem is absolutely different from roots and radicles. Bulbs and tubers are rhizomes. Plants with roots or radicles may be rhizomorphic in other respects altogether: the question is whether plant life in its specificity is not entirely rhizomatic. … Principles of connection and heterogeneity: any point of a rhizome can be connected to anything other, and must be. This is very different from the tree or root, which plots a point, fixes an order. … A rhizome ceaselessly establishes connections between semiotic chains, organizations of power, and circumstances relative to the arts, sciences, and social struggles. A semiotic chain is like a tuber agglomerating very diverse acts, not only linguistic, but also perceptive, mimetic, gestural, and cognitive: there is no language in itself, nor are there any linguistic universals, only a throng of dialects, patois, slangs, and specialized languages. There is no ideal speaker-listener, any more than there is a homogeneous linguistic community. (Gilles Deleuze and Felix Guattari, *A Thousand Plateaus: Capitalism and Schizophrenia*, trans. Brian Massumi, London: Athlone Press, 1988, pp. 6–7.)

The form of communication suggested in this extract is strikingly like that subsequently developed on the Internet; rhizomatic structures prefigure that system's practised ability to generate ever-new networks. There is yet another swerve away from the concept of central authority to be noted in such ideas, with difference being claimed as the natural state of affairs. Ideal speakers, listeners or language communities are taken to be illusions fostered by those who want to centralise power for their own political ends. To opt for rhizomatic networks is to make a declaration of incredulity against all existing structures of power.

Another important aspect of Deleuze's and Guattari's thought is their commitment to 'nomadism'. For them, this becomes a process by which human beings reject fixed narratives:

> [E]ven though the nomadic trajectory may follow trails or customary routes, it does not fulfill the function of the sedentary road, which is to *parcel out a closed space to people*, assigning each person a share and regulating the communication between shares. The nomadic trajectory does the opposite: *it distributes people (or animals) in an open space*, one that is indefinite and noncommunicating. … [N]omads have no points, paths, or land, even though they do by all appearances. If the nomad can be called the Deterritorialized[7] par excellence, it is precisely

> because there is no reterritorialization *afterward* as with the migrant, or upon *something else* as with the sedentary (the sedentary's relation with the earth is mediatized by something else, a property regime, a State apparatus). With the nomad, on the contrary, it is deterritorialization that constitutes the relation to the earth, to such a degree that the nomad reterritorializes on deterritorialization itself. It is the earth that deterritorializes itself, in a way that provides the nomad with a territory. (Deleuze and Guattari, *A Thousand Plateaus*, pp. 380, 381.)

In this extended metaphor, we are to consider nomadism as a model for how we relate as individuals to central authority; refusing to allow ourselves to be sidetracked into passive support for metanarratives (sedentary existence), and maintaining our freedom to drift around (both physically and mentally). To drift around in nomadic fashion is to maximise our chances of creating new rhizomatic structures that bypass central authority altogether, and thus serve eventually to render it powerless. It is a characteristically postmodern move enacted by a wide range of theorists, from Lyotard through to the feminist movement. Authority is not so much confronted as ignored.

Lyotard has been at the forefront of theorisation about the postmodern, with his now famous claim that our entry into postmodernity has been marked by a mass reaction against the dominant grand narratives of modern culture. 'Incredulity toward metanarratives' is, for Lyotard, the defining feature of the postmodern condition, and he wishes to encourage it through the development of a host of counter-cultural little narratives. Little narratives have specific objectives, and no one of them is to be considered superior to the others. They function much like the American notion of 'issue politics', in which a particular issue (such as environmental abuse perpetrated by a multinational corporation) is addressed, and they can cut across existing party political lines in a similar coalition-oriented way. A few nomads band together in a common cause, then drift away from each other when the task in hand is completed, refusing to allow themselves to turn into a new metanarrative in the aftermath of their success.

Lyotard has received his share of criticism, with Terry Eagleton being particularly hostile to the notion that no one particular narrative has any greater claim on our attention than any other, and that the success of a narrative is a matter of rhetorical technique and audience manipulation rather than any moral considerations:

> In *The Postmodern Condition*, a work which despite its nervousness of totalities is immodestly sub-titled 'A Report on Knowledge', Lyotard urges us to abandon the *grands récits* of the Enlightenment and model our knowledge instead on the self-legitimating narratives of the Cashinahua Indians of the upper Amazon, whose stories, so we are told, apparently certify their own truth in the pragmatics of their transmission. It is difficult, therefore, to see how there can be for Lyotard any real distinction between truth, authority and rhetorical seductiveness: the one who has the smoothest tongue or the raciest story has the power. It is also hard to see how this move would not, for example, authorize the narratives of Nazism, provided they are grippingly enough recounted. Nazism, for Lyotard as for some other postmodern thinkers, is one lethal destination of the Enlightenment's *grands récits*, the tragic consummation of a terroristic Reason and totality. He does not understand it as the upshot of a barbarous anti-Enlightenment irrationalism which, like certain aspects of postmodernism, junked history, refused argumentation, aestheticized politics and staked all on the charisma of those who told the stories. There is no comment in *The Postmodern Condition* on the contemporary women's movement, which in its simultaneous belief in political emancipation, and in the need to be liberated from a dominative male rationality, somewhat complicates any simple response to the Enlightenment. Nor is there any consideration of the national liberation movements which, since the American defeat in Vietnam, have inflicted on global imperialism a series of staggering rebuffs, and which often enough operate by the 'metalanguages' of freedom, justice and truth. These movements have not, apparently, heard of postmodernism, or of the epistemological illusions of meta-narrative. There is an interesting parallel in *The Postmodern Condition* between a 'good' pragmatism and a 'bad' one: just as those succeed best who tell the finest stories, so (as Lyotard himself remarks) he who has the fattest research grant is most likely to be right. The Confederation of British Industry, did they but know it, are postmodernists to a man. (Terry Eagleton, *The Ideology of the Aesthetic*, Oxford and Cambridge, MA: Blackwell, 1990, p. 396.)

This is a common criticism of the postmodernist enterprise – that it has opted out of the process of value judgement and embraced an extreme relativism that renders it politically suspect. To the traditional left, politics is above all the practice of making value judgements, of justifying their own beliefs over those of their enemies.

Christopher Norris, writing at the time of the collapse of the Soviet empire in the late 1980s, makes a similar point to Eagleton:

> To assume that we can, in some sense, 'learn from history' is either a species of category-mistake or – as Lyotard would have it – a negative lesson in the sheer contingency of all such events. If there is one thing we should have learned by now (he thinks) it is the message spelled out by Lyotard's catalogue of failed revolutions, twisted ideals, workers' states turning against the workers, communist regimes becoming a vicious parody of communist principles and so forth. On the other hand we should be wrong, he argues, to take these episodes as empirical data that somehow *proved* the bankruptcy of communist or socialist ideas, their historical obsolescence or manifest failure to come up with the promised goods. Such thinking ignores the crucial difference between arguments belonging to the phrase-regime of speculative reason – that is to say, judgements of an ethical, political or social-evaluative character – and those that claim a grounding in past or present historical realities. ...
>
> But of course there is another side to the argument, one that would rule against anyone who wanted to treat those events as 'proof' that Eastern bloc communism was working its way through the errors and distortions characteristic of its early development, and was now – at last – within sight of achieving a genuine form of socialist participatory democracy. For in Lyotard's view this could only be another species of 'transcendental illusion', a desire to take the will for the deed, or to treat the current 'spectacle' as something other than a strictly *sublime* event, one that by its nature cannot give rise to truth-claims or probative arguments of any kind. All that we are given to read in such episodes is a 'sign' of progress, justice, liberty, socialist values or whatever. A sign, that is to say, which remains necessarily ambivalent, which may indeed point toward a better, more enlightened state of affairs, but which can always turn out to bear no relation to the longer-term march of historical events. So what Lyotard gives with one hand he promptly snatches away with the other. If political ideals have validity only for reason in its speculative aspect, then there is nothing that could count as an adequate ground for treating this or that 'great historical episode' as an indicator of progress or human emancipation. (Christopher Norris, *What's Wrong with Postmodernism: Critical Theory and the Ends of Philosophy*, Hemel Hempstead: Harvester Wheatsheaf, 1990, pp. 12–13.)

Lyotard's supporters have replied that to read Lyotard as a relativist is to misunderstand him quite drastically. Bill Readings, for example, offers a spirited defence of Lyotard on this issue:

> Knowledge may take the form of narrative, but it can only do this as an instrument of a subjective consciousness which is itself abstracted from the narrative, which does not itself require to be narrated.
>
> Crucially, this allows us to distinguish between relativism and postmodernism. Relativism, which classicism dismisses as 'bad faith', appears as modernism's negative moment, a nihilism in the face of the recognition that knowledge is 'only' subjective narration, just 'telling stories'. Relativism says that any claim to classical objectivity is just 'one way of looking at things'. However, relativism must legitimate its own claim to be more than just 'one way of looking at things' by imposing its subjective consciousness as a metanarrative, the way of describing all ways of looking at things. Thus it still answers (poorly) to a non-narrative criterion of efficient communication. Relativism is not so much a break with metalanguage as the preservation of metalanguage even at the price of relinquishing any content to the transcendent subject it installs. *Cogito* becomes *dubito*, but *ergo sum* remains.
>
> The characteristic of both classicism and modernism is thus to erect one instance of narrative to the point where it governs narration from outside, becomes a metanarrative. If classicism privileges the referent, if modernism privileges the sender, then the postmodern condition is one in which no single instance of narrative can exert a claim to dominate narration by standing beyond it. If modernism has suggested against classicism that there is no referent that can be abstracted from the condition of narrative, *Just Gaming* and *The Postmodern Condition* introduce the instances of Judaism and the Cashinahua in order to disrupt modernism by insisting that there is no subject-position that is ultimately outside narration. (Bill Readings, *Introducing Lyotard: Art and Politics*, London and New York: Routledge, 1991, p. 67.)

Lyotard himself has been at pains to refute the charge of moral relativism and, more than most postmodernists, has sought to confront the problem of value judgement head on. One of the results of this engagement is his theory of 'paganism', whereby each moral dilemma is to be approached without preconceptions and dealt with on its own merits.

Judgements are made, but, in Lyotard's terms of reference, one is always judging 'without criteria'. To introduce such criteria would be to lapse back into the metanarrative mode:

> One works 'case by case' even when one is producing a constitution: after all, it can only be implemented in the light of practice, that is, one will realize that practice constitutes a new context for the statements of the constitution, and that this context requires that such and such a thing be prescribed, which had not been prescribed in the constitution, and the latter is therefore amended. In this sense, I think that, inasmuch as there is no reference to the presumption of a metalanguage that is shaping society in conformity to itself, one can say that there is paganism whenever there is this very curious representation wherein he who states the just is himself as caught in the very sphere of language as those who will be the recipients of his prescriptions, and may eventually be judged by the judge. The judge is in the same sphere of language, which means that he will be considered just only by his actions, if it can be seen that he judges well, that he is really just. And he will really be just only if his actions are just. And his actions can be judged to be just only when one adds up all the accounts. But in matters of opinion there is no adding up of accounts, no balance sheet. (Jean-François Lyotard and Jean-Loup Thébaud, *Just Gaming*, trans. Wlad Godzich, Manchester: Manchester University Press, 1985, p. 28.)

Effectively, what Lyotard is propounding is what is called a 'consequentialist' theory of ethics, whereby we decide from the effects of a judge's ruling whether it was the best course of action to have taken. Utilitarianism is probably the best-known example of a consequentialist theory, with its reliance on the 'Greatest Happiness Principle', which says that in any moral dilemma we are advised to follow the course of action that leads to the greatest happiness of the greatest number. Good and evil are not fixed categories, therefore, but judgements to be applied retrospectively. As in Lyotard's case, we are expected to assess the moral dilemma in question without preconceptions. Whether this resolves the problem of value judgement is a moot point (Utilitarianism's many critics certainly deny that it does), but it shows that judgements can still be made even in the absence of grand narrative rules and regulations. Pagan judgements neither conform to an established code nor set a precedent for future judgements. They are, instead, what Lyotard calls 'events' –

that is, responses to a situation within the situation's own terms of reference.

Richard Rorty, too, has rejected the charge of relativism, answering his many critics as follows:

> The ... objection is that what I have been calling 'postmodernism' is better named 'relativism', and that relativism is self-refuting. Relativism certainly is self-refuting, but there is a difference between saying that every community is as good as every other and saying that we have to work out from the networks we are, from the communities with which we presently identify. Post-modernism is no more relativistic than Hilary Putnam's suggestion that we stop trying for a 'God's-eye view' and realize that 'We can only hope to produce a more rational conception of rationality or a better conception of morality if we operate from within our tradition'. The view that every tradition is as rational or as moral as every other could be held only by a god, someone who had no need to use (but only to mention) the terms 'rational' or 'moral', because she had no need to inquire or deliberate. Such a being would have escaped from history and conversation into contemplation and metanarrative. To accuse postmodernism of relativism is to try to put a metanarrative in the postmodernist's mouth. One will do this if one identifies 'holding a philosophical position' with having a metanarrative available. If we insist on such a definition of 'philosophy', then postmodernism is post-philosophical. But it would be better to change the definition. (Richard Rorty, 'Postmodernist Bourgeois Liberalism', *Journal of Philosophy*, 80, 1983, pp. 583–9 (p. 589).)

Rorty's pragmatic approach to philosophical problems has a definite postmodern cast to it. For this thinker, the search for grand narratives, and thus for some ultimate 'truth' about the world, is a misguided activity always doomed to failure:

> If we could bring ourselves to accept the fact that no theory about the nature of Man or Society or Rationality, or anything else, is going to synthesize Nietzsche with Marx or Heidegger with Habermas, we could begin to think of the relations between writers on autonomy and writers on justice as being like the relation between two kinds of tools – as little in need of synthesis as are paintbrushes and crowbars.

> ... For most contemporary intellectuals, questions of ends as opposed to means – questions about how to give a sense to one's own life or that of one's community – are questions for art or politics, or both, rather than for religion, philosophy, or science. This development has led to a split within philosophy. Some philosophers have remained faithful to the Enlightenment and have continued to identify themselves with the cause of science. They see the old struggle between science and religion, reason and unreason, as still going on, having now taken the form of a struggle between reason and all those forces within culture which think of truth as made rather than found. These philosophers take science as the paradigmatic human activity, and they insist that natural science discovers truth rather than makes it. They regard 'making truth' as a merely metaphorical, and thoroughly misleading, phrase. They think of politics and art as spheres in which the notion of 'truth' is out of place. Other philosophers, realizing that the world as it is described by the physical sciences teaches no moral lesson, offers no spiritual comfort, have concluded that science is no more than the handmaiden of technology. These philosophers have ranged themselves alongside the political utopian and the innovative artist.
>
> Whereas the first kind of philosopher contrasts 'hard scientific fact' with the subjective or with 'metaphor', the second kind sees science as one more human activity, rather [than] as the place at which human beings encounter a 'hard', nonhuman reality. On this view, great scientists invent descriptions of the world which are useful for purposes of predicting and controlling what happens, just as poets and political thinkers invent other descriptions of it for other purposes. But there is no sense in which *any* of these descriptions is an accurate representation of the way the world is in itself. These philosophers regard the very idea of such a representation as pointless. (Richard Rorty, *Contingency, Irony, and Solidarity*, Cambridge: Cambridge University Press, 1989, pp. xiv, 3–4.)

For 'description' here, we can read 'narrative' in Lyotard, and such entities will be judged, not by their truth-value (which is indeterminable as far as thinkers like Rorty and Lyotard are concerned), but by their effects. The attitude we are encouraged to adopt towards life, if we are in agreement with the second kind of philosopher mentioned by Rorty, is that good old postmodern standby, irony. Ironists are those who recognise 'the contingency and frailty' of our existence in the world, and therefore cannot take the claims of grand narratives very seriously; they know that other descriptions, other narratives, are always available to them (Ibid., p. 74). There is an attitude of irony towards the practice of philosophy in general, with Rorty contending, not unreasonably, that it is only philosophers who worry about foundations or legitimation procedures. The rest of humanity tends to find pragmatic solutions to the problems of socio-political existence, and to be unconcerned about their philosophical shortcomings. In Rorty's opinion, philosophy should follow suit.

Rorty is often described as post-philosophical in terms of his approach to his subject, and that tag is frequently applied to postmodern thought. Gianni Vattimo interprets this to mean that postmodernism strives to be post-metaphysical, and that this imperative is most evident in the arts:

> If we leave aside … matters of macrosociology, and turn instead to the field of the arts, here too we are struck by the dissolution of the value of the new. This is the meaning of the postmodern, to the degree in which it cannot be reduced to a mere fact of cultural fashion. From architecture to the novel to poetry to the figurative arts, the postmodern displays, as its most common and imposing trait, an effort to free itself from the logic of overcoming, development, and innovation. From this point of view, the postmodern corresponds to Heidegger's attempt to prepare a post-metaphysical kind of thought which would not be an *Uberwindung* [conquest] but rather a *Verwindung* [transformation, distortion] of metaphysics. … Seen in the light … of Heidegger's post-metaphysical ontology, the postmodern experience of art appears as the way in which art occurs in the era of the end of metaphysics. … In the phantasmagoric (as Adorno calls it) play of a society built around the marketplace and technological mass media, the arts have experienced without any further metaphysical mask (such as the search for a supposedly authentic foundation of existence) the experience of the value of the new as such. This experience occurs in a purer and more visible way than it does for science and technology, which are still to a degree tied to truth-value or use-value. For the arts, the value of the new, once it has been radically unveiled, loses all possibility of foundation or value. The crisis of the future which permeates all late-modern culture and social life finds in the experience of art a privileged locus of expression. Such a crisis, obviously, implies a radical change in our way of experiencing history and time, as is somewhat obscurely anticipated by Nietzsche

> in his 'doctrine' of the eternal return of the Same. ... If in this way, the very notion of artistic revolution, caught up in this game of ungrounding, loses some of its meaning, at the same time it perhaps supplies a means of establishing a dialogue between philosophical thought and poetry, in view of that which in contemporary philosophy continually reasserts itself as the possible – though problematical – overcoming of metaphysics. (Gianni Vattimo, *The End of Modernity: Nihilism and Hermeneutics in Post-modern Culture*, trans. Jon R. Snyder, Cambridge and Oxford: Polity Press and Blackwell, 1988, pp. 105–7.)

Metaphysics is seen to be yet another source for metanarratives, with modernism being caught up in modernity's metanarrative of progress. Postmodernism involves a rejection of such notions – that is, of the idea that any one narrative is to be privileged over any other. Originality and experimentation, the mainstays of modernist artistic practice, lose their aesthetic value from this perspective, with the arts becoming an area where the authority invested in such concepts and practices simply evaporates.

Marxists have been particularly critical of postmodernism, feeling that they still have a viable grand narrative to defend, despite Marxism's mixed fortunes over the course of the twentieth century. One of the most trenchant attacks from this quarter has been from Alex Callinicos, who refuses to believe that postmodernism has any basis in socio-political reality:

> This then is the terrain defined by talk of postmodernism – a transformed social world which Postmodern art and poststructuralist philosophy reflect, but in which they also participate, and which requires a different kind of politics. Now I reject all this. I do not believe that we live in 'New Times', in a 'postindustrial and postmodern age' fundamentally different from the capitalist mode of production globally dominant for the past two centuries. I deny the main theses of poststructuralism, which seem to me in substance false. I doubt very much that Postmodern art represents a qualitative break from the Modernism of the early twentieth century. ... It often seems as if the issue between postmodernists and their opponents turns on what one thinks of the merits or otherwise of recent writing, painting or architecture when compared with the Modernist masterworks of Joyce, Picasso or Mies. But there is a prior question, which is inde-

> pendent of such judgements of value, and which is one of my main concerns in this book, namely whether one can indeed sharply distinguish between Modernism and Postmodernism as two separate epochs in the history of the arts. If, as I argue, one cannot, and if indeed the various claims for the existence or emergence of a postmodern era are false, as I further contend, then we are led to a further question: whence this proliferating discourse on postmodernity? Why is it that in the past decade so large a portion of the Western intelligentsia become convinced that both socio-economic system and cultural practices are undergoing a fundamental break from the recent past?
>
> This book sets out to answer this question, as well as to refute the arguments advanced in support of the idea of such a break. It thus rather uneasily occupies a space defined by the convergence of philosophy, social theory and historical writing. Fortunately, there is an intellectual tradition which is characterized precisely by the synthesis it effects of these genres, namely the classical historical materialism of Marx himself, Engels, Lenin, Trotsky, Luxemburg and Gramsci. … I seek here not simply to demonstrate the intellectual inadequacy of postmodernism, understood as the claim, justified by appeal to Postmodern art, poststructuralist philosophy and the theory of post-industrial society, that we are entering a postmodern epoch, but to set it in historical context. Postmodernism, then, is best seen as a symptom. (Alex Callinicos, *Against Postmodernism: A Marxist Perspective*, Cambridge and Oxford: Polity Press and Blackwell, 1989, pp. 4–6.)

Callinicos adheres uncritically to the grand narrative of Marxism that Lyotard, among a host of postmodernist philosophers, has long since rejected, and regards postmodernism as essentially a failure of understanding. It is a false problem, a symptom of what is wrong with our society rather than a harbinger of cultural change, a crude attempt to distract us from the exploitation that is still all around us in a world dominated more than ever by the capitalist ethic. Far from the theories of the past being a barrier to resolving the problems of the present (as postmodernists firmly believe), they are in fact the answer to these, if only we would go back to the classics of Marxism and study them with greater care. For a classical Marxist such as Callinicos, postmodernism is little more than a counsel of despair that prevents us from taking decisive action against a repressive political system. Postmodernism is simply the current name for the disease that Marxism has set out to cure.

Fredric Jameson's critique of postmodernism also has a distinctly Marxist bias. Here again, postmodernism is treated more as a symptom than a remedy, with Jameson regarding it as a critical constituent feature (the 'cultural logic') of a late capitalism striving to maintain its global dominance in the face of a new generation of adversaries:

> Despite the delirium of some of its celebrants and apologists (whose euphoria, however, is an interesting historical symptom in its own right), a truly new culture could only emerge through the collective struggle to create a new social system. The constitutive impurity of all postmodern theory, then (like capital itself, it must be at internal distance from itself, must include the foreign body of alien content), confirms the insight of a periodization that must be insisted on over and over again, namely, that postmodernism is not the cultural dominant of a wholly new social order (the rumor about which, under the name of 'postindustrial society', ran through the media a few years ago), but only the reflex and the concomitant of yet another systemic modification of capitalism itself. No wonder, then, that shreds of its older avatars – of realism, even, fully as much as of modernism – live on, to be rewrapped in the luxurious trappings of their putative successor.
>
> But this unforeseeable return of the narrative as the narrative of the end of narratives, this return of history in the midst of the prognosis of the demise of historical telos, suggests a second feature of postmodernism theory which requires attention, namely, the way in which virtually any observation about the present can be mobilized in the very search for the present itself and pressed into service as a symptom and an index of the deeper logic of the postmodern, which imperceptibly turns into its own theory and the theory of itself. How could it be otherwise where there no longer exists any such 'deeper logic' for the surface to manifest, and where the symptom has become its own disease (and vice versa, no doubt?). But the frenzy whereby virtually anything in the present is appealed to for testimony as to the latter's uniqueness and radical difference from earlier moments of human time does indeed strike one sometimes as harboring a pathology distinctively autoreferential, as though our utter forgetfulness of the past exhausted itself in the vacant but mesmerized contemplation of a schizophrenic present that is incomparable virtually by definition. ... [E]very position on postmodernism in culture – whether apologia or stigmatization – is also at one and the same time, and *necessarily*, an implicitly or explicitly political stance on

> the nature of multinational capitalism today. (Fredric Jameson, *Postmodernism, or, The Cultural Logic of Late Capitalism*, London and New York: Verso, 1991, pp. xii, 3.)

Jameson finds postmodernism a more interesting historical symptom than Callinicos does (he wrote the introduction to the English edition of Lyotard's *The Postmodern Condition*, for example). He is even willing to find merit in some postmodern works of art. Yet there is still that underlying commitment to a Marxist scheme in his analysis, as well as a hint of conspiracy theory where postmodernism serves to distract us from the real state of socio-political affairs. We are not yet in a brave new world; it is more the case that we are caught up in the dying throes of the old. Nor is postmodernism to be considered the inevitable outcome of that latter event, and all claims to be so are reduced to the level of mere 'rumour'. Those who take their ideology critique seriously, the implication goes, know to discount these.

Against the re-statements of the Marxist creed that we find in the work of Callinicos and Jameson there have been various attempts to postmodernise Marx. Terrell Carver, for example, has sought to do just this in his study *The Postmodern Marx*, in which he outlines a new agenda for dealing with Marx in the aftermath of the collapse of communism in Europe. Carver calls for the following:

- A shift in what Marx is read. The traditional organisation of Marx-texts, from which the traditional 'Marxist' reading arose, is not the only possible one. New texts have been discovered and published, and the doctrinal and biographical defences for selecting and ordering Marx's texts in the familiar manner have collapsed. In my account, Marx's critical work on contemporary democratic and authoritarian movements takes centre stage, along with his critique of the categories of contemporary economic life, read in a 'post-modern' way.
- A shift in how Marx is read. The hermeneutics of Gadamer and Ricoeur, Derridean deconstruction, and the Cambridge 'contextualists' have profoundly altered the way that reading is conceived, as well as views on authorial intention, the status and import of language itself, and the role of the writer. Interpretive work on Marx needs to catch up with the postmodern intellectual age.
- A shift in why Marx is read. Marx has been read as a revolutionary, a scientist, a philosopher, an economist, and no doubt as other

> *personae*. I read him as something of a politician. Marx's interventions into left-liberal and left-socialist politics are precisely relevant to the free market/mixed economy debates that are crucial to the future everywhere. I look for a context of political action and political audience that can be reconstructed around each text as a way of drawing contemporary politics into focus. (Terrell Carver, *The Postmodern Marx*, Manchester: Manchester University Press, 1998, p. 2.)

Postmodernism is used here as a way of reconstructing our relationship to the past in order to render it more relevant to present-day politics. In effect, Marx is 'rescued' from the Marxist grand narrative and opened up to reinterpretation within a new cultural paradigm. There are now 'multiple Marxes' to contend with instead, on the grounds that,

> An authoritative commentator producing a single Marx (even a single 'schizophrenic' one) has long been the norm. This seems to me to confront the reader with an attempted closure in terms of 'what to think about Marx'. More crucially, it seems to discourage any further engagement between the reader and Marx, and to leave the issues that he raised firmly in the past. ... The continued recovery of 'classic' thinkers is an important element in the way that politics is actually done. Re-assessments are periodically in order, and the new interpretative methodologies of postmodernism provide an intellectual reason for doing this. The new political situation globally provides another more pressing political one. Re-reading Marx is itself an important way of moving on intellectually and politically. (Carver, *The Postmodern Marx*, p. 5.)

This is postmodernism presented in its most positive light – as a method of liberating ourselves from outmoded ways of thought (essentially, the Enlightenment heritage that Western culture is founded upon). Marx is not so much discarded as recycled. To a classical Marxist, however, that is little short of heresy – Marx is not simply one interpretation among many, he is *the* interpretation that subsumes all others. Marxism and pluralism are mutually exclusive from that perspective, and Carver is asking for the impossible.

Derrida, too, has attempted to rescue Marx from the clutches of the Marxist grand narrative and to argue for 'multiple Marxes' who can be applied to a changing socio-political context in a creative fashion:

> Upon re-reading the *Manifesto* and a few other great works of Marx, I said to myself that I know of few texts in the philosophical tradition, perhaps none, whose lesson seemed more urgent *today*, provided that one take into account what Marx and Engels themselves say (for example, the Engels' 'Preface' to the 1888 re-edition) about their own possible 'aging' and their intrinsically irreducible historicity [historical character]. What other thinker has ever issued a similar warning in such an explicit fashion? Who has ever called for the *transformation* of his own theses? ... It will always be a fault not to read and reread and discuss Marx – which is to say also a few others – and to go beyond scholarly 'reading' or 'discussion'. It will be more and more a fault, a failing of theoretical, philosophical, political responsibility. When the dogma machine and the 'Marxist' ideological apparatuses (States, parties, cells, unions, and other places of doctrinal production) are in the process of disappearing, we no longer have any excuse, only alibis, for turning away from this responsibility. There will be no future without this. Not without Marx, no future without Marx, without the memory and the inheritance of Marx: in any case of a certain Marx, of his genius, of at least one of his spirits. For this will be our hypothesis or rather our bias: *there is more than one of them, there must be more than one of them*. (Jacques Derrida, *Specters of Marx: The State of the Debt, the Work of Mourning, and the New International*, trans. Peggy Kamuf, New York and London: Routledge, 1994, p. 13.)

Surveying the contemporary geopolitical situation after the collapse of the Soviet empire and the end of the Cold War, Derrida finds a world desperately in need of Marxist radicalism, but not of Marxist dogmatism:

> For it must be cried out, at a time when some have the audacity to neo-evangelize in the name of the ideal of liberal democracy that has finally realized itself as the ideal of human history: never have violence, inequality, exclusion, famine, and thus economic oppression affected as many human beings in the history of the earth and of humanity. Instead of singing the advent of the ideal of liberal democracy and of the capitalist market in the euphoria of the end of history, instead of celebrating the 'end of ideologies' and the end of the great emancipatory discourses, let us never neglect this obvious macroscopic fact, made up of innumerable singular sites of suffering: no degree of progress allows one to ignore that never before, in absolute figures, never have so many men, women, and children been

> subjugated, starved, or exterminated on the earth. (Derrida, *Specters of Marx*, p. 85.)

If this is a true picture of our current world, then it has been failed by Marxism in its traditional guise, and the argument for a more open-ended postmodern Marxism gains considerable momentum in consequence. The socio-political problems Marx identified are still with us, but not the same consciousness; the new consciousness requires a fundamental revision of attitude towards the grand narratives of the past – Marxism included. In a prototypically postmodern move, pragmatism replaces dogmatism. Yet again, however, we have to recognise that any 'transformation' of Marx's basic theses would be anathema to the classical Marxist constituency. What is dogma to Derrida is to the latter the key to humankind's socio-political salvation. It is hard to see how any compromise can be brokered between such fundamentally divergent viewpoints.

The topic of Marxism remains a site where some of the most bitter exchanges have taken place about the value of postmodernism as a cultural ethos. Marxism may have its faults, but for many those faults pale beside those of which postmodernism is guilty:

> 'Without memory of morning or hope of night' (Beckett), without lost paradises or imminent collapses, antagonistic classes go on fighting a most disorderly and unpredictable struggle. Now we see what Marxism so fears in postmodernism and poststructuralism and why in its fear it has been unable to distinguish between its friends and its adversaries. It fears itself, or rather its own practice, whose image it cannot bear to contemplate. Marxist theory has confronted its inadequacy to its own practice and thus its own unequal development, its own contradictions. Just when we thought we had escaped our destiny, we ran right into its arms.
>
> Perhaps all of us in one way or other have been duped by the subjectless cunning of the struggle in theory. A rationalist fantasy of order, a dream of logical guarantees that would guide our practice and validate our theory, disarmed and prevented us from grasping the conflict of forces internal to the field that remains inescapably ours. For there is no metanarrative, no transcendentality. We act within a specific conjuncture only to see that conjuncture transformed beneath our feet, perhaps by our intervention itself, but always in ways that ultimately escape our intention or control,

> thereby requiring new interventions *ad infinitum*. On a field of conflicting forces whose balance of power shifts endlessly, we have no fixed reference points, nothing to guide us but the knowledge of our own errors. One such error, the knowledge of which ought by now to have emerged clearly enough, is the very concept of postmodernism itself. In its totalizing, transcendental pretensions, this concept precisely forecloses progress in thought by denying the possibility that the fissures, disjunctions, breaks in contemporary social reality are symptoms of an impending crisis. For the signal feature of postmodernism most inimical to historical materialism is its claim to be the end of all crises, the end of all narratives, the end of resistance and revolutionary transformation. The debate on postmodernism will prove to have been productive to the extent that it awakens in us the consciousness of its own limits, which are not the limits of history itself (as the partisans of postmodernism claim), but rather the boundaries of that territory where Marxist theory has always intervened most effectively: the present conjuncture. The only truly irremediable error would be to believe that this present will endure forever. (Warren Montag, 'What is at Stake in the Debate on Postmodernism?', in E. Ann Kaplan, ed., *Postmodernism and its Discontents: Theories, Practices*, London and New York: Verso, 1988, pp. 88–103 (pp. 101–2).)

This is an interesting reading in that it treats postmodernism, ostensibly an anti-totalising enterprise, as a totalising theory itself, and thus as a check on cultural debate. While it may have helped us to identify some of the flaws in Marxism (most importantly, the discrepancy between theory and practice that has bedevilled the movement over the course of the twentieth century), it has nothing of substance with which to replace it. But although this view of postmodernism is thought-provoking, it is also very biased, focusing on the work of some of the more nihilistic postmodernist thinkers (Baudrillard, for example) who are not necessarily to be taken as entirely representative of postmodern thought. Some postmodernist thinkers, drawing on postmodern scientific concepts such as 'the edge of chaos' (see Chapter four for more detail), would argue that postmodernism is a theory of crisis – or at least, of near-crisis – and that this is one of its strong points. Crisis can be good for us, if it generates creative new modes of thought and action. Yet for all that, Montag has pinpointed some dubious practices in some areas of postmodern thought, and his claim that postmodernism is a metanarrative trying to disguise the fact is worth taking seriously. Even some of the most committed postmodernist thinkers worry whether this might be so.

The phenomenon of post-Marxism has involved several attempts to cross-reference Marx with poststructuralist and postmodernist thought – most notably, perhaps, in the work of Ernesto Laclau and Chantal Mouffe, whose critiques (both jointly and singly authored) of the classical Marxist heritage have served to polarise debate on the left in recent years. Writing in the mid-1980s, before the final collapse of the Eastern bloc, Laclau and Mouffe argue that Marxism will only continue to have any cultural value if it takes on board the insights offered by poststructuralism and postmodernism:

> Left-wing thought today stands at a crossroads. The 'evident truths' of the past – the classical forms of analysis and political calculation, the nature of the forces in conflict, the very meaning of the Left's struggles and objectives – have been seriously challenged by an avalanche of historical mutations which have riven the ground on which those truths were constituted. Some of these mutations doubtless correspond to failures and disappointments: from Budapest to Prague and the Polish coup d'etat, from Kabul to the sequels of Communist victory in Vietnam and Cambodia, a question-mark has fallen more and more heavily over a whole way of conceiving both socialism and the roads that should lead to it. This has recharged critical thinking, at once corrosive and necessary, on the theoretical and political bases on which the intellectual horizon of the Left was traditionally constituted. But there is more to it than this. A whole series of positive new phenomena underlie those mutations which have made so urgent the task of theoretical reconsideration: the rise of the new feminism, the protest movements of ethnic, national and sexual minorities, the anti-institutional ecology struggles waged by marginalised layers of the population, the anti-nuclear movement, the atypical forms of social struggle in countries on the capitalist periphery – all these imply an extension of social conflictuality to a wide range of areas, which creates the potential, but no more than the potential, for an advance towards more free, democratic and egalitarian societies. (Ernesto Laclau and Chantal Mouffe, *Hegemony and Socialist Strategy: Towards a Radical Democratic Politics*, London: Verso, 1985, p. 1.)

As the authors go on to remark, we are clearly 'situated in a post-Marxist terrain' at such points (Ibid., p. 4). We are also situated in a postmodern terrain, in which traditional authority is seen to fragment all around us. Rather than bemoan the passing of the old verities, Laclau and Mouffe want to take advantage of the new situation to revitalise revolutionary politics. For them, the postmodern world is a series of exciting opportunities that should not be allowed to go to waste, particularly in the name of defending a worn-out theoretical paradigm such as Marxism had become by the late twentieth century. Marxism RIP, would seem to be the message.

Laclau and Mouffe's argument against Marxism is quite a technical one philosophically speaking, hinging as it does on a detailed critique of the concept of hegemony. Hegemony was developed by Marxist theorists in the earlier twentieth century as a way of describing why the predicted collapse of capitalist society was taking longer to occur than expected. The delay could be explained in a number of ways (the success of the dominant ideology in propagating its ideals through the media and the arts, for example), but the point of the exercise was to protect the theory at the expense of historical reality. If history refused to conform to the theory, that did not invalidate the theory for the Marxist faithful, but merely delayed its eventual, inevitable, success. The grand narrative derived from Marx and Engels was taken to be inviolate; its authority remaining intact regardless of the survival of capitalism past its crisis point. Postmodernism, of course, has no interest in shoring up old theories and discourses, and Laclau and Mouffe regard themselves as being in the vanguard of a movement to drag the left into the postmodern world, where it will have to be far more pragmatic about what it does and who it supports. Classical Marxism's grand narrative no longer has any role to play in a world in which the old certainties have disappeared under the pressure of widespread, and disorienting, cultural change. Marxism is to be repositioned to meet a new set of cultural challenges, as defined by postmodernism. If that means supporting movements that do not meet Marxist criteria of what constitutes a revolutionary cause, then so be it.

As an example of the criticism that Laclau and Mouffe faced from Marxism's defenders, we can cite Norman Geras's long, impassioned, polemic against the authors in the *New Left Review*. Geras is dismissive of the notion that we have crossed over into a new phase of culture where Marxism in its classical guise has lost most of its relevance, and regards Laclau and Mouffe's postmodernist-influenced arguments as so much vain posturing:

> I want to discuss Ernesto Laclau and Chantal Mouffe's *Hegemony and Socialist Strategy: Towards a Radical Democratic Politics* – which styles itself 'post-Marxist'. This is not because I consider the book to be theoretically worthwhile in any substantive respect. I do not. Indeed, it is a product of the very advanced stage of an intellectual malady … and it is theoretically profligate, dissolute, … more or less any ideational combination or disjunction being permitted here, without regard for normal considerations of logic, of evidence or of due proportion. But the book is interesting nevertheless for at least two reasons. The first is that, as Ellen Meiksins Wood has said, it is 'beautifully paradigmatic': it brings together virtually all the key positions of a sector of the European left moving rightwards, and the second is the post-Marxism claim itself.
>
> This has, let it be noted … a certain plain-speaking accuracy. The authors announce a clear break. They are now beyond Marxism. There is a bit more to be said about it, however. For, they do also insist on reminding us that Marxism is where they come from. Whilst allowing that their present conclusions could have been arrived at by other paths and ones 'alien to the socialist tradition' – to which one can only say: verily! – they are mindful of their own past and have chosen, therefore, to proceed from 'certain intuitions and discursive forms' within it. Could they be mindful too in this of links they are for the time being content to preserve? I shall suggest, in any event, that the tendency in recent Marxism most germane to the construction of their current outlook is merely the bad side of something which was two-sided in the hands of its originator. And then there is the exact meaning in which they may be said now to be 'beyond' Marxism. At the point in time, thought and politics they have so far reached, the post-Marxist tag no doubt has a nicer ring to Laclau and Mouffe's ears than would the alternative, 'ex-Marxist'. It evokes an idea of forward movement rather than a change of colours, what purports to be an advance or progress, and all decked out in the finery of discourse theory. My contention will be that at the heart of this post-Marxism there is an intellectual vacuum … both a theoretical and a normative void. (Norman Geras, 'Post-Marxism?', *New Left Review*, 163, 1987, pp. 40–82 (pp. 42–3).)

Geras's was only one of a series of responses, both negative and positive (although initially mainly the former), to *Hegemony and Socialist Strategy*. However, its charges against Laclau and Mouffe turn it into a highly symbolic example of the defence of grand narrative against the challenge posed by postmodernism.[8] There is, first of all, the suggestion that post-Marxism is a symptom of what is wrong with our society rather than a cure, an 'intellectual malady' rather than a radically new perspective on culture that calls into question existing assumptions. Then there is the accusation of a neoconservative bias, as if any movement that queried the authority of the grand narrative of the left could only be reactionary at base – the 'you are either with us or you are against us' syndrome. These are familiar objections to the postmodernist project, as is the claim that it is intellectually vacuous – a series of gestures rather than a reasoned philosophical programme. For Geras, Laclau and Mouffe are little better than intellectual charlatans, lazy thinkers fooled into latching on to a fashionable trend that disrupts the real critical work taking place on the left. Post-Marxism, like postmodernism in general, is condemned for striking attitudes rather than engaging in rigorous critical debate. The 'post-' is treated as little more than an affectation.

The charge of political conservatism has been made against postmodernism by many others, most notably by Habermas:

> At first the expression 'postmodern,' as it was applied in America during the 1950s and 1960s to literary trends that wanted to set themselves apart from works of the early modern period, was also used merely to designate new variants within the broad spectrum of late modernism. 'Postmodernism' became an emotionally loaded outright political battle cry only in the 1970s, when two opposing camps seized the expression: on the one side the *neoconservatives*, who wanted to get rid of the supposedly subversive contents of a 'hostile culture' in favor of revived traditions; and on the other side the radical *critics of growth* for whom the *Neues Bauen*, the New Architecture, had become a symbol for the destruction produced by modernization. Only then did postavant-garde movements, which had formerly shared the orientation of modern architecture – and were correctly described by Charles Jencks as representative of 'late modernism' – become caught up in the conservative mood of the 1970s, paving the way for an intellectually playful but provocative repudiation of the moral principles of modern architecture. (Jürgen Habermas, *The New Conservatism: Cultural Criticism and the Historians' Debate*, ed. and trans. Shierry Weber Nicholsen, Cambridge and Oxford: Polity Press and Blackwell, 1989, pp. 4–5.)

The postmodern movement in general becomes caught up in this rightward drift (which also includes such thinkers as the post-industrial theorist Daniel Bell), a drift that, for Habermas, is characterised by intellectual confusion and lack of ideological coherence. If anything holds this disparate movement together it is the rejection of modernity and Enlightenment, but Habermas for one is unpersuaded by the quality of the arguments being advanced:

> The thesis of a post-Enlightenment, furthermore, is anything but convincing. Certainly, metaphysical and religious world-views have disintegrated. The empirical sciences do not provide a substitute for them. Yet the wide distribution of popular scientific literature indicates that cosmological findings regarding the origin and development of the universe, biochemical discoveries about the mechanisms of heredity, and especially anthropological and ethnological insights into the natural history of human behavior and the evolution of our species; that psychological findings on the development of intelligence in children, the development of the moral consciousness, affects, and motivations of the child, the psychology of mental illness, and social-scientific insights into the origin and development of modern societies – that all this still touches the self-understanding of contemporary subjects. These findings also alter the standards for the discussion of life problems for which the empirical sciences themselves have no ready answers. Ultimately, one would have to ask the neoconservatives, who want to put science and scholarship at such a distance, how they plan to justify their glib answers to the much lamented crisis of orientation – if not with arguments that stand up to scientific examination. (Habermas, *The New Conservatism*, p. 39.)

In other words, there is still a desire for knowledge and explanations within the population at large that cuts against the scepticism associated with critics of the Enlightenment project; mere interpretations do not suffice. Science, for Habermas, is still an Enlightenment-orientated enterprise capable of improving the quality of human life through its collective endeavours, and the general public both realises, and appreciates, this.

Habermas differentiates between 'old', 'new' and 'young conservatives', and although these groups do differ in terms of objectives, their common suspicion of modernity – or at least significant aspects of that phenomenon – helps to create a climate of anti-modernism. Even if postmodernists in the main see themselves as left-wing in their political sympathies, the effect of their turn from modernity is to reinforce the conservative cause in general. Meanwhile, hovering over French postmodernism ('young conservatives', in Habermas's classification) is, 'of course, the spirit of Nietzsche, newly resurrected in the 1970s'.[9] Under Nietzsche's baleful influence, radicalism declines into irrationalism – to the ultimate benefit, Habermas claims, of the forces of reaction. With the memory of Germany's Nazi past still relatively fresh in European culture, Habermas can only deplore such a state of affairs. Postmodernism, from this perspective, is an almost entirely negative development, the spread of which must be vigorously opposed lest it thrusts us into a new dark age, leaving us with nothing rather than everything. As far as Habermas is concerned, modernity is far from being exhausted and still eminently worthy of our support. The Enlightenment project is not yet dead.

Another thinker to have doubts about the politics of postmodernism is Slavoj Žižek, whose brand of post-Marxism involves returning to Hegel to find a more antagonistic model of dialectics that supports 'difference and contingency' – characteristics that Marxism itself had tried to eradicate from its world-view. On the face of it, Hegel's dialectic of history is deterministic, with the 'World Spirit' inexorably developing towards its highest state of expression, or 'true' freedom (see note 8 from Chapter one, page 255). Žižek wants to abandon the notion of a predetermined end to history, arguing that the Hegelian dialectic could never lead us there anyway. The dialectic is simply a process for the production of contradictions; as thesis generates antithesis in the progression of the dialectic. Žižek's claim is that the application of Lacanian psychoanalytical theories to Hegel reveals that final resolution of the dialectic remains an impossible dream. Just as the Lacanian individual subject has a permanent condition of 'lack' at the centre of his or her being (desires that can never be met), so the Hegelian dialectic has a contradiction. In neither case can the desired object be reached, and we are left with the experience of difference and contingency instead. It is a realisation with important implications for the practice of political philosophy:

> [T]his Lacanian reading of Hegel and the Hegelian heritage opens up a new approach to ideology, allowing us to grasp contemporary ideological phenomena (cynicism, 'totalitarianism', the fragile status of democracy) without falling prey to any kind of 'postmodernist' traps

> (such as the illusion that we live in a 'post-ideological' condition). (Slavoj Žižek, *The Sublime Object of Ideology*, London and New York: Verso, 1989, p. 7.)

Despite the criticism of postmodernism, there is a sense in which Žižek, too, can be regarded as a postmodern thinker. Grand narrative certainly comes under attack in his work, and the authority it claims is revealed to be illusory. In Žižek's reading, grand narrative has precisely the authority that we as subjects invest in it – which suggests that in real terms grand narratives are very fragile entities:

> [W]e have established a new way to read the Marxian formula 'they do not know it, but they are doing it': the illusion is not on the side of knowledge, it is already on the side of reality itself, of what people are doing. What they do not know is that their social reality itself, their activity, is guided by an illusion, by a fetishistic inversion. What they overlook, what they misrecognize, is not the reality but the illusion which is structuring their reality, their real social activity. They know very well how things really are, but still they are doing it as if they did not know. ...
>
> If our concept of ideology remains the classic one in which the illusion is located in knowledge, then today's society must appear post-ideological: the prevailing ideology is that of cynicism; people no longer believe in ideological truth; they do not take ideological propositions seriously. The fundamental level of ideology, however, is not of an illusion masking the real state of things but that of an (unconscious) fantasy structuring our social reality itself. And at this level, we are of course far from being [a] post-ideological society. Cynical distance is just one way – one of many ways – to blind ourselves to the structuring power of ideological fantasy: even if we do not take things seriously, even if we keep an ironical distance, *we are still doing them*. ... If the illusion were on the side of knowledge, then the cynical position would really be a post-ideological position, simply a position without illusions: 'they know what they are doing, and they are doing it'. But if the place of the illusions is in the reality of doing itself, then this formula can be read in quite another way: 'they know that, in their activity, they are following an illusion, but still, they are doing it'. For example, they know that their idea of Freedom is masking a particular form of exploitation, but they still continue to follow this idea of Freedom. (Žižek, *The Sublime Object of Ideology*, p. 33.)

Žižek's target is the Marxist doctrine of false consciousness: 'They do not know it, but they are doing it' – that is, acting against their own best interests by supporting the dominant ideology. In Žižek's view, it is a much more complex situation than that – a case of *wanting* to believe in the ideals of the dominant ideology, even though we are aware that those ideals do not work out in reality. To make that connection, as Žižek does, is to create the basis for 'incredulity toward metanarratives'. There is a postmodernist slant to Žižek's analysis, therefore, even if he does insist that reaching the state of incredulity may be more difficult than some postmodernists are suggesting. However, it is something of a slur on the work of such figures as Lyotard to dub postmodernism as 'post-ideological'; there is possibly greater political sophistication in the movement than Žižek is willing to acknowledge.

Where the philosophy of the postmodern fits into the feminist enterprise is a contentious issue. Feminists can be very ambivalent about the postmodern, and some regard it as inimical to their general project. As a prelude to the first part of the next chapter, therefore, we might briefly reflect on the relationship between American feminism and recent continental philosophy through some introductory remarks to a volume of essays on the topic:

> When women enter into philosophy in this era of post-structuralist challenge to the subject, they often advocate the destabilization of those gender-marked norms governing language and the subject which have been left in place by much of male post-structuralist theory. The reflections offered by these women drift away from the currently recognized conceptual terrain, and in so doing, undermine male-defined theory. The movement which brings phallogocentrism to an end is called, by Hélène Cixous, a starting on all sides at once, and by Monique Wittig, a fracturing and extension into space that is like Pascal's circle, whose center is everywhere and whose circumference is nowhere. …
>
> Much feminist philosophy, along with existentialism, is inclined to focus on the freedom of the subject. Many feminists find the post-structuralist injunction to relinquish the notion of the subject dangerous. A politics that seeks to enact social change needs a concept of agency. … From the point of view of political action, however, post-structuralism can appear to dissolve the world into a system of signs. …

> The distance of feminist philosophy in the United States from much postmodern debate manifests … a circumspect attitude towards its assumptions concerning textuality. Post-structuralist prioritization of the text, its emphasis on intertextual interpretation and its claim that language and ideology develop in the conflicts, discrepancies, and gaps between texts, intrigues and concerns feminist philosophers. The conviction that 'the personal is political,' which has motivated much of the women's movement in the United States and most feminist scholarship, has some affinity with the emphasis that existential phenomenology has given to lived experience in an effort to circumvent the grasp of Western metaphysics. Feminist philosophy understands the slogan, 'the personal is political,' as valorizing individual and collective experience and showing why philosophy must engage in an unfolding of local narratives. In contrast, the postmodern focus on the text tends to leap over experience and to privilege a literacy that, by its racist and heterosexist presuppositions, ignores and misrepresents the lives, languages, and philosophizing, of many women. Here feminist philosophy seeks to dismantle the philosophical textuality of the West, which erects a truth or certainty cut off from history, and especially, from women's histories and experience. (Jeffner Allen and Iris Marion Young, eds, *The Thinking Muse: Feminism and Modern French Philosophy*, Bloomington and Indianapolis, IN: Indiana University Press, 1989, Introduction, pp. 2–17 (pp. 7, 10, 11).)

Clearly, all is not well in the relationship between American feminism and postmodern philosophy. Indeed, the latter seems to be challenging the very basis of the former, which depends so heavily on the concept of personal experience. From an American feminist perspective, postmodern philosophy, far from having escaped from the world of metanarratives, is instead part of the long-running metanarrative that is Western masculinist philosophy. With perceptions of the discipline so much at variance, there is considerable room for disagreement – just how much we will explore in more detail in the next chapter.

CHAPTER THREE

The Sociology and Politics of the Postmodern

Postmodernism has made critical inroads into the social sciences, which for the purposes of this study will be condensed into the following general areas of enquiry:

- Feminism – pp. 90–102
- Social Theory – pp. 102–37, and
- Political Theory – pp. 137–49.

We have already seen C. Wright Mills's reference to the postmodern age as the 'Fourth Epoch', and that signals the beginning of a long, and often rancorous, debate within the social sciences as to whether or not an irreversible paradigm shift actually has occurred. Some will argue that it has, some that it has not; and of those who argue that it has, some will welcome the event, some will not. There is a wide spectrum of opinion, therefore, with many possible positions to be taken within it – ambivalence being a very common response. What is clear, however, is that the phenomenon of the postmodern has exercised minds within the social sciences to a very considerable degree over the last few decades. It has become a topic that is hard to avoid, a topic that demands engagement.

Before proceeding to explore the nature of that engagement, a rationale might be offered for treating feminism as a separate area for study, and also for the selection of extracts in the section entitled 'Social Theory'. Feminism is not a discipline as such and its concerns extend to all areas of intellectual endeavour. It will, in fact, put in an appearance in some form or another in most chapters of this volume. However, most of its enquiries are probably conducted within the social sciences, hence its placement here. As for social theory, this will be interpreted in a fairly broad manner, taking in a diversity of subject areas and disciplines such as human geography, business studies, religious studies and even history.

Although this may initially appear to make for a somewhat diffuse grouping, there are common interests and methods to be noted that hold it together. All the areas included are informed to a significant degree by sociological principles, and evince an abiding concern with social relations. The contexts may differ, but the researches of those working within such fields as human geography, business studies and religious studies share a sociological orientation. History may seem to be something of a special case. It can be claimed for either the humanities or the social sciences, but when it comes to social history, the points made earlier about orientation and methods certainly apply. Whether the topic is society at large or the institutions within it (cities, business organisations, church movements and so on), the character of the social relations involved looms large in the ensuing enquiry.

Feminism

One of the major criticisms advanced by feminists against postmodernism is that it is more philosophical than social-critical in its orientation – a considerable disadvantage, given that in feminist circles philosophy is taken to be an essentially masculinist activity. This is the line argued by Nancy Fraser and Linda J. Nicholson, who go on to speculate how a mutually advantageous accommodation between the two enterprises might nevertheless be reached:

> Feminists, like postmodernists, have sought to develop new paradigms of social criticism that do not rely on traditional philosophical underpinnings. They have criticized modern foundationalist epistemologies and moral and political theories, exposing the contingent, partial, and historically situated character of what have passed in the mainstream for necessary, universal, and ahistorical truths. And they have called into question the dominant philosophical project of seeking objectivity in the guise of a 'God's eye view' which transcends any situation or perspective.
>
> However, whereas postmodernists have been drawn to such views by a concern with the status of philosophy, feminists have been led to them by the demands of political practice. This practical interest has saved feminist theory from many of the mistakes of postmodernism: women whose theorizing was to serve the struggle against sexism were not about to abandon powerful political tools merely as a result of intramural debates in professional philosophy. (Nancy Fraser and

Linda J. Nicholson, 'Social Criticism without Philosophy: An Encounter between Feminism and Postmodernism', in Andrew Ross, ed., *Universal Abandon?: The Politics of Postmodernism*, Edinburgh: Edinburgh University Press, 1989, pp. 83–104 (pp. 91–2).)

We have already seen in Chapter two just how dense and abstract those intramural debates can be, especially when it comes to deconstruction. Feminists, with their unashamedly political agenda, will only want to follow these so far; after a certain point, it could be claimed, there is little of value to their cause to be found. One could argue that Fraser and Nicholson underestimate the political motivation that lies behind much postmodern philosophical enquiry. However, their task, as they perceive it, is to ensure that the postmodern is politicised with feminist intent:

> How can we combine a postmodernist incredulity towards metanarratives with the social-critical power of feminism? How can we conceive a version of criticism without philosophy that is robust enough to handle the tough job of analyzing sexism in all its 'endless variety and monotonous similarity'?
>
> A first step is to recognize, *contra* Lyotard, that postmodern critique need forswear neither large historical narratives nor analyses of societal macrostructures. The point is important for feminists, since sexism has a long history and is deeply and pervasively embedded in contemporary societies. Thus, postmodern feminists need not abandon the large theoretical tools needed to address large political problems. There is nothing self-contradictory in the idea of a postmodern theory.
>
> However, if postmodern-feminist critique must remain 'theoretical', not just any kind of theory will do. Rather, theory here would be explicitly historical, attuned to the cultural specificity of different societies and periods and to that of different groups within societies and periods. Thus, the categories of postmodern-feminist theory would be inflected by temporality, with historically specific institutional categories like 'the modern, restricted, male-headed nuclear family' taking precedence over ahistorical, functionalist [that is, defined by function] categories like 'reproduction' and 'mothering'. Where categories of the latter sort were not eschewed altogether, they would be genealogized, that is, framed by a historical narrative and rendered temporally and culturally specific.
>
> Moreover, postmodern-feminist theory would be nonuniversalist.

When its focus became cross-cultural or transepochal, its mode of attention would be comparativist rather than universalist, attuned to changes and contrasts instead of to 'covering law'. Finally, post-modern-feminist theory would dispense with the idea of a subject of history. It would replace unitary notions of 'woman' and 'feminine gender identity' with plural and complexly constructed conceptions of social identity, treating gender as one relevant strand among others, attending also to class, race, ethnicity, age, and sexual orientation.

In general, postmodern-feminist theory would be pragmatic and fallibilistic.[1] It would tailor its methods and categories to the specific task at hand, using multiple categories when appropriate and forswearing the metaphysical comfort of a single 'feminist method' or 'feminist epistemology'. In short, this theory would look more like a tapestry composed of threads of many different hues than one woven in a single color.

The most important advantage of this sort of theory would be its usefulness for contemporary feminist political practice. Such practice is increasingly a matter of alliances rather than one of unity around a universally shared interest or identity. It recognizes that the diversity of women's needs and experiences means that no single solution – on issues like child care, social security, and housing – can be adequate for all. Thus, the underlying premise of this practice is that, whereas some women have some common interests and face some common enemies, such commonalties are by no means universal; rather, they are interlaced with differences, even with conflicts. This, then, is a practice made up of a patchwork of overlapping alliances, not one circumscribable by an essential definition. One might best speak of it in the plural as the practice of 'feminisms'. In a sense, this practice is in advance of much contemporary feminist theory. It is already implicitly postmodern. It would find its most appropriate and useful theoretical expression in a postmodern-feminist form of critical inquiry. Such inquiry would be the theoretical counterpart of a broader, richer, more complex, and multilayered feminist solidarity, the sort of solidarity that is essential for overcoming the oppression of women in its 'endless variety and monotonous similarity'. (Fraser and Nicholson, 'Social Criticism without Philosophy', pp. 100–2.)

Postmodernism in this analysis provides the most sympathetic cultural model for the development of the feminist enterprise, being non- (and even anti-)hierarchical, multicultural and very flexible. The lack of any central doctrine to postmodern thought appeals to many feminists, whose preference is for a tactical rather than a doctrinaire approach to overcoming social prejudice against women.

In the same year as the above essay was published, a more problematical view of the relationship between feminism and postmodernism was being put forward by Meaghan Morris:

> In a number of recent discussions of postmodernism, a sense of intrigue develops around a presumed absence – or withholding – of women's speech in relation to what has certainly become one of the boom discourses of the 1980s. Feminists in particular, in this intrigue, have had little or nothing to say about postmodernism. … In addressing the myth of a postmodernism still waiting for its women we can find an example of a genre, as well as a discourse, which in its untransformed state leaves a woman no place from which to speak, or nothing to say. For by resorting to the device of listing 'excluded' women, women excluded for no obvious reason except that given by the discourse – their gender – I have positioned myself in a speech-genre all too familiar in everyday life, as well as in pantomime, cartoons, and sitcoms: the woman's complaint, or *nagging*. One of the defining generic rules of 'nagging' is unsuccessful repetition of the same statements. It is unsuccessful, because it blocks change: nagging is a mode of repetition which fails to produce the desired effects of difference that might allow the complaint to end. … A traditional method has always been for the nagger somehow to lose interest, and so learn to change her subject (and her addressee). One possibility in this context is to follow up Dana Polan's suggestion that postmodernism is a 'machine for producing discourse'.[2] Polan argues that as the input to the machine begins to determine what it is possible to say in its name, so it becomes increasingly difficult to generate as output anything non-repetitive. Participants in a postmodernism debate are 'constrained' to refer back to previous input, and to take sides in familiar battles on a marked-out, well-trodden terrain ('Habermas v. Lyotard', for example). The solution to feminist complaint might then be a simple one – switch position from nagger to nagged, then switch off.
>
> But assuming a calculated deafness to discussion about postmodernism is not much of a solution for feminist women. To choose to *accept* a given constraint is not to challenge, overcome, or transform anything. … A different gesture worth making would be, it

> seems to me, to make a generically feminist gesture of reclaiming women's work, and women's names, as a context in which debates about postmodernism might further be considered, developed, transformed (or abandoned). (Meaghan Morris, *The Pirate's Fiancée: Feminism, Reading, Postmodernism*, London and New York: Verso, 1988, pp. 11, 15–16.)

Morris's point is that, yet again, women are being judged in terms of a male discourse, and that they should feel themselves under no obligation to enter into dialogue with this. Postmodernism may or may not be of use to feminists in furthering their cause, but it certainly should not be allowed to set the terms of reference for the debate: feminism must come first, postmodernism second – and a very distant second at that.

Sabina Lovibond makes the interesting point that feminism is a product of modernity, and that this heritage inevitably creates a certain degree of tension in its relationship with postmodernism:

> One of the first thoughts likely to occur in the course of any historical reflection on feminism is that it is a typically *modern* movement. The emergence of sexual equality as a practical political goal can be seen as one element in the complex course of events by which *tradition* has given way, over a matter of centuries, to a way of life that is deeply *untraditional* – in fact, to 'modernity' … Now it is difficult to see how one could count oneself a feminist and remain indifferent to the modernist promise of social reconstruction. From a female point of view, 'tradition' has (to put it mildly) an unenviable historical record. Yet it is in the area of sexual relations that 'traditional values' (marriage, home ownership, wholesome family life, etc.) are proving hardest to shift. Perhaps no other feature of the pre-modern scene has persisted so stubbornly as male dominance – the class system constructed on the basis of biological sexual difference; certainly the thought of a time when concepts such as 'wife' and 'husband', with all the moral atmosphere they evoke, will be as obsolete as 'villein' or 'lord of the manor' is apt to set off a landslide in the mind. Still, if we assess without prejudice the implications for gender (I mean, for masculinity and femininity as cultural constructs) of the 'modern' repudiation of unearned privilege, we may well conclude that this development is an integral part of the package; and if so, it will follow that feminists have at least as much reason as the rest of the world for regarding the 'project of modernity', at the present time, as

> incomplete. … [F]eminists should continue to think of their efforts as directed not simply towards various local political programmes, but ultimately towards a global one – the abolition of the sex class system, and of the forms of inner life that belong with it. This programme is 'global' not just in the sense that it addresses itself to every corner of the planet, but also in the sense that its aims eventually converge with those of all other egalitarian or liberationist movements. … [I]t follows that the movement should persist in seeing itself as a component or offshoot of Enlightenment modernism, rather than as one more 'exciting' feature (or cluster of features) in a postmodern social landscape. (Sabina Lovibond, 'Feminism and Postmodernism', in Roy Boyne and Ali Rattansi, eds, *Postmodernism and Society*, Basingstoke and London: Macmillan, 1990, pp. 154–86 (pp. 160, 161, 178, 179).)

Having made clear its substantive differences from postmodernism, Lovibond is also at pains to ensure that feminism is not subsumed under 'some central authority' within Enlightenment modernism itself (Ibid., p. 179). This is the kind of fear often voiced by Marxist feminists, who see their programme being relegated – by a predominantly male leadership – to secondary status behind the supposedly superior objectives of the class struggle and the dictatorship of the proletariat. For Lovibond, feminism's universality is non-authoritarian in nature, and thus not susceptible to the kind of cultural critique that postmodernist theory is offering. Inasmuch as postmodernism qualifies as a 'liberationist' movement (and opinions do vary quite dramatically on this point), feminists will be interested in what it has to say about our culture; but it will remain only one of several possible alliances for feminism to explore, and can claim no special relationship.

Feminist theorists are much exercised by what they see as the limitations of postmodernism as a cultural theory – limitations that would hold back feminism were they unequivocally to endorse a postmodernist programme:

> Were it to ally itself with postmodernism, feminist theory would be faced with the problem of defending its truth claims as it presents arguments and formulas for the very deconstruction of those claims as well as for the idea of gender itself. How can it write a radical politics from so many different sites, with so many decentered subjects? The movement has to ask if it is possible to assume a bipolarity of gender without buying into the very dualism it has criticized as central to

women's subjugation. Does a bipolar view of gender eliminate the very diversity of being a woman that has enriched the movement and allowed it to go beyond the white, middle-class orientation it was accused of having in its early days? Or is there something in the experiences of all women that unites them and pits them against those who share a similar unity of status? Is there a culturally dominant set of sex roles that persons have to adopt, or is there more fluidity than arguments incorporating attacks on a heterosexist and masculinist hegemony suggest?

The analysis presented here detects certain serious consequences for the Women's Movement were there to be a wholesale adoption of postmodern tenets. These consequences would produce unsettling results for feminist theory and, in turn, for the movement with which it is in liaison. There is an understandable attraction to postmodernism, given its emphasis on turning away from abstractions and towards particular experiences of everyday life. It taps into the sociality of lived experience, including areas that are not in the realm of the rational, scientific, and bureaucratic. It is very much at home with ambiguity. At the same time, by emphasizing differences – the multiple ways of ordering, experiencing, and giving meaning to life – postmodernism makes the task of political organization more difficult. We need a politics built on carefully articulated moral choices that defy deconstruction. Postmodernism does not resolve the epistemic quagmire of how to choose which demon to follow, although it confronts the political person with far more demons than previously imagined. It does not establish the criteria we would use for evaluating knowledge, nor does it specify how to justify the struggles in which we are engaged.

Insofar as feminist theory has set itself the task of uncoupling truth and power, it would seem, then, that any more sustained liaison with postmodernism is unadvisable. (Sondra Farganis, 'Postmodernism and Feminism', in David R. Dickens and Andrea Fontana, eds, *Postmodernism and Social Inquiry*, London: UCL Press, 1994, pp. 101–26 (pp. 122–3).)

'Serious consequences', 'epistemic quagmire', 'demons', 'unadvisable': this is strong language, communicating the depth of unease in the feminist movement as to the implications of postmodernism's agenda. Postmodernism stands as a temptation that the feminist movement must resist if it is to retain the integrity necessary to carry through its political programme. Apart from anything else, feminism requires value judgements to be made; and as we have noted before, value judgement is where postmodern theory is at its weakest.

As the interventions of critics like Morris, Lovibond and Farganis indicate, the feminist response to postmodernism is often ambivalent, yet there is still a widespread interest in exploring how to appropriate postmodernism's transgressive power for feminist objectives:

> [P]ostmodernism teaches us how to play subversive games with traditional codes. In Canada, a perfume factory recently published an ad which showed a woman in her bloomers embracing a man from behind. In the Netherlands, van Gils, a producer of suits, advertises a naked boy in the arms of a fully dressed woman wearing a man's suit. In France, 'little Arthur' shows his knickers while being supported by a tall naked woman. We could regard advertising these disjunctions as sign crimes, namely the endowing of a woman with the attributes of the phallocentric man from the fifties. Should they be forbidden, or are they fun? Forbidden games are surely the most exciting. And which girls in the fifties ever dreamt of being able to adopt the signs and symbols of men?
>
> There are many feminists who are not particularly enthusiastic about the advent of postmodernism, though sometimes for reasons other than mine. For those feminists, feminism is still a serious enterprise that will not tolerate postmodernism interfering with or mocking its goals. However, for the social sciences postmodernism seems to be nothing less or more than a fashionable disguise for good old theories like social constructivism, symbolic interactionism and critical cultural analysis.[3] If this new outfit provides them with a new stimulus with respect to the analysis of gender relations, it has done its job already.
>
> It is often alleged that constructivism, symbolic interactionism, critical cultural analysis and various forms of the sociology of knowledge, both on the level of morality and of political practice, could end in a sterile and passive relativism. Yet these approaches and postmodernism can also prepare the way for going beyond the simple issues of equality or difference. They allow us to replace unitary notions of 'women' and 'gender identity' by plural and complex conceptions of social identity. This is because postmodernism is more than merely a perspective on difference. It is the celebration of playful plurality. Thus, on the level of political practice, it becomes clear

> that the diversity of women's needs calls for different solutions ... Being equal instead of being dealt with in a uniform way will then imply that women should be approached in a differentiated way, attuned to their various changing needs and identities. (Lieteke van Vucht Tijssen, 'Women Between Modernity and Postmodernity', in Bryan S. Turner, ed., *Theories of Modernity and Postmodernity*, London: Sage, 1990, pp. 147–63 (pp. 161–2).)

The author goes on to suggest that such personal differentiation can then also be applied to men by women – a practice that could be 'a major step in breaking down the barriers between the sexes and creating a situation in which equality means the possibility of being' (Ibid., p. 162). Postmodernism is adapted to a feminist programme, without the latter losing its sense of inner integrity – thus meeting the conditions laid down by Morris. Games with codes can be turned to feminist advantage, if feminism will allow itself to be pragmatic enough to join in.

Other thinkers have been more sceptical of the nature of feminism's supposed debt to modernity and the Enlightenment project:

> The anomalous position of feminism *vis-à-vis* the modernist-postmodernist debate is of enormous importance for the future of the feminist enterprise. The issues at stake are far from trivial. Postmodernism is challenging, among other things, the fundamental dichotomies of Enlightenment thought, dichotomies such as rational/irrational and subject/object. It is questioning the homocentricity of Enlightenment knowledge and even the status of 'man' himself. These are not issues on which feminism can be ambiguous. If all the 'feminisms' have anything in common it is a challenge to the masculine/feminine dichotomy as it is defined in western thought. It is this dichotomy that informs all the dichotomies the postmoderns are attacking, even though they do not always make this explicit. Similarly, challenging the priority of 'man' in the modern episteme [belief-system or ideology, with all its attendant rules and conventions] must be fundamental to any feminist program. On these key issues, as well as on many others, feminism has much to gain from an alliance with postmodernism. An alliance with modernism, on the other hand, can only result in a perpetuation of the Enlightenment/modernist epistemology that inevitably places women in an inferior position.
>
> Advancing an argument for a postmodern approach to feminism is by no means simple. The modernist legacy of feminism is not a

> superficial aspect of contemporary feminism. Questions such as whether a postmodern feminism offers an adequate political program and whether the emancipatory impulse of both liberalism and Marxism must be abandoned are of central importance. Discussions of postmodernism and feminism are already seeking to resolve these questions. It is my intention to contribute to that resolution by constructing an argument for a postmodern approach to feminism. This argument has several aspects. First, it involves chronicling similarities between postmodernism and feminism. Second, it involves arguing that a postmodern position can resolve some of the key issues debated in contemporary feminism, issues such as the existence of woman's 'nature'. Third, it involves the argument that feminism can contribute to the postmodern position by adding the dimension of gender, a dimension lacking in many postmodern accounts. ... The Enlightenment defined 'epistemology' as the study of knowledge acquisition that was accomplished through the opposition of a knowing subject and a known object. ... Feminists reject the opposition of subject and objects because inherent in this opposition is the assumption that only men can be subjects, and, hence, knowers. (Susan J. Hekman, *Gender and Knowledge: Elements of a Postmodern Feminism*, Cambridge and Oxford: Polity Press and Blackwell, 1990, pp. 2–3, 9.)

From this perspective, modernism is the enemy of the feminist project in that its liberationist ideals are seen to be almost exclusively for the benefit of men. Feminism is presented as the missing ingredient that will enable postmodernism to realise its objective of overcoming the Enlightenment ethos. And the feminist cause will also become more effective, once in alliance with postmodern theory.

Linda Hutcheon additionally notes a dialectical relationship between feminism (or 'feminisms', as she, like many of her peers, prefers to characterise the field) and postmodernism, particularly when it comes to the politics of representation. Postmodernism teaches us that all representations are constructed, a point with which feminists are only too familiar when it comes to the subject of the female body:

> Feminisms are not really either compatible with or even an example of postmodern thought, as a few critics have tried to argue; if anything, together they form the single most powerful force in changing the direction in which (male) postmodernism was heading but, I think, no longer is. It radicalized the postmodern sense of difference

> and de-naturalized the traditional historiographic separation of the private and the public – and the personal and the political ...
>
> The reason for the none the less quite common conflation of the feminist and the postmodern may well lie in their common interest in representation, that purportedly neutral process that is now being deconstructed in terms of ideology. In shows like *Difference: On Representation and Sexuality*, held at the New Museum of Contemporary Art in New York in 1985, sexual difference was shown to be something that is continuously reproduced by cultural representations normally taken for granted as natural or given. Few would disagree today that feminisms have transformed art practice: through new forms, new self-consciousness about representation, and new awareness of both contexts and particularities of gendered experience. They have certainly made women artists more aware of themselves as women and as artists; they are even changing men's sense of themselves as gendered artists. They have rendered inseparable feminisms as socio-political movements and feminisms as a (plural) phenomenon of art history. Temporally, it is no accident that they have coincided with the revival of figurative painting and the rise of conceptual art, of what I have called photo-graphy [photographs which include verbal text] as a high-art form, of video, alternative film practices, performance art – all of which have worked to challenge both the humanist notion of the artist as romantic individual 'genius' (and therefore of art as the expression of universal meaning by a transcendent human subject) and the modernist domination of two particular art forms, painting and sculpture. But feminisms have also refocused attention on the politics of representation and knowledge – and therefore also on power. They have *made* postmodernism think, not just about the body, but about the female body; not just about the female body, but about its desires – and about both as socially and historically constructed through representation. (Linda Hutcheon, *The Politics of Postmodernism*, London and New York: Routledge, 1989, pp. 142–3.)

Postmodernism is once again identified as having a distinctly male bias, and thus as standing in need of feminist critique. But there are at the least common interests between the areas of discourse that deserve to be fostered. Both are challenging existing systems of value and the authority that accretes to these over the years. As presented here, feminism might even be the catalyst that propels postmodernism into realising its full potential as a radical theory. In Hutcheon's reading, anyway, postmodernism would seem to have more to gain from co-operation than feminism does. What feminism does is to make explicit the politics that are often only implicit in postmodernist discourse. A feminism that makes use of the insights and techniques (irony, parody and so on) of postmodern thought, looks set to be a very powerful analytical method.

An interesting recent development of the postmodern age has been the advent of postfeminism, which, like postmodernism, can be regarded as a reaction against metanarrative – in this case the metanarrative of second-wave feminism. Like postmodernism, too, there is disagreement as to postfeminism's exact meaning, terms of reference and ultimate objectives:

> 'Postfeminism' is a term that is very much in vogue these days. In the context of popular culture it's the Spice Girls, Madonna and the *Girlie Show*: women dressing like bimbos, yet claiming male privileges and attitudes. Meanwhile, those who wish to maintain an allegiance to more traditional forms of feminism circle around the neologism warily, unable to decide whether it represents a con trick engineered by the media or a valid movement. ...
>
> Much of this distrust is to do with the fact that, outside of its infinitely flexible media definition, exactly what postfeminism constitutes – even whether it exists at all as a valid phenomenon – is a matter for frequently impassioned debate. As Vicki Coppock, Deena Haydon and Ingrid Richter put it in *The Illusions of 'Post-feminism'*, 'post-feminism has never been defined. It remains the product of assumption'. It is a characteristic postfeminism shares with its semantic relative, postmodernism, which has been similarly described as 'an amorphous thing'.
>
> Indeed, even the most cursory reading of texts tagged with the 'postfeminist' label reveals that there is little agreement among those with whom it is popularly associated as to a central canon or agenda. Very generally speaking, however, postfeminist debate tends to crystallise around issues of victimisation, autonomy and responsibility. Because it is critical of any definition of women as victims who are unable to control their own lives, it is inclined to be unwilling to condemn pornography and to be sceptical of such phenomena as date-rape: because it is skewed in favour of liberal humanism, it embraces a flexible ideology which can be adapted to suit individual needs and desires. Finally, because it tends to be implicitly heterosexist in orientation,

> postfeminism commonly seeks to develop an agenda which can find a place for men, as lovers, husbands and fathers as well as friends.
>
> The term 'postfeminism' itself originated from within the media in the early 1980s, and has always tended to be used in this context as indicative of joyous liberation from the ideological shackles of a hopelessly outdated feminist movement. ...
>
> In fact, to accept the inherently theoretical nature of the post-feminist project perhaps offers the most convincing way in which the term can be used. In this context, postfeminism becomes a pluralistic epistemology dedicated to disrupting universalising patterns of thought, and thus capable of being aligned with postmodernism, post-structuralism and postcolonialism. (Sarah Gamble, 'Postfeminism', in Sarah Gamble, ed., *The Routledge Companion to Feminism and Post-feminism*, London and New York: Routledge, 2001, pp. 43–54 (pp. 43–4, 50); originally published as *The Icon Critical Dictionary of Feminism and Postfeminism*, Cambridge: Icon Books, 1998.)

Second-wave feminists have been predictably outraged by the development of postfeminism, with many treating it as an outright betrayal of their cause. Whether it represents a paradigm shift on the model of post-modernism is a more open question, but it certainly shares some of the iconoclasm we have come to associate with postmodern thought. It is, if you like, feminism for a postmodern age. That is not likely to recommend it, however, to those second-wave feminists who regard post-modernism as an essentially male-dominated phenomenon that actively hinders the progress of their own project. Given the degree of ambivalence in feminist circles to postmodernism itself, it is not to be wondered at that postfeminism has had such a generally frosty reception within the second-wave community. The latter tend to see themselves as fighting against a metanarrative rather than building up one of their own. Post-feminism can appear as if it is part of a reactionary-minded backlash against feminism itself – another form of neoconservatism, perhaps. To be 'post-' continues to be the most contentious of positions to inhabit.

Social Theory

One of the most acute analysts of the postmodern condition has been the sociologist Zygmunt Bauman. Although broadly sympathetic to the post-modern ethos, Bauman also notes the problems that have come in the wake of the collapse of modernity, and he has his doubts about the supposed advantages of postmodern culture over modern. Even the fall of communism is not an unqualified good, he points out, if it leaves us in a world with no alternative to an apparently all-conquering capitalism:

> Throughout its history, communism was modernity's most devout, vigorous and gallant champion – pious to the point of simplicity. It also claimed to be its only true champion. Indeed, it was under communist, not capitalist, auspices that the audacious dream of modernity, freed from obstacles by the merciless and seemingly omnipotent state, was pushed to its radical limits: grand designs, unlimited social engineering, huge and bulky technology, total transformation of nature. Deserts were irrigated (but they turned into salinated bogs); marshlands were dried (but they turned into deserts); massive gas-pipes criss-crossed the land to remedy nature's whims in distributing its resources (but they kept exploding with a force unequalled by the natural disasters of yore); millions were lifted from the 'idiocy of rural life' (but they got poisoned by the effluvia of rationally designed industry, if they did not perish first on the way). Raped and crippled, nature failed to deliver the riches one hoped it would; the total scale of design only made the devastation total. Worse still, all that raping and crippling proved to be in vain. Life did not seem to become more comfortable or happy, needs (even ones acknowledged by the state tutors) did not seem to be satisfied better than before, and the kingdom of reason and harmony seemed to be more distant than ever.
>
> What the affluent west is in fact celebrating today is the official passing away of its own past; the last farewell to the modern dream and modern arrogance. If the joyous immersion in postmodern fluidity and the sensuous bliss of aimless drift were poisoned by the residues of modern conscience – the urge to do something about those who suffer and clamour for something to be done – they seem unpolluted now. With communism, the ghost of modernity has been exorcised. Social engineering, the principle of communal responsibility for individual fate, the duty to provide commonly for single survivals, the tendency to view personal tragedies as social problems, the commandment to strive collectively for shared justice – all such moral precepts as used to legitimise (some say motivate) modern practices have been compromised beyond repair by the spectacular collapse of the communist system. No more guilty conscience. No scruples. No supra-individual commitments contaminating individual enjoyment. The past has descended to its grave in disgrace.

> (Zygmunt Bauman, *Intimations of Postmodernity*, London: Routledge, 1992, pp. 179–80.)

In this reading, the postmodern world is one where the weak are even more vulnerable than they were under an admittedly deeply flawed modernity. What Bauman identifies is a lack of any moral centre to postmodernity. In the absence of Enlightenment ideals, there is little check on the excesses of free market capitalism. The grand narrative of modernity was certainly abused (particularly by communism), but something is lost in the transition to postmodernity that we should mourn the passing of – namely, the moral vision of modernity. Bauman does not look back in irony, but in an awkward and deeply qualified regret for what might have been. Postmodernity is for Bauman a state in which dissent from the capitalist ethic has effectively been annihilated, and he finds that extremely worrying – his recognition of communism's many faults notwithstanding. 'The world without an alternative', he notes, 'needs self-criticism as a condition of survival and decency' (Ibid., p. 186). But he is forced to admit that postmodernity is unpropitious territory for the development of such a critical ethos. The postmodern future looks somewhat ominous.

Bauman's rather bleak vision has been contested, with critics yet again rehearsing the line that reports of modernity's death have been grossly exaggerated:

> The question arises, of course, whether Bauman's description of the postmodern habitat and its postmodern agents does indeed apply to the whole of what he sees as the postmodern world – 'the affluent countries of Europe and of European descent'. One is inclined to accept its validity with regard to certain, fairly well-circumscribed, sectors of the urban population – the politically sensitive sector of the new middle classes of Featherstone and Lash, for instance, and the loose 'neo-tribal' groupings at the heart of the various youth cultures[4] – but these (still) constitute usually small minorities in any given national culture. If there is a postmodernity, in Bauman's sense, it is still engulfed by a much larger modernity, or perhaps is it better to say that a still representable and predictable modernity is shot through with an unrepresentable, unpredictable and indeterminate postmodernism. Similarly, traditional politics have far from disappeared, even though their appeal has undeniably diminished, and they continue to dominate the political scene. Indeed, the traditional

> politics of modernity as often as not successfully incorporate the moral and existential concerns of the new postmodern micropolitics, in some cases even acquiring a new (and unforeseen) élan. (Hans Bertens, *The Idea of the Postmodern: A History*, London and New York: Routledge, 1995, p. 236.)

In this kind of perspective, then, modernity is an altogether more resilient creature than commentators like Bauman would seem to believe, and postmodernity something less than the all-conquering new cultural paradigm they can make it out to be. Bertens is critical of those who have been so quick to jump on the postmodern bandwagon: 'That … so many theorists argue that we have entered a new postmodern era, must be ascribed to their tendency to overrate the importance of the cultural changes of the recent past.' (Ibid., p. 247.) Postmodernism is symptomatic of a crisis within modernity, which modernity might well manage to resolve, rather than of modernity's collapse as such. It could be that a new 'radicalized' modernity awaits us (Ibid., p. 248). The future need not be so ominous as Bauman fears.

The resilience of modernity is captured in a different way by Philip Cooke, for whom 'postmodernism is the continuation of modernism by other means' (Philip Cooke, *Back to the Future: Modernity, Postmodernity and Locality*, London: Unwin Hyman, 1990, p. x). Given that status, Cooke feels he can deflect much of the criticism that has been made of the postmodern ethos:

> Postmodernism can seem, as Jameson and others have said elsewhere, depthless, eclectic and disoriented. Moreover, in architecture especially, it seems highly complicit with the power structure of consumer society. Unquestionably, many postmodern buildings and even wider segments of the urban landscape such as the waterfront developments that have become commonplace in large cities, cater to the tastes and lifestyles of the rich and famous. Corporate capital was amongst the earliest purchasers of the fashionably new styles. And although it is important not to overlook the role of the public sector in commissioning the work of some of the leading newer architects such as [Ricardo] Bofill, [Michael] Graves, [Charles] Moore and [Leon] Krier, it can still, as a critic in the *Architectural Review* put it, 'look like little more than the pretty plaything of rampant capitalism'.
>
> It is not clear why this should surprise the critics. Corporate capital quickly appropriated virtually every fashionable new architectural

> style that preceded postmodern architecture. It is difficult to see why postmodernism should be any different. In this respect it can be argued that these styles are no more or less complicit with the values of the corporate elite than any other.
>
> ... There are striking similarities between modernism's Janus-face, looking backwards in order to move forward, and that of post-modernism in which there is, if anything, a stronger desire to vault backwards over the austere hermeticism of the late modern era in order to move forward into a renewed, more accessible aesthetic regime.
>
> ... [Critics] fail to recognize the ambiguity in postmodern art and architecture between working within the cultural and wider socio-economic system and simultaneously subverting aspects of it. Irony is mistaken for oppositionism, and local sensitivity – where it exists – for a rejection of universal and transcendent norms. Even Jameson does not deny the possibility that progressive cultural and social insights and practices can arise from within the postmodern perspective. Perhaps undue attention has been paid to postmodernism's historical coincidence with the rise of neoconservative politics and the crisis of progressive institutions such as the Keynesian welfare state and Fordist modes of regulation and forms of accumulation. The undoubted reductionism in Jameson's analysis ... is testimony to the problems of engaging in a totalizing form of modern discourse. Postmodernism's own critique questions precisely the monolithic, totalizing perspective. (Cooke, *Back to the Future*, pp. 110–11, 112.)

Postmodernism is the victim rather than the accomplice of capitalism in this interesting reading, where 'coincidence' replaces 'collusion' in terms of the development of each system. Critics, and Marxist critics in particular, have simply missed the subtlety of the subversive strategies in which postmodern practitioners have been engaging. What those critics have also missed, in Cooke's interpretation of recent cultural history, is the real nature of postmodernism's relationship to modernism – that it is 'an internal critique of modernism' set on correcting its deficiencies (Ibid., p. x). Postmodernism constitutes the basis of modernism's renewal, and we should welcome that outcome.

Sociologists have shown a particular interest in how postmodernism works as a form of cultural production and consumption. Mike Featherstone's enquiry into this topic is concerned to establish whether postmodernism really does express radical changes in the cultural grass-roots:

> The questions we face in trying to understand postmodern culture sociologically, therefore, revolve around understanding how these two aspects [–] the production and circulation of postmodern theories (many of which have a sense of end of history, albeit non-tragic finality, about them), and the wider production and circulation of everyday cultural experiences and practices [–] are related. Here we need not be for or against postmodernism, rather we have to explain sociologically how postmodernism is possible, and how an interest in the loose family of notions associated with it [has] come into being. ... In brief, then, we seek to understand and point toward the need for an explanation of these two aspects[:] the theoretical, and everyday, of the claimed movement toward the postmodern, in which *postmodernism*, which is theorized and expressed in intellectual and artistic practices, can be seen as an index or harbinger of a broader *postmodern culture*, a wider set of changes in the production, consumption, and circulation of cultural goods and practices. (Mike Featherstone, *Consumer Culture and Postmodernism*, London: Sage, 1991, pp. 33–4.)

While Featherstone sees potential benefits to postmodernism as a form of cultural production, he urges that we must maintain a sense of proportion in our consumption of the theories involved:

> The question is whether these tendencies, which have been labelled postmodern, merely point to a collapse of an established hierarchy, a temporary phase, a cultural intermezzo of intensified competition, varied standards and value complexes, before a re-monopolization by a new establishment. Or should we see the extension of the current tendencies *ad infinitum* – the end of history? In this context it is salutary to refer to similar historical ages of cultural turmoil and incoherence. If it is proclaimed today that there is no fashion, only fashions, then we should bear in mind that Simmel discovered similar tendencies in Florence around 1390 when the styles of the social elite were not met with imitation and each individual sought to create his own style.[5] Fashion and other lifestyle pursuits, to use Simmel's metaphor, are used as 'bridges and doors' to unite and exclude. If these functions appear to decline does it mean that we are merely in a temporary intermezzo? Or does the extension of the game to draw more

> groups, cultures and nations into a widened global system mean that the conditions for particular dominant elites to exercise global hegemony over taste and culture are destroyed with the unlikelihood of foreseeable re-monopolization, thus pointing us towards a historical development in which some of the impulses detected and labelled postmodern may become more widespread? (Featherstone, *Consumer Culture and Postmodernism*, p. 111.)

An altogether more sceptical voice about the consumption of cultural theories in our society is that of Dick Hebdige, for whom Biff cartoons (familiar to the general public in Britain through a widely distributed postcard series, and from the 1980s into the new millennium in weekend strips in the *Guardian* newspaper) take on a deeply symbolic import:

> Biff are two graphic artists, Mick Kidd and Chris Garratt, who formed a partnership in 1980. Kidd and Garratt produce cartoons in a heavily ironic style – an instantly identifiable pastiche of visual banalities and conversational clichés. ... Art criticism in the Age of Biff is something quite different, something quite new. Perhaps, along with all the other posts to which people are currently tying their critical or post-critical colours: post Marxism, post feminism, post industrialism, post structuralism, post modernism, one last post is called for – one last stake to be driven Dracula-style through the heart of the serious pundit, to lay to rest the ghost of the hollow-eyed, earnest critic once and for all – post-Biffism. ... Art criticism in the age [that] semiotics originally endowed (or so some of its proponents used to claim) with a corrosive (or at the very least) revelatory edge, threatens to become little more than signs and meanings for young consumers. ... The Biffites: those budding Humphrey Bogarts with Art & Design degrees who are willing to go unaided by religious and political convictions down these mean airwaves armed with a keen eye for detail, are going to be alert first and foremost not to the nuances of right and wrong, to the flapping of the Right and the Left wings of the established political parties; they are going to be sensitive not to the Big Issues of the day, but rather to the 'pointless' play of social and aesthetic codes. An army of 'private eyes' is being called up in the 1980s to wander freely through the labyrinth of signs and Biff supply the draft cards. There are no cases left to solve in the whacky world of Biff, no murders to investigate beyond the 'death of the author' (and all the evidence suggests that either He did Himself

> in anyway or never really existed in the first place – that the 'author' was nothing but an alias for the text). There is no monster at the centre of the labyrinth of signs, no Minotaur ... no clues because no crimes. And when you put the cards away, what happens if it doesn't seem enough? When you want at last, just for a change, to cast off the quotation marks, when you finally decide that you don't want to live out the rest of your life in parenthesis? (Dick Hebdige, *Hiding in the Light: On Images and Things*, London and New York: Routledge, 1988, pp. 148, 149–50, 154.)

Hebdige's sense of humour enables him to appreciate the joke when he finds one of his own lectures on popular culture being satirised in a Biff comic strip. Yet his serious point remains: Biff's appeal is to a post-modern constituency, which consumes cultural theory in a very uncritical, very eclectic, manner where anything and everything goes. Value judgement and political sensibility are sacrificed in the cause of a highly self-regarding, self-congratulating irony, which for Hebdige ultimately registers as the most superficial of responses to the problems that beset our culture. In the 'Age of Biff', cultural consumption has imploded in on itself. Clever and witty though they undoubtedly are (and Hebdige fully acknowledges this), Biff has become a symbol of our current cultural malaise: if there is one thing the Biffites are not, Hebdige insists, it is political radicals. Self-congratulation does not lead to social revolution.

Although many sociologists share Hebdige's opinion of the superficiality of postmodernism, they find themselves unable to deny how powerful a hold it has come to exert on the contemporary imagination. Scott Lash, for example, while making it clear he is no postmodernist himself, still feels compelled to admit that postmodernism has become our culture's new paradigm. It is a paradigm that operates on a principle of 'de-differentiation' (in which activities blend into each other rather than being kept separate) which has a profound effect on both consumption and production:

> If cultural modernization was a process of differentiation [separating out], then postmodernization is one of de-differentiation. ... There are four main components to a given cultural paradigm. They are: (1) the relationship among types of cultural object produced – i.e. aesthetic, theoretical, ethical, etc.; (2) the relationship between the cultural as a whole and the social; (3) its 'cultural economy', whose elements in turn are conditions of production and consumption, the

> institutions of culture, mode of circulation, and the cultural product or good itself; and (4) the mode of signification: i.e. relations among signifier, signified, and referent. If modernization presupposed differentiation on all of these counts, then postmodernization witnesses de-differentiation on each of these four components.
>
> First of all, the three main cultural spheres lose their autonomy, in a process in which, for example, the aesthetic realm begins to colonize both theoretical and moral-political spheres. Second, the cultural realm is no longer 'auratic', in [Walter] Benjamin's sense; that is, it is no longer systematically separated from the social.[6] This has to do with the partial breakdown of the boundaries between high and popular culture and the concomitant development of a mass audience for high culture. But it is also a matter of a new immanence in the social of culture, in which representations also take on the function of symbols. Third, the 'cultural economy' becomes de-differentiated. On the production side is the famous disintegration of the author celebrated by poststructuralists, or alternatively the merging of author into the cultural product as in the late 1980s biographical novels or performance art … On the consumption side, de-differentiation takes place in, for example, the tendency of some types of theatre since the mid 1960s to include the audience itself as part of the cultural product. One of the most important 'institutions' of culture is criticism, which mediates between cultural product and consumer. And a number of critics have come to dispute the distinction between literature and criticism, which is the same as the distinction between institutions and cultural objects. Other 'institutions' include those which commercially circulate cultural objects, and [the] use of advertisements in doing so. With the advent of the pop video … one is hard put to say where the commercial institution stops and where the cultural product starts. (Scott Lash, *Sociology of Postmodernism*, London and New York: Routledge, 1990, pp. 11–12.)

There can, however, be sceptical voices as to whether postmodernism really *is* the new cultural paradigm in the wider world. Jim McGuigan maintains that, for the mass of the population in their daily lives, the picture is very different. Speaking of Lyotard's thesis of the collapse of metanarratives, McGuigan points out that,

> It is unclear … to what extent this sudden loss of conviction in rational grounds for criticising and changing the world represents the

experience of ordinary people. … [T]he uncritical drift in this field of study derives largely from an inversion of hyper-criticism, exemplified by the dominant ideology thesis in relation to modern media and popular culture.[7] Linked to this inversion is the fashionable procedure, sometimes given a Derridean imprimatur, of deconstructing cherished radical assumptions by, ostensibly, out-radicalising them. Such a mutating (mute? mutilating?) of intellectual practice probably says more about the competitive academy in the postmodern era than it does about the clash of contending forces in the world at large, which is another story.

In short, the study of culture is nothing if it is not about values. A disenchanted, anti-moralistic, anti-judgemental stance constructed in opposition to cultural and political zealotry only takes you so far. The posture may be cool, detached and irreverent but it is not value-free. New revisionism is rooted in populist sentiments of an increasingly slippery kind. And it is striking how a pact has been made, overtly or covertly, with economic liberalism, rediscovering the virtues of the market as a cultural provider and incitement to pleasure. Curiously, much less interest has been shown in political liberalism, by which I mean the discourse of rights, citizenship and democracy. (Jim McGuigan, *Cultural Populism*, London and New York: Routledge, 1992, pp. 172–3.)

McGuigan is committed to cultural populism, which he sees as a positive force in society, and considers that it is, in general, ill-served by postmodern theory.[8] The gist of his argument is that whatever is happening on the ground, postmodernism is not really recording it: theory and reality diverge.

Human geography is also deeply concerned with social relations, this time as they are affected by our physical environment – as in our cities. In common with their peers in so many other areas of the social sciences, for human geographers postmodern theory represents a means by which to challenge the dominant assumptions about social relations in their field. Edward W. Soja is one of the prime exponents of the new 'postmodern geography', which he feels should replace Marxist geography as the new radical paradigm in the discipline:

Just as contemporary Western Marxism seems to have exploded into a heterogeneous constellation of often cross-purposeful perspectives,

> Modern Geography has also started to come apart at its seams, unravelling internally and in its old school ties with the other nineteenth-century disciplines that defined the modern academic division of labour. The grip of older categories, boundaries, and separations is weakening. What was central is now being pushed to the margins, while the once tactful fringes boldly assert a new-found centrality. The shifting, almost kaleidoscopic, intellectual terrain has become extremely difficult to map for it no longer appears with its familiar, time-worn contours.
>
> This unsettled and unsettling geography is, I suggest, part of the postmodern condition, a contemporary crisis filled, like the Chinese pictograph for crisis and Berman's vaporous description of modernity in transition, with perils and new possibilities; filled with the simultaneous shock of the old and the new.[9] … [A]nother culture of time and space seems to be taking shape in this contemporary context and it is redefining the nature and experience of everyday life in the modern world – and along with it the whole fabric of social theory. I would locate the onset of this passage to postmodernity in the late 1960s and the series of explosive events which together marked the end of the long post-war boom in the capitalist world economy. (Edward W. Soja, *Postmodern Geographies: The Reassertion of Space in Critical Social Theory*, London: Verso, 1989, pp. 60–1.)

Soja's postmodernism is anchored in leftist thought and is concerned to avoid what he sees as a regrettable tendency among many other postmodernists to drift towards neoconservatism (a charge to be made by Habermas also):

> The development of a radical political culture of postmodernism will accordingly require moving beyond rigorous empirical descriptions which imply scientific understanding but too often hide political meaning; beyond a simplistic anti-Marxism which rejects all the insights of historical materialism in the wake of an exposure of its contemporary weaknesses and gaps; beyond the disciplinary chauvinisms of an outdated academic division of labour desperately clinging to its old priorities; beyond a Marxist geography that assumes that a historical geographical materialism has already been created by merely inserting a second adjective. A new 'cognitive mapping' must be developed, a new way of seeing through the gratuitous veils of both reactionary postmodernism and late modern historicism to

> encourage the creation of a politicised spatial consciousness and a radical spatial praxis. The most important postmodern geographies are thus still to be produced. (Soja, *Postmodern Geographies*, p. 75.)

A certain nostalgia for grand narrative – of the Marxist variety – can be observed in Soja, but also a desire to break free of traditional restraints: 'radical' no longer simply means 'left' in the old sense of the term. Human geography is yet another area in which established authority is being subjected to vigorous challenge that takes no account of established reputations.

Soja's involvement with the neo-Marxist 'L.A. School' comes through strongly in *Postmodern Geographies*, in which Los Angeles is presented as almost the archetype of the postmodern city, with all the advantages and disadvantages that such a condition entails. Mike Davis has queried the group's ethos in this respect:

> During the 1980s the 'L.A. School' (based in the UCLA planning and geography faculties, but including contributors from other campuses) developed an ambitious matrix of criss-crossing approaches and case-studies. Monographs focused on the dialectics of de- and re-industrialization, the peripheralization of labor and the internationalization of capital, housing and homelessness, the environmental consequences of untrammeled development, and the discourse of growth. Although its members remain undecided whether they should model themselves after the 'Chicago School' (named principally after its *object* of research), or the 'Frankfurt School' (a philosophical current named after its *base*), the 'L.A. School' is, in fact, a little bit of both.[10] While surveying Los Angeles in a systematic way, the UCLA researchers are most interested in exploiting the metropolis, à la Adorno and Horkheimer, as a 'laboratory of the future'. They have made clear that they see themselves excavating the outlines of a paradigmatic postfordism, an emergent twenty-first century urbanism.[11] Their belief in the region as a crystal ball is redoubled by Fredric Jameson's famous evocation (in his 'Cultural Logic of Late Capitalism') of Bunker Hill as a 'concrete totalization' of postmodernity.
>
> By exposing the darkest facets of the 'world city' (Los Angeles's 'new Dickensian hell' of underclass poverty in the words of UCLA geographer Alan Scott) the 'L.A. School' ridicules the utopias of *L.A. 2000* [a city-commissioned planning report, published in 1988]. Yet, by hyping Los Angeles as the paradigm of the future (even in a

> dystopian vein), they tend to collapse history into teleology and glamorize the very reality they would deconstruct. Soja and Jameson, particularly, in the very eloquence of their different 'postmodern mappings' of Los Angeles, become celebrants of the myth. The city is a place where everything is possible, nothing is safe and durable enough to believe in, where constant synchronicity [concurrent existence of different ways of life and so on] prevails, and the automatic ingenuity of capital ceaselessly throws up new forms and spectacles. (Mike Davis, *City of Quartz: Excavating the Future in Los Angeles*, London: Verso, 1990, pp. 84–6.)

As such sentiments suggest, Davis is fairly sceptical about the radical political potential being claimed for 'postmodern' Los Angeles:

> [M]ost current, giddy discussions of the 'postmodern' scene in Los Angeles neglect entirely these overbearing aspects of counter-urbanization and counter-insurgency. A triumphal gloss – 'urban renaissance', 'city of the future', and so on – is laid over the brutalization of inner-city neighborhoods and the increasing South Africanization of its spatial relations. Even as the walls have come down in Eastern Europe, they are being erected all over Los Angeles. (Davis, *City of Quartz*, p. 227.)

Faith in postmodernism is in short supply in this account of the politics of the Los Angeles cityscape. To be postmodern in this context is to gloss over the reality of a city that is divided against itself. Spatial consciousness here is anything but radical in form. When one investigates, ghettoisation is what will be found on the ground.

One of the most influential interventions into postmodernism from the field of human geography has come from David Harvey, who retains far more of a Marxist bias than does Soja, setting out the basic argument of his study, *The Condition of Postmodernity*, in the following uncompromising terms:

> There has been a sea-change in cultural as well as in political-economic practices since around 1972.
>
> This sea-change is bound up with the emergence of new dominant ways in which we experience space and time.
>
> While simultaneity in shifting dimensions of time and space is no proof of necessary or causal connection, strong a priori grounds can

> be adduced for the proposition that there is some kind of necessary relation between the rise of postmodernist cultural forms, the emergence of more flexible modes of capital accumulation, and a new round of 'time–space compression' in the organization of capitalism.
>
> But these changes, when set against the basic rules of capitalistic accumulation, appear more as shifts in surface appearance rather than as signs of the emergence of some entirely new postcapitalist or even postindustrial society. (David Harvey, *The Condition of Postmodernity: An Enquiry into the Origins of Cultural Change*, Cambridge, MA and Oxford: Blackwell, 1990, p. vii.)

For Harvey, postmodernism is a consequence of capitalism's most recent crisis and, as such, still explicable by means of classical Marxist theory:

> Aesthetic and cultural practices are peculiarly susceptible to the changing experience of space and time precisely because they entail the construction of spatial representations and artefacts out of the flow of human experience. They always broker between Being and Becoming. … Since crises of overaccumulation typically spark the search for spatial and temporal resolutions, which in turn create an overwhelming sense of time–space compression, we can also expect crises of overaccumulation to be followed by strong aesthetic movements.
>
> The crisis of accumulation that began in the late 1960s and which came to a head in 1973 has generated exactly such a result. The experience of time and space has changed, the confidence in the association between scientific and moral judgements has collapsed, aesthetics has triumphed over ethics as a prime focus of social and intellectual concern, images dominate narrative, ephemerality and fragmentation take precedence over eternal truths and unified politics, and explanations have shifted from the realm of the material and political-economic groundings towards a consideration of autonomous cultural and political practices.
>
> The historical sketch I have here proposed suggests, however, that shifts of this sort are by no means new, and that the most recent version of it is certainly within the grasp of historical materialist enquiry, even capable of theorization by way of the meta-narrative of capitalist development that Marx proposed.
>
> Postmodernism can be regarded, in short, as a historical-geographical condition of a certain sort. (Harvey, *The Condition of Postmodernity*, pp. 327–8.)

Postmodernism is reduced to a localised socio-historical phenomenon, which manifests itself as a collective loss of nerve with regard to the claims of metanarrative theories in general. However, Harvey remains confident that the moment will pass – and possibly already has. For this theorist, the age of metanarrative is alive and well, and his own faith in Marxism is undimmed by the experience of postmodernity. What theorists like Laclau and Mouffe would want to know, however, is why the Marxist historical scheme is taking so long to fall into place. Harvey seems like one of the hegemony theorists in calling for yet more time for capitalism's final crisis to materialise. Post-Marxists, however, have given up waiting (or listening to excuses), and moved on to new theoretical pastures. We might say that Harvey is precisely the kind of thinker with whom they have lost patience.

Another sociologist to argue that modernity is not yet dead is Keith Tester:

> Quite simply, if post-modernity is the intimation of a transcendent condition without the bounds of modernity then, consequently, it is also the intimation of the condition in which questions of the status of what has or has not happened become quite beyond the asking. After all, post-modernity means a transcendence of the boundaries which constitute the basis of any knowing of what might be (without the boundaries it is distinctly possible that there can be no understanding). As such, post-modernity as transcendence of modern boundaries implies a condition in which the existent cannot be explained or interpreted. It can only be confronted as a simple and unalterable fact. In the post-modern condition, the existent is without bounds (after all there are no bounds for it to be within; no bounds to contain it). A situation is intimated in which the existent might swamp and perpetually escape any and every attempt to represent and understand it. It is a dull fact about which it might well be hermeneutically impossible to allow for any alternative.
>
> Consequently, in so far as post-modernity pushes the social and the cultural beyond the social and societal understanding, so the social and the cultural might also be beyond the social and the societal interference. And that is actually tantamount to saying that post-modernity intimates nothing other than the construction of a new natural artifice. It might betray a tendency towards a denial of human freedom. It is certainly a refusal to face up to the full consequences of freedom (but it has been known, albeit for extremely different

> reasons, since Kant and the existentialists, that for some the abrogation of freedom might be a very attractive proposition indeed. Freedom is not easy, and neither is it necessarily very pleasant. But it is the most we can have). (Keith Tester, *The Life and Times of Post-Modernity*, London and New York: Routledge, 1993, pp. 157–8.)

Like Bauman, Tester fears that postmodernity is a condition in which alternative viewpoints cannot be formulated, and criticism and dissent simply disappear. When that happens, freedom is all too likely to disappear as well. All the more reason, Tester feels, to persevere with modernity:

> The post-modern condition implies a mere ability to register and record the existent but without any chance of the legitimate posing of the question of 'why?' It is in other words, a rendering of the existent as a purely empirical fact and quite without any meaning other than the material compunction of its being.
>
> Any sociology which retains a commitment to the enterprises, lessons and interests of modernity is simply overwhelmed by the intimations of post-modernity. But any sociology which gives up on the problems and possibilities of modernity and which instead, attempts to deal head on with the post-modern condition and contingency, ceases to be able to make any judgement whatsoever. It is instead, reduced to the level of a simple and a more or less insignificant description. Empiricism takes the place of evaluation, however hesitant and embarrassed that evaluation might be. But some ability to evaluate is necessary. It is a denial of our responsibility to others to give up on the ability to condemn some practices and support others. ...
>
> It might be said from the post-modern point of view, there is actually nothing left to happen. The last word might indeed have been said. Post-modernity holds out the prospect of the universality of humanity. Of course, the universality is in no small measure a product of the implications of technology and indeed, of the mundane metaphysical wager of immortality. But it remains a universality of a far more likely and practical sort than any of the philosophers were able to imagine in their wildest speculations.
>
> Post-modernity can perhaps be seen as something like the culmination of human history and moreover, as something like the final fulfilment of all of the hopes and ambitions which have been expressed so desperately and so longingly since the birth of philosophy. So long as no attention is paid to the ragged remains of the

> pre-historical and the historical who lurk outside the glittering arcades of post-modernity it might seem as if the world has been rendered finally and fully clear. It might well seem as if the mysteries of the world have been solved once and for all. But in any case, what do the dirty and tattered masses mean? From a post-modern point of view, they actually mean nothing because there is nothing for them to mean. All the inhabitants of post-modernity can do now is register their presence. At most they can simply ask the poor what it feels like to be shabby. There is no longer anything that can be done since the presence of the poor no longer implies any social and cultural process of the happening. They are grubby and pathetic and that is all they are. (Tester, *The Life and Times of Post-Modernity*, pp. 158, 159–60.)

Tester sees this socio-political lassitude as a product of postmodernism's obsession with the sublime, given that the sublime demonstrates to us our powerlessness. From that acknowledgement of powerlessness proceeds a collapse of value judgement and, in Tester's reading, a sense of fatalism regarding human action. While he can see some benefits in post-modernity in making us realise the virtues and vices of modernity, Tester is deeply worried about its longer-term political impact. Behind such a reading lies the fear we have noted being expressed by commentators in many other fields of enquiry – that postmodernism, through its abdication from value judgement, plays into the hands of the political conservaives. For anyone concerned to improve the condition of the poor and the exploited – that is, for any left-wing thinker of conscience at all – there can be no excuse for opting out of political action. Only the reactionaries will gain when that happens.

Other social theorists are quite willing to concede the death of the modernist project, as well as the necessity for this event to occur, while refusing to accept its postmodernist alternative. Stephen Crook, for example, is particularly critical of what is being offered in the name of the latter:

> Social theory becomes radical in taking up the responsibility of giving reasons why change is required, of making the demand for change accountable in terms of some standards of judgement. Modernist radicalisms attempt to carry out this task through the foundationalist integration of the two dimensions of theoretical and social change, this integration portrayed as the completion of modernity. This

> response to the requirements of radicalism may not be acceptable, but at least it represents a serious attempt to grapple with the problem. When radical social theory loses its accountability, when it can no longer give reasons, something has gone very wrong. But this is precisely what happens to postmodern theory, and it seems appropriate to use the over-stretched term 'nihilism' as a label for this degeneration. The nihilism of postmodernism shows itself in two symptoms: an inability to specify possible mechanisms of change, and an inability to state why change is better than no change.
>
> The first symptom afflicts a wide range of projects. Most notoriously, Foucault's model of 'Power/Knowledge' seems able to articulate 'resistance' only as an embodiment of the power which it is supposed to resist.[12] Jameson concludes his account of the new age of postmodernity with the remark that it is an open question whether any sources of opposition to the new age will be found[13] ... Baudrillard offers a vision of a 'one dimensional' system impenetrable to change, of 'all secrets, spaces and scenes abolished in a single dimension of information' (Baudrillard, 1983, p. 131).[14] The only paradoxical hope he offers is of a hopeless 'challenge' which is both 'unremitting and invisible' (Baudrillard, 1980, p. 107).[15]
>
> ... The dilemma facing postmodernism is that it must either allow that modernism was once valid, but is no longer, in which case it begins to look like an orthodox historicism, or it must insist that modernism (and pre-modernism) were always false, in which case it seems to be advancing claims to represent a timeless truth. This problem arises because postmodernism makes only half a break with modernism ... [P]ostmodernism breaks with modernist answers, but not with the (equally modernist) questions which prompt them. (Stephen Crook, 'The End of Radical Social Theory?: Notes on Radicalism, Modernism and Postmodernism', in Boyne and Rattansi, eds, *Postmodernism and Society*, pp. 46–75 (pp. 58–9, 68).)

Postmodernism becomes a self-defeating exercise, therefore, and it is accordingly rejected as having no relevance to the project of radical social theory in which nihilism can have no part to play. Indeed, nihilism can only be looked on with extreme distaste by the left as the antithesis of their essentially optimistic world-view, with its belief in the possibility of change for the better.

As an example of where abdication from value judgement of the kind feared by theorists like Tester and Crook can lead, we can turn to

Baudrillard's somewhat infamous 'coffee table' volumes, *America* and *Cool Memories*, with their studiedly post-critical and post-political pose:

> We fanatics of aesthetics and meaning, of culture, of flavour and seduction, we who see only what is profoundly moral as beautiful and for whom only the heroic distinction between nature and culture is exciting, we who are unfailingly attached to the wonders of the critical sense and transcendence find it a mental shock and a unique release to discover the fascination of nonsense and of this vertiginous disconnection, as sovereign in the cities as in the deserts. To discover that one can exult in the liquidation of all culture and rejoice in the consecration of in-difference.
>
> I speak of the American deserts and of the cities which are not cities. No oases, no monuments; infinite panning shots over mineral landscapes and freeways. Everywhere: Los Angeles or Twenty-Nine Palms, Las Vegas or Borrego Springs ...
>
> No desire: the desert. Desire is still something deeply natural, we live off its vestiges in Europe, and off the vestiges of a moribund critical culture. Here the cities are mobile deserts. No monuments and no history: the exaltation of mobile deserts and simulation. There is the same wildness in the endless, indifferent cities as in the intact silence of the Badlands. Why is LA, why are the deserts so fascinating? It is because you are delivered from all depth there – a brilliant, mobile, superficial neutrality, a challenge to meaning and profundity, a challenge to nature and culture, an outer hyperspace, with no origin, no reference-points. (Jean Baudrillard, *America*, trans. Chris Turner, London and New York: Verso, 1988, pp. 123–4.)

America becomes the perfect postmodern setting, where traditional culture (that identified with Europe, as Baudrillard hints) is 'liquidated', taking with it the critical faculty. The observer no longer makes aesthetic judgements on his environment, but simply drifts through it uncritically – or nomadically, we might say, recalling Deleuze and Guattari. Ultimately, it is a manner of existence that leads to extreme passivity:

> [T]here is a charm and a particular freedom about letting just anything come along, with the grace – or ennui – of a later destiny. ... There are things one can no longer talk about or cannot yet talk

> about again. Their ghosts have not yet been stabilized. Marxism? (Jean Baudrillard, *Cool Memories*, trans. Chris Turner, London and New York: Verso, 1990, pp. 3, 232.)

Politics disappears at such points, with the individual opting out of action or debate and refusing to take any particular stance on any particular issue. Tester's fears about what a world without evaluation would be like are realised here in the atrophy of Baudrillard's political sensibility. For the left, post-political equals apolitical – yet another invitation to those in power to do whatever they want to without any threat of counter-action (the particular fear that we saw haunting Bauman in the aftermath of communism's collapse). Baudrillard may find 'release' in this condition; the traditional left will interpret it as nihilism dressed up to look fashionable.

The left has certainly taken issue with Baudrillard's post-aesthetic vision. Douglas Kellner, for example, finds *America* to be conceptually trite and theoretically superficial:

> Baudrillard suggests at the beginning of his study that one should read America as a fiction (A[merica], p. 59). But one could well read Baudrillard's own study as a fiction about America, as pataphysical projection of his own fantasies about America.[16] More uncharitably, one could read the book as a whole as symptomatic of the decline of Baudrillard's theoretical powers and the collapse of social analysis and critique – as well as politics – in favor of highly uneven social observation and metaphysical ruminations. While some of the earlier parts of the book (especially pp. 55–126) contain some acute observations and while the project of analyzing the signs and constellations of America is certainly fascinating, Baudrillard fails to pull it off.
>
> In fact, the same basic limitation in Baudrillard's metaphysics is apparent in his analysis of America: his subject matter is under-theorized, and his attempts at theory are uneven and problematical. Novel and original ideas cohabit promiscuously with banal stereotypes (America as a desert, as primitive). The problem with using these concepts as expressive of the very essence of America is that his treatment falls prey to a dull essentialism. Moreover, it is not just the pejorative and condescending tone of his particular concepts, but the very status of the key concepts themselves that is problematical. As Lyotard argued long ago, the very concept of 'the primitive' is an ideological construct with racist and imperialist overtones. And 'the desert'

> is a rather stereotyped European cliché for modernity (see Antonioni's film *Red Desert*) or for the emptiness of the soul in a fallen world. Not much is gained by resurrecting such worn-out concepts. (Douglas Kellner, *Jean Baudrillard: From Marxism to Postmodernism and Beyond*, Cambridge and Oxford: Polity Press and Blackwell, 1989, p. 170.)

Others have been more charitable in their assessment than Kellner, with Bryan S. Turner arguing that *America* and *Cool Memories* are perfect exemplifications of a particular kind of postmodern temperament:

> What is the nature of the offence of *America* (1989) and the autobiographical *Cool Memories* (1990)? ... *America* and *Cool Memories* are offensive to academics, especially serious academics like Callinicos and Kellner, because they are politically uncommitted, whimsical, and depthless. *Cool Memories* reads as a clever, but disconnected, set of notes on Baudrillard's personal experience of America. The parallel text of *America* appears to have more organization and is self-consciously designed as a text with an audience in mind. If we think about these two volumes from the point of view of their style, they are postmodern in the limited sense that they exhibit the characteristics of 'cruising'. A cruise is a trip or voyage typically undertaken for pleasure; it is a trivial exercise. The tourist on a cruise attracts a negative response from those who are local inhabitants, because, like Simmel's 'The Stranger', they are marginal and in that sense dangerous. The stranger (*der Fremde*) is detached and rootless, expressing a general human estrangement (*Entfremdung*), and a nostalgia for settlement and security. Cruising is pointless, aimless and unproductive. It leaves no residue, no evidence, no archive. It does not intend to interpret; it is post-anthropological. ... The travel theme gives the text a perfect feeling of depthlessness, of skating over the surface. The maxim condenses this mood, by contrast, into the stylized phrase or sentence. Of these sentences we might, à la Baudrillard himself, say that they are completely memorable, wholly forgettable. But this observation should be taken as praise, because it is precisely this sense of fleeting reality which expresses the postmodern mood. (Bryan S. Turner, 'Cruising America', in Chris Rojek and Bryan S. Turner, eds, *Forget Baudrillard?*, London and New York: Routledge, 1993, pp. 146–61 (pp. 152–3, 160).)

Superficiality from this perspective is a positive characteristic – a refusal to become bogged down in tired old metanarrative debates that have long since outlived their usefulness (has capitalism reached its final crisis?, and so on). Cruising is a form of nomadism, and as such a justifiable response to a culture that has turned its back on meaning. Where Kellner seeks ideological engagement and searching critique, Turner appreciates the sheer lack of these, taking it to be more true to the postmodern ethos to swerve away from judgement in this manner. Their sharply divided responses are only too typical of postmodernism's reception in the intellectual community.

Postmodernism's insistence that we examine all narrative treatments of cultural history very carefully for any evidence of metanarrative 'contamination' has had a profound effect on historical scholarship in general. Hayden White was one of the first to draw attention to the ideological implications of the narrative frameworks of traditional history writing with his concept of 'metahistory':

> I treat the historical work as what it manifestly is: a verbal structure in the form of a narrative prose discourse. Histories (and philosophies of history as well) combine a certain amount of 'data,' theoretical concepts for 'explaining' these data, and a narrative structure for their presentation as an icon of sets of events presumed to have occurred in times past. In addition, I maintain, they contain a deep structural content which is generally poetic, and specifically linguistic, in nature, and which serves as the precritically accepted paradigm of what a distinctively 'historical' explanation should be. This paradigm functions as the 'metahistorical' element in all historical works that are more comprehensive in scope than the monograph or archival report. (Hayden White, *Metahistory: The Historical Imagination in Nineteenth-century Europe*, Baltimore, MD and London: Johns Hopkins University Press, 1973, p. ix.)

The notion of a 'precritically accepted paradigm' suggests the workings of ideology on the historical consciousness, in which case we should be sceptical of all claims that history represents a truthful and accurate record of the past. History is rather metahistory – history written from a particular point of view, which dictates that certain concerns will dominate the narrative to the exclusion of other, potentially equally valid, ones. What White has done is to introduce the notion of relativism into historical writing, something to be developed further by postmodernist historians eager to attack the *status quo* of their discipline.

A specifically postmodern approach to history has indeed emerged in recent years with figures such as James Vernon and Patrick Joyce to the fore. Vernon's work on nineteenth-century English constitutional history is unashamedly enthusiastic in its adoption of a postmodern perspective:

> In these historic times politics are back in fashion. The apparent about turn of the forward march of labour, the Right's electoral successes on both sides of the Atlantic during the 1980s and 1990s, and the collapse of the Berlin Wall in 1989, have led many to reassess their understanding of politics. For some there is a distinct millennial feel to this postmodern world, one in which all the narratives we need to explain and understand politics have disintegrated before our very eyes; while for others these events represent not so much a defeat as a triumph, a triumph of just one narrative, liberalism. Critical to this rethinking of politics has been our understanding of the ways in which political identities, subjectivities, and constituencies of support are created. Just as commentators have chronicled the increasing power of the media in shaping our perceptions of politics, so postmodernist critical theory has turned our attention to the decentred subject and the discursive techniques by which the narrative forms of language construct political subjectivities as stable and coherent. As ever somewhat belatedly, and certainly in Britain somewhat begrudgingly, a new 'cultural history' which critically engages with such postmodernist insights has begun to emerge, one which offers us the possibility of expanding our concept of politics and political history. Although, like a bad smell they wished would go away, most political historians have tried to ignore these new developments, they do have far-reaching implications for the study of nineteenth-century English politics …
>
> One of the attractions of such a cultural approach is as a remedy for the deficiencies of the current narratives of nineteenth-century political history, with their triumphalist accounts of the development of England's democratic and libertarian constitution. (James Vernon, *Politics and the People: A Study in English Political Culture, c. 1815–1867*, Cambridge: Cambridge University Press, 1993, p. 1.)

Vernon's objective, therefore, is to undermine the established meta-narratives of nineteenth-century English political history on the grounds that these have hidden ideological agendas that continue to affect our perception of our world. What he has in mind particularly are those 'tory narratives' which have set out to

> reject the liberal fiction that nineteenth-century politics was about the seemingly ceaseless progression to a liberal democratic constitution. Instead, for tories, England's libertarian tradition lies not in the struggle for democracy, but in the struggle for a prosperous, entrepreneurial Protestant nation. (Vernon, *Politics and the People*, p. 2.)

In other words, tory narratives function as metahistories and it is the task of the postmodern historian to counter these by drawing our attention to all the various little narratives of the historical period in question. The postmodern historian takes on the political consensus that, in the traditional manner of metanarratives, is marginalising alternative viewpoints. In the process of resurrecting these excluded little narratives, history becomes a site of ideological conflict and historians like Vernon treat it as their duty to 'expand' the range of political history as much as possible. No matter what its detractors may say, the postmodern is the political for a thinker like Vernon. Relativism takes on a specifically political edge from this perspective, far removed from the mere iconoclasm of anti-postmodernist legend.

As Vernon indicates, the introduction of postmodernist theory into historical research has upset traditionalists quite considerably. One such is the eminent social historian of early modern society, Lawrence Stone, whose critical remarks on the subject in the prestigious journal *Past and Present* sparked off a controversy in the early 1990s:

> During the last twenty-five years, the subject matter of history – that is events and behaviour – and the data – that is contemporary texts – and the problem – that is explanation of change over time – have all been brought seriously into question, thus throwing the profession, more especially in France and America, into a crisis of self-confidence about what it is doing and how it is doing it. The first threat comes from linguistics, building up from Saussure to Derrida, and climaxing in deconstruction, according to which there is nothing besides the text, each one wide open to personal interpretation irrespective of the intentions of the author. Texts thus become a mere hall of mirrors reflecting nothing but each other, and throwing no light upon the 'truth', which does not exist. …

> The second development, at first enormously liberating and finally rather threatening, comes from the influence of cultural and symbolic anthropology as developed by a brilliant group of scholars headed by Clifford Geertz, Victor Turner, Mary Douglas and others. Their work has influenced many of the best historians of the last decade, especially in America and France. But the cultural historian and the symbolic anthropologist part company where the latter says 'the real is as imagined as the imaginary'. This presumably means that both are merely a set of semiotic codes governing all representations of life; that the material is dissolved into meaning; and that the text is left unconnected with the context.
>
> The third threat comes from New Historicism. At first sight a welcome return to a study of the text in its geographical, temporal, social, economic and intellectual context, it has turned out to be a variant of the symbolic and semiotic view of cultural productions, in which language is 'the medium in which the real is constructed and apprehended'. As a result, New Historicism treats political, institutional and social practices as 'cultural scripts', or discursive sets of symbolic systems or codes. (Lawrence Stone, 'History and Post-Modernism', *Past and Present*, 131, May 1991, pp. 217–18.)

Stone's language suggests this is much more than just a standard professional disagreement over approaches to history and history writing; for him, the very future of the subject is at stake. Taking up the challenge, he presents himself as someone willing to fight the notion that 'history might be on the way to becoming an endangered species' (Ibid., p. 218). As so often in the traditionalist response to postmodern theory, we have the sense of a siege mentality; of the barbarians being at the gates.

That stance soon came under attack, with Patrick Joyce taking up the fight on behalf of the postmodernists. The polemical tone of Joyce's rejoinder reminds us of just how high passions can run in debates over the postmodern:

> It is good that postmodernism has at last been brought into open view in the pages of *Past and Present*. Whether a one-and-a-half page polemical 'note' is the best way to have initiated debate is another matter. In fact, Stone is not interested in debate, but in denunciation. …
>
> The major advance of 'post-modernism' needs to be registered by historians: namely that the events, structures and processes of the

> past are indistinguishable from the forms of documentary representation, the conceptual and political appropriations, and the historical discourses that construct them. Once this is conceded the foundations of the 'social history' paradigm are greatly weakened, the paradigm that arguably informs much of the rationale of *Past and Present*. A recognition of the irreducibly discursive character of the social undermines the idea of social totality. There is no overarching coherence evident in either the polity, the economy or the social system. What there are are instances (texts, events, ideas, and so on) that have social contexts which are essential to their meaning, but there is no underlying structure to which they can be referred as expressions or effects. Thus with the notion of social totality goes the notion of social determination, so central to 'social history'. The certainty of a materialist link to the social is likewise broken. Gone too are the grand narratives that historicized the notion of social totality. Responding to the anti-reductionist logic of post-modernism means, therefore, thinking about new versions of the social, ones that require historians to be the inquisitors and perhaps the executioners of old valuations. Whatever the outcome, what must be questioned is the sanctity of 'history' as a distinct form of knowledge predicated upon the autonomy of the social. Stone's pre-emptive strike on 'post-modernism' is not a defence of history *per se*, but of one particular approach to the past. New approaches and new kinds of history are now on the agenda. (Patrick Joyce, 'History and Post-Modernism', *Past and Present*, 133, November 1991, pp. 204–9 (pp. 204, 208–9).)

Stone's 'crisis of confidence' is argued to be merely the crisis of a particular metanarrative, which is facing a paradigm shift. Such shifts, as we will discover when we turn to Thomas Kuhn's model of scientific history in Chapter four, demand the adoption of one position and the rejection of the other: *either* traditional social history *or* postmodernist social history. Paradigms do *not* speak unto paradigms, and a belief in foundations of discourse and a commitment to relativism cannot co-exist. As we have seen in so many other areas of discourse, postmodernism has a tendency to divide disciplines. You follow Stone and his associates, or you follow Joyce, Vernon and theirs; and whichever route you choose, you find yourself with a ready-made body of bitter enemies within your own profession.

In a companion piece to that of Joyce, the case is put for an anti-traditionalist, postmodern approach to the subject of women's history:

> An aggressive attitude may have to be adopted towards the sources themselves, concentrating not on the most obvious interpretation, but on secondary layers of meaning. Reading historical material for information about women automatically means reading against the grain, since many sources share Stone's conviction that 'events and behaviour' are the proper subject of history, relegating the repetitive and everyday matters in which most women were involved to the margins, if their existence is acknowledged at all. (Catriona Kelly, 'History and Post-Modernism', *Past and Present*, 133, November 1991, pp. 209–13 (pp. 212–13).)

Kelly's complaint is that women have never really been part of the metanarrative process, and that anything that calls the latter into question, as postmodernism plainly does, can only be for the benefit of those engaged in the task of writing women's history. The positive political role of postmodern theory comes to the fore yet again – as does its potential to split disciplines into opposing camps.

Social relations are a key concern of business theorists, too – in this case, social relations as they apply within business organisations. In the modern era, these relations tend to be very hierarchical in form, and most business theory is designed to reinforce this model. In recent years, however, postmodernism has provided more radical practitioners with the impetus for a wide-ranging reconsideration of existing methods of research into organisational structures. K. Gergen, for example, regards postmodern theory as the basis for a new conception of organisations and the social relations obtaining within them:

> For the greater part of the twentieth century the major approach to organizational study has been modernist, mixing both romanticist and modernist metaphors of human functioning, but in general attempting to lay bare the essentials. Or, in Lyotard's ... terms, organizational theorists have participated in the grand modernist narrative of progress. It is a story we repeat to ourselves in order to justify what we do, one that says that with a combination of rigorous rationality and methodology we can move ever closer to knowledge of the object (and thus toward rational decisions regarding its welfare). It is the seriousness of this grand narrative that postmodernists would challenge, for not only is it mystifying, but it generates zero-sum conflicts and suppresses a multitude of alternative voices. Rather than founders

of the 'last word' (where in the beginning was the word of God), we should perhaps view ourselves as balloon craftsmen – setting aloft vehicles for public amusement. ...

Finally, means must be sought for opening the organizational doors to alien realities. For example, minority voices, voices of dissensus within the organization, must be invited to speak out; and, although unsettling the fluid operation of the organization, their messages must be made intelligible, absorbed and integrated. Organizational members should also be encouraged in alternative pursuits – to master alternative argots, from various fields of study, politics, sports, the arts, foreign cultures, specialty clubs, and the like. Instead of detracting from the time devoted to organizational ends, and engendering 'peculiar' points of view, such extraneous pursuits will enrich the realm of signification within. Minority hiring should not be viewed as an obligation so much as an opportunity for expanding the discursive (and practical) capacities of the organization. And organizations might wisely invite criticism – from various political, intellectual and moral corners – not with an intent to improve their defensive skills, but to understand and incorporate alternative realities. Again, constant challenges to the smooth coordination of internal realities are essential to organizational vitality. Or, more bluntly, if everything is running smoothly the organization is in trouble.

The result of this constant challenge to naturally occurring tendencies toward consensus will be, from the present standpoint, the prevention of hegemonic tendencies of various sub-units (including high-level management) within the firm and the more complete integration of the organization into the surrounding environment. (K. Gergen, 'Organization Theory in the Postmodern Era', in M. Reed and M. Hughes, eds, *Rethinking Organization: New Directions in Organizational Theory and Analysis*, London: Sage, 1992, pp. 207–26 (pp. 215–16, 223).)

Organisations (and traditional organisational theory) are equated with modernity, thus becoming subject to postmodern critique, with Gergen arguing the case for an 'edge of chaos' model for organisational existence: '[I]f everything is running smoothly the organization is in trouble.' In this particular postmodern turn, internal tension is a marker of successful operation rather than, as traditionalists (with their unshakeable commitment to order) would tend to see it, a threat to the organisation's very existence. What Gergen is calling for is a complete recasting of organisational structure such that it more closely resembles the world outside, with all the latter's many disorders and social tensions; as he puts it, a deliberate blurring of the 'misleading distinction between *inside* and *outside* the organization' (Ibid., p. 223). From this perspective, organisations are currently repressive institutions that present a barrier to necessary social change. But as with much postmodern thought, there is a highly idealistic quality to Gergen's analysis. One wonders just how receptive market-orientated organisations would be to such potentially disorienting procedures, especially if they affected profit margins adversely for any length of time.

Steve Linstead's deconstructive approach to the study of organisations argues that new conceptions of subjectivity, as well as of the way in which meaning is produced by individuals, demand that we 'read' organisations in a different way than we have done in the past:

> Organizations, as texts, are ... partially constitutive of the subjectivity of those who are involved in their production. Similarly, they seek to constitute the subjectivity of this readership, their style, strategy and context 'interpellating' them [attracting their attention], inviting participation in a certain way. Nevertheless, 'readers' bring their awareness of other texts, other cultural forms, other evocations and explosions of meaning to their reading of any text, and enter into the text, changing its nature and re-producing it as they consume it. ... Current approaches to organizational analysis are dominated by the oppositional approach which sets integrated, whole self-conscious and centred individuals against each other, hierarchically arranging and aggregating them in groups, subgroups, subcultures and cultures, and many of the problems of organizational analysis are a logical outcome of this analytical practice. This is recognizable as the embodiment of logocentrism, the philosophy of presence that assumes 'natural' categories (for example individual, organization, group structure, function) which become prioritized and normalized.
>
> This habit is deeply engrained in the social sciences, in theorizing, research practice, and pedagogy, and in the study of organizations [it] becomes emblematic in one form in the overwhelming concentration on the concept of 'shared meaning' as definitive of cultural forms; as does the alternative but complementary formulation of subcultural fragmentation. Supplementarity indicates that 'shared meaning' is impossible, always incomplete;[17] differance that it [shared meaning] exists in continual fluidity with its own negation, paradox and ambi-

guity being its essential qualities rather than occasional surprises or problems at the margin. *'Shared meaning' is nothing more than the deferral of differance*. Viewing 'organizational culture' in this way we should *expect* it to be paradoxical, being unsurprised by Young's (1989)[18] observation that strong cultures may mark strong internal division – this embodies the supplementary principle of return that is entirely to be expected. However, we must look elsewhere than to the aggregation of self-conscious rational minds pursuing their interests at a group level to explain or respond to its emergence.

Organization then is continuously emergent, constituted and constituting, produced and consumed by subjects who, like organizations, are themselves fields of the trace, sites of intertextuality. The emphasis in investigation then must be away from oppositional, interpretative strategies towards supplementary, representational ones, towards those processes which *shape* subjectivity rather than the process by which individual subjects act upon the world. (Steve Linstead, 'Deconstruction in the Study of Organizations', in John Hassard and Martin Parker, eds, *Postmodernism and Organisations*, London: Sage, 1993, pp. 49–70 (pp. 59, 60).)

Again, it is a case of postmodern thought providing the opportunity to rethink how structures function and whether they are being held back by the weight of received authority in their own particular area of operation. The metanarrative of business practice, with its essentially top-down approach to organisation and operation (higher management handing out directives to middle management for implementation at the levels underneath them in turn), is being challenged by commentators such as Linstead, who stand as representative of a rapidly growing body of literature.[19]

The implication for religion of the rise of postmodernism has also been a topic of some debate of late, especially in the area of the sociology of religion. The Church has traditionally seen itself as a centre of authority. Postmodern theory, as we know, poses problems for all structures of authority, encouraging a sceptical attitude towards these. While some Christian theologians have felt threatened by postmodern scepticism and relativism, others have been more sympathetic to its critique of modernity and its works:

What is the true task of theology? What are the conditions for meeting that task? These questions can appear unanswerable in the present

> situation of disarray in normative reflection. Currently theology appears to lack a common framework of normative concepts and meanings with which to proceed. The problem of the perceived *loss of framework* is widely recognised as severe, because postmodern criticism of the principle of subjectivity and its successor concepts seem to undercut any possibility for clearing a foundation on which a framework could be constructed. This situation leads back to literature because the first step in moving beyond the impasse of the loss of a framework becomes that of telling the story of the loss of framework. Many suppose that constructing the narrative of the demise of theology's framework itself can orientate our questions concerning the task of theology. …
>
> As I understand theology's plight, it involves more than the loss of framework. Even if the framework problem were solved, theology's problem would remain: if theology's task is construed as to speak authentically of God and so to contribute to cultural and social reintegration in a world whose values are in disarray, theology has not yet faced the tragic quality of its defeat in the modern world. Theology has been defeated as a voice having something to contribute to the modern social system. Theology has not, however, been defeated by postmodern criticism, and it misconstrues its situation if it thinks so. If theology has an adversary, it is not postmodern discourse.
>
> On the contrary, theology has been defeated by the lawfulness inherent in the modern global economy. Even if theology does have something to say to or about those within the modern world system, they have no ears to hear. Why? In the highly competitive market economy, certain traits of character, deliberation and action come to prevail because they provide advantages. These traits assume the force of necessity and drive out other possibilities. (David E. Klemm, 'Back to Literature – and Theology?', in David Jasper, ed., *Postmodernism, Literature and the Future of Theology*, Basingstoke and London: Macmillan, 1993, pp. 180–90 (pp. 180–1).)

There is a sense here that theology and postmodernism share an enemy; both dislike modernity's promotion of conformity and eradication of difference. It is just possible that the postmodern mind could be more open to dialogue with theology than the modern has tended to be. Certainly, excessive rationality has never been a friend to religion. Co-existence, and dialogue, with the postmodern might be the preferable option for contemporary theology.

The postmodern certainly seems to encourage such dialogue:

> [T]he practitioners of postmodern theorization appear to incorporate quasi-religious thematics into their texts. ... Characteristically, modern thought seeks to reduce the burden of what it identified as 'irrational' phenomena by showing that they are traceable to an error, a failure of reason, or else that they secretly subserve rational purposes: for example, Freud traced pathological mental phenomena to failures of self-recognition, but also showed how irrational manifestations help us to cope with the subjectively intolerable. Yet Nietzsche and his contemporary French followers do not, on the whole, seek to show that the apparently strange and arbitrary is not purely arbitrary. On the contrary, they seek to demonstrate almost the reverse: that apparently rational, common-sense assumptions about self-identity, motivation and moral values themselves disguise historically instituted mythological constructs. So, for example, the whole complex of attitudes to do with free will and guilt is but a rationalization of a low degree of power, and plebeian *ressentiment* [resentment]. Where modernity lifted the burden of power and obscurity in favour of a light-travelling reason, postmodern hyper-reason makes arbitrary power into the hydra-headed but repetitious monster whose toils we can never escape, yet whom we should joyfully embrace.[20]
>
> ... [E]very socially instituted creed and code of practice must lack foundations beyond the essence that it creates through its own self-elaboration. Religion will not depart, because *all* social phenomena are arbitrary and therefore 'religious'. (John Milbank, 'Problematizing the Secular: The Post-postmodern Agenda', in Philippa Berry and Andrew Wernick, eds, *Shadow of Spirit: Postmodernism and Religion*, London and New York: Routledge, 1992, pp. 30–44 (pp. 30, 31).)

There is a mystical quality to postmodern thought, therefore, that brings it close to the religious outlook. Faith, after all, lacks rational foundations, which puts it at odds with modernity no less than postmodern relativism. Then, too, postmodernism's emphasis on the power of the sublime echoes the religious concept of divine omnipotence, both inaccessible to the human. In each case, the limits of human reason are being acknowledged.

Ernest Gellner considers the paradox of the co-existence of postmodernism and Islamic fundamentalism in our world, and concludes that collectively they provide an excellent advertisement for the benefits of the Enlightenment project, or 'Enlightenment Rationalist Fundamentalism' as he chooses to call its method. Postmodernism, in this reading, is an extreme form of relativism for which no philosophical or sociological case whatsoever can be made. Unattractive though it is in most ways to the Enlightenment supporter, religious fundamentalism is less reprehensible. It can even be said to 'deserve our respect' for having created the cultural conditions in which the Enlightenment could occur (Ernest Gellner, *Postmodernism, Reason and Religion*, London and New York: Routledge, 1992, p. 95). However, no such benefit of the doubt is extended to postmodernism:

> Postmodernism is a contemporary movement. It is strong and fashionable. Over and above this, it is not altogether clear what the devil it is. In fact, clarity is not conspicuous amongst its marked attributes. It not only generally fails to practise it, but also on occasion actually repudiates it. But anyway, there appear to be no 39 postmodernist Articles of faith, no postmodernist Manifesto, which one could consult so as to assure oneself that one has identified its ideas properly.
>
> ... Postmodernism would seem to be rather clearly in favour of relativism, in as far as it is capable of clarity, and hostile to the idea of unique, exclusive, objective, external or transcendent truth. Truth is elusive, polymorphous, inward, subjective ... and perhaps a few further things as well. Straightforward it is not. My real concern is with *relativism*: the postmodernist movement, which is an ephemeral cultural fashion, is of interest as a living and contemporary specimen of relativism, which as such is of some importance and will remain with us for a long time.
>
> ... Postmodernism as such doesn't matter too much. It is a fad which owes its appeal to its seeming novelty and genuine obscurity, and it will pass soon enough, as such fashions do. But it is a specimen of relativism, and relativism does matter. Relativism isn't objectionable because it entails moral nihilism (which it *does*); moral nihilism may be hard to escape in any case. It is objectionable because it leads to *cognitive* nihilism, which is simply false, and also because it possibly misrepresents the way in which we actually understand societies and cultures. It denies or obscures tremendous differences in cognition and technical power, differences which are crucial for the understanding of current developments of human society. A vision which

> obscures that which matters most cannot be sound. (Gellner, *Postmodernism, Reason and Religion*, pp. 22–3, 24, 71–2.)

Equally, Islamic fundamentalism is a living and contemporary specimen of religious fundamentalism, although it has an inner integrity that is signally lacking in the postmodern project:

> Muslim fundamentalism is an enormously simple, powerful, earthy, sometimes cruel, absorbing, socially fortifying movement, which gives a sense of direction and orientation to millions of men and women, many of whom live lives of bitter poverty and are subject to harsh oppression. It enables them to adjust to a new anonymous mass society by identifying with the old, long-established High Culture of their own faith, and explaining their own deprivation and humiliation as a punishment for having strayed from the true path, rather than a consequence of never having found it. (Gellner, *Postmodernism, Reason and Religion*, p. 72.)

Islamic fundamentalism is, quite unashamedly, a metanarrative, and Gellner is more able to countenance this than what is to him the nihilistic relativism of the postmodern cause. The former may not be to the personal taste of an Enlightenment rationalist fundamentalist, but the latter has no social utility at all that Gellner can detect. On the one hand we have deep, if misguided, faith; but on the other, there is mere fashion which will soon pass.

Gellner's book was originally intended to be part of a joint project with the Islamic scholar Akbar S. Ahmed, which the publisher eventually decided to put out as two separate volumes. Ahmed is far less critical of postmodernism than Gellner, and even argues that Islam must come to an accommodation with it – for its own ultimate benefit:

> Faith versus scepticism, tradition versus iconoclasm, purity versus eclecticism – it is difficult to relate Islamic postmodernism to Western postmodernism in any coherent or direct manner, or even to establish a causal relationship between the two. Although Muslims may employ some of the conceptual tools of [Jean-]François Lyotard or Jean Baudrillard for analysis, there must be a parting of company on certain crucial points. While Muslims appreciate the spirit of tolerance, optimism and the drive for self-knowledge in postmodernism, they also recognize the threat it poses them with its cynicism and

> irony. This is a challenge to the faith and piety which lies at the core of their world-view. …
>
> The postmodernist age in the 1990s hammers at the doors of Muslim *ijtihad* [innovation]; Muslims ignore the din at their peril. Before they creak open the door, however, they must know the power and nature of the age and for that they must understand those who represent it. These include figures they do not admire, like the singer Madonna and the writer [Salman] Rushdie. More important, Muslims must understand why these figures represent the age. The onslaught comes when Muslims are at their weakest: corrupt rulers, incompetent administrators and feeble thinkers mark their societies. For all the rhetoric and symbolic form, the spirit of Islam is often palpably missing from their endeavours, while, more than ever, *ijtihad* is urgently needed where women, education and politics are involved. The old methods and the old certainties will not hold the forces swirling and eddying around Muslim societies; there can be no edulcoration [purification] of Muslim society without a comprehension of the non-Muslim age we live in. (Akbar S. Ahmed, *Postmodernism and Islam: Predicament and Promise*, London and New York: Routledge, 1992, pp. 5–6, 260.)

Religious fundamentalism is explained away by Ahmed as part of a larger pattern of fundamentalism that has insinuated itself into the contemporary world:

> One truth has emerged in our postmodernist world: that the concept of fundamentalism, as the media applies it, cannot be restricted to religion. Although Marxism-Leninism, fundamentalist communism, is disintegrating, for more than half a century it dominated large parts of the world. … Market fundamentalism has also influenced the World Bank and the International Monetary Fund in their prescriptions for poorer economies. As with the Christian fundamentalists, the values most prized by messianic capitalists are discipline, sobriety and hard work. (Ahmed, *Postmodernism and Islam*, p. 16.)

Islamic fundamentalism is not unique, therefore, and like all other current forms of fundamentalism it needs to be exposed to postmodernism's tolerance, optimism and commitment to self-knowledge. Ultimately, postmodernism represents a stimulating challenge to Islam, which needs to engage with this movement of thought if it is to revitalise itself. It is a conclusion that has an even greater sense of urgency to it now than it did when its author put it forward a decade ago, with various groups around the globe openly calling for *jihad*, or holy war, against the West.

We will return to the topic of Islamic fundamentalism in a postmodern world at the end of this chapter. As we will discover, opinions on its value as a metanarrative have become even more sharply divided than they were when Ahmed's book was published.

Political Theory

In political terms, postmodernism represents not just the rise of pluralism but the end of the fixed positions of left and right that had characterised the culture of modernity. The result is a situation that is very fluid, yet also very bewildering to anyone used to the clear-cut divisions of modernist politics in which all knew where they stood:

> The otherwise misty term 'post-structuralism' also has a political meaning in post-modernity: it indicates the social and political prevalence of the functional over the structural, the gradual weakening, if not total disappearance of, a politics based solely on class interests and class perceptions. This statement is not an assertion of (non-existing) social harmony in today's western society. Rather it is a comment upon the character of its internal conflicts. The traditional social collisions, mostly economic in nature, remain virulent in all inconsistently welfarist countries or in countries where a neo-conservative trend tends to weaken the welfarist character of society. Above all, state and trade[s] unions are bitterly enmeshed in them, and violent economic conflicts between state and class-based organizations characterize modern politics *sui generis*. However, alongside the mainstream, unmistakable trends of postmodern politics emerge both on the right and the left which are function-based and function-targeted in a double sense. They are, in the first place, aiming at the strengthening or elimination respectively of a single function of modernity. These are the movements which overwhelmingly appear as single-issue actions and which are the epitomes of functionalist-postmodern politics. Secondly, once again both on the right and the left, there are more general attempts at rearranging the given network of functions in a particular society. The trends and upheavals in today's politics simply cannot be understood in modernist-class categories, for their interpretation in strictly structural (class) terms would lead to absurd

> results. Paradigmatic examples of such postmodernist-functionalist trends are [Margaret] Thatcher's project of a 'popular capitalism' on the extreme right end of the political spectrum and May 1968 in Paris on the radical-leftist end. … 'Being after', therefore, means in this sense, 'being after the class scenarios'. …
>
> The dominant temporality of post-modernity has serious political implications as well. Redemptive politics of any kind are incompatible with the postmodern political condition. … The postmodern self-limitation to the present as our one and only eternity also excludes experiments with 'leaps into *nihil*', that is, attempts at the *absolute* transcendence of modernity. At the same time, the postmodern political condition is tremendously ill at ease with Utopianism of even a non-Messianic type, which makes it vulnerable to easy compromises with the present as well as susceptible to 'doomsday myths' and collective fears stemming from the loss of future. (Agnes Heller and Ferenc Fehér, *The Postmodern Political Condition*, Cambridge and Oxford: Polity Press and Blackwell, 1988, pp. 2–3, 4.)

The volatile nature of politics in a postmodern age is well captured by this analysis. When class ceases to be a significant factor of political life, as most postmodern commentators seem to have agreed it has in the West, then new networks of interests certainly become possible; but without any larger goal than the mere supersession of modernity, politics takes on a worryingly *ad hoc* quality. Heller and Fehér go on to speak of postmodernism as involving an 'anything goes' mentality (Ibid., p. 139). There is a moral vacuum in the postmodern political condition that the left is going to find very problematical. The authors conclude, however, that postmodernism cannot be positioned in conventional political terms as either reactionary or radical, and that in fact it renders such labels largely 'irrelevant' (Ibid.). Like it or not, we are in new socio-political terrain and will have to learn to make significant adjustments.

For Iris Marion Young, the main adjustment required from us in this new terrain is a move away from the notion of community towards a deconstruction-derived 'politics of difference', in which a multiplicity of viewpoints is given the opportunity to flourish:

> Radical theorists and activists often appeal to an ideal of community as an alternative to the oppression and exploitation they argue characterize capitalist patriarchal society. Such appeals often do not explicitly articulate the meaning of the concept of community, but

> rather tend to evoke an affective value. Even more rarely do those who invoke an ideal of community as an alternative to capitalist patriarchal society ask what it presupposes or implies, or what it means concretely to institute a society that embodies community. I raise a number of critical questions about the meaning, presuppositions, implications and practical import of the ideal of community.
>
> I criticize the notion of community on both philosophical and practical grounds. I argue that the ideal of community participates in what Derrida calls the metaphysics of presence or Adorno calls the logic of identity, a metaphysics that denies difference. The ideal of community presumes subjects who are present to themselves and presumes subjects can understand one another as they understand themselves. It thus denies the difference between subjects. The desire for community relies on the same desire for social wholeness and identification that underlies racism and ethnic chauvinism, on the one hand, and political sectarianism on the other. …
>
> The ideal of community … totalizes and detemporalizes its conception of social life by setting up an opposition between authentic and inauthentic social relations. It also detemporalizes its understanding of social change by positing the desired society as the complete negation of existing society. It thus provides no understanding of the move from here to there that would be rooted in an understanding of the contradictions and possibilities of existing society.
>
> I propose that instead of community as the normative ideal of political emancipation, that radicals should develop a politics of difference. A model of the unoppressive city offers an understanding of social relations without domination in which persons live together in relations of mediation among strangers with whom they are not in community. … The social differentiation of the city also provides a positive inexhaustibility of human relations. The possibility always exists of becoming acquainted with new and different people, with different cultural and social experience; the possibility always exists for new groups to form or emerge around specific interests. (Iris Marion Young, 'The Ideal of Community and the Politics of Difference', *Social Theory and Practice*, 12, 1986, pp. 1–26 (pp. 1, 2, 22).)

Postmodern culture demands a 'politics of difference' as far as Young is concerned, and it is in the city – or an idealised form of it that may not exist everywhere as yet – that the inspiration for this practice will be found. We might say that a politics of difference represents a more formalised version of Lyotard's notion of 'little narratives', through which we seek to create the right conditions for such narratives to thrive. It also seems to draw on Deleuze and Guattari's rhizomatic models, with new connections being constructable between any two points of the social whole, without reference to any central mechanism of control.

There are many other adjustments that need to be made to our world-view by the close of the twentieth century. For Paul Virilio, for example, the changing nature of politics in a postmodern world is intimately bound up with the notion of speed. Virilio sees late twentieth-century life as an extension of trends traceable back into modernity, when speed of response (by the military, for example) became one of the major objectives of industrialised Western societies. The logical outcome of this obsession with speed of response is a culture dominated by its technology:

> The reduction of distances has become a strategic reality bearing incalculable economic and political consequences, since it corresponds to the negation of space. ... Contraction in time, the disappearance of the territorial space, after that of the fortified city and armor, leads to a situation in which the notions of 'before' and 'after' designate only the future and the past in a form of war that causes the 'present' to disappear in the instantaneousness of decision.
>
> The final power would thus be less one of imagination than of anticipation, so much so that to govern would be *no more than* to foresee, simulate, memorize the simulations ...
>
> The loss of material space leads to the government of nothing but time. ... In this precarious fiction speed would suddenly become a destiny, a form of progress. (Paul Virilio, *Speed and Politics: An Essay on Dromology*, trans. Mark Polizzotti, New York: Semiotext(e), 1986, pp. 140–1.)

Virilio's is a nightmare vision, prefiguring Lyotard's *The Inhuman* in its suspicion of the goals of techno-science.[21] Speed has the capacity to destroy all criticism and dissent, and in that sense represents the logical culmination of modernity's desire for total control over humanity and all its actions – or, as Virilio puts it, our destiny. The end of history beckons, with geopolitics meanwhile being reduced to time-management as a way of gaining the advantage over one's enemies. In such a society we would have the instant gratification of which Daniel Bell was so critical, but this time around for far more sinister purposes than personal pleasure. What

Virilio sketches out is a form of society in which the human dimension is eclipsed by technology, simply because the latter is more efficient (that is, quicker) at decision-making. Nuclear war with humanity as powerless onlookers is only one of the alarming prospects raised by such a scenario.[22]

However, for many theorists postmodern theory holds out the possibility of a more creative approach to geopolitical affairs than previously. In the field of international relations theory, for example, Rob Walker has been particularly enthusiastic about the impact postmodernism has the potential to make:

> As a theory, or complex of theories, constituted through claims about sovereign identity in space and time, international relations simply takes for granted that which seems to me to have become most problematic. I prefer to assume that any analysis of contemporary world politics that takes the principle of sovereign identity in space and time as an unquestioned assumption about the way the world is – as opposed to an often tenuous claim made as part of the practices of modern subjects, including the legitimation practices of modern states – can only play with analogies and metaphors taken from discourses in which this assumption is also taken for granted …
>
> While my explicit focus is on modern Anglo-American theories of international relations, and on attempts to develop a critical posture towards them, I am also concerned with broader theoretical analyses of the rearticulation of spatiotemporal relations in late or postmodernity, and with what the specific experiences of international relations theory might tell us about the limits of our ability to comprehend and respond to contemporary spatiotemporal transformations more generally. Reading theories of international relations as a constitutive horizon of modern politics in the territorial state, I want to clarify some of the difficulties besetting attempts to envisage any other kind of politics, whether designated as a world politics encompassing the planet, as a local politics arising from particular places, or as somehow both at once – the possibility that seems to me to be both the most interesting but also the one that is explicitly denied by modernist assumptions about sovereign identity in space and time. …
>
> To pursue speculations about the transformative quality of contemporary trajectories with any theoretical rigour … is necessarily to put in doubt the spatial resolution of all philosophical options that is expressed by the principle of state sovereignty – a resolution which is in any case always in doubt and subject to constant deferral,[23] as well

> as subject to constant attempts to affirm its natural necessity. To put the point as succinctly as possible: if it is true that contemporary political life is increasingly characterised by processes of temporal acceleration, then we should expect to experience increasingly disconcerting incongruities between new articulations of power and accounts of political life predicated on the early-modern fiction that temporality can be fixed and tamed within the spatial coordinates of territorial jurisdictions. (R. B. J. Walker, *Inside/Outside: International Relations as Political Theory*, Cambridge: Cambridge University Press, 1993, pp. 8, 9, 13–14.)

Postmodern theory enables Walker to challenge the assumptions that lie behind modernity's concept of state sovereignty (which, interestingly enough, Ahmed saw as one of the West's most poisoned gifts to an Islamic world that had never really thought in those terms before). Rather like Lyotard, Walker identifies a legitimation crisis as the root of the problem: state sovereignty is simply taken on trust by the general public and has no ultimate ground for its authority. In other words, state sovereignty, as traditionally conceived, acts in the manner of a grand narrative, thus preventing creative thought about territorial disputes. Given how many disputes around the world turn on the issue of who wields sovereign control (for example, the Middle East, Cyprus, Northern Ireland, the former Yugoslavia and various first nation claims),[24] Walker is right to draw our attention to the need for fresh thinking in this area. The general critique of ideological authority and its legitimation methods in postmodern theory provides the basis for such a new perspective to be constructed. The postmodern turn enables us to escape the clutches of traditional modes of political discourse.

Andrew Linklater has also argued for the need to go beyond existing paradigms in international relations, dominated as the field has been by Marxist and 'realist' models of analysis. Realists adopt an empirical approach to geopolitical problems, whereas Marxists and neo-Marxists operate according to their theory's universal scheme (with its commitment to class struggle and so on). For Linklater, neither theory offers a totally satisfactory account of relations between states, and he argues for a post-Marxist approach instead:

> A critical sociology of moral development in the sphere of intersocietal relations may be regarded as post-Marxist for the following reasons. Marx's social theory pointed to tensions between universal

> norms and particularistic practices in production relations. At no point did Marx develop an account of how similar tensions developed in other social relations involving the sexes, races, nations or ethnic groups, states and other independent political communities. Nor did Marx consider the modes of political conduct which would free subjects from the tensions which existed in these spheres of social interaction. The crucial point for present purposes is that Marx did not consider how the tension between universalism and particularism emerged in relations between independent political communities; and his social and political theory made no comment on how this tension might be resolved. For this reason Giddens is right to argue that Marx's thought is the starting-point for an emancipatory politics – nothing more and nothing less.[25] The significance of this remark is only now being recognised in the field of international relations. When its full import has been recognised, the study of international relations and critical social theory may merge in a comprehensive historical analysis of the struggle between universalising and particularising processes. (Andrew Linklater, *Beyond Realism and Marxism: Critical Theory and International Relations*, Basingstoke and London: Macmillan, 1990, p. 164.)

Although there is still a certain amount of sympathy displayed for Marxism in this account, the concern with the particular (as in the reference to the various 'social relations' ignored by Marx) brings to mind the postmodern emphasis on little narratives at the expense of grand. In its metanarrative form, Marxism is inhibiting progress in this area of enquiry – as it has in so many others. Marx's researches may provide a basis for geopolitical analysis, but they are not to be treated as holy writ. No theory from the past can be considered to hold all the answers for problems of the present, never mind those of the future.

The critic and cultural theorist Edward W. Said has identified a more general metanarrative to inhibit social progress, one that has also left a legacy of geopolitical problems. It is the metanarrative of the West, as applied in this instance to the Middle East. Said's term for this process of ideological domination is 'orientalism', and he is scathing of the detrimental impact it has had on Arab culture over the last few centuries:

> The Orient was almost a European invention, and had been since antiquity a place of romance, exotic beings, haunting memories and

> landscapes, remarkable experiences. ... The Orient is not only adjacent to Europe; it is also the place of Europe's greatest and richest and oldest colonies, the source of its civilizations and languages, its cultural contestant, and one of its deepest and most recurring images of the Other. In addition, the Orient has helped to define Europe (or the West) as its contrasting image, idea, personality, experience.
>
> ... Taking the late eighteenth century as a very roughly defined starting point Orientalism can be discussed and analyzed as the corporate institution for dealing with the Orient – dealing with it by making statements about it, authorizing views of it, describing it, by teaching it, settling it, ruling over it: in short, Orientalism as a Western style for dominating, restructuring, and having authority over the Orient. I have found it useful here to employ Michel Foucault's notion of a discourse, as described by him in *The Archaeology of Knowledge* and in *Discipline and Punish*, to identify Orientalism. My contention is that without examining Orientalism as a discourse one cannot possibly understand the enormously systematic discipline by which European culture was able to manage – and even produce – the Orient politically, sociologically, militarily, ideologically, scientifically, and imaginatively during the post-Enlightenment period. Moreover, so authoritative a position did Orientalism have that I believe no one writing, thinking, or acting on the Orient could do so without taking account of the limitations on thought and action imposed by Orientalism. In brief, because of Orientalism the Orient was not (and is not) a free subject of thought or action. (Edward W. Said, *Orientalism: Western Conceptions of the Orient*, 2nd edn, Harmondsworth: Penguin, 1995, pp. 1–2, 3.)

Orientalism is a product of the Enlightenment project and is a vital part of its metanarrative, which views the world according to its own ideas of material and technological progress. The Orient helps the West to define what that metanarrative is – the former's failure to meet Western standards of material and technological progress reinforcing the West's sense of socio-political superiority. As such, in a postmodern world it is a conception ripe for deconstruction; it is one more metanarrative that has outlived its time and whose repressive effects are only too plain to see in contemporary Middle Eastern politics.

Postmodernism may have rejected grand narratives, but the latter clearly still have their supporters. We have already seen in Chapter two how

Marxists are continuing to defend their own grand narrative against the onslaught of postmodern theorists. Similar spirited defences can also be found at the opposite end of the ideological spectrum. The political scientist Francis Fukuyama has famously argued that the fall of communism in Europe represents the ultimate victory of the Enlightenment project as embodied by Western liberal democracy. He also argued that we have reached the 'end of history', by which he means history in the 'clash of civilisations' sense, in which opposing ideologies attempt to triumph over each other. In Fukuyama's view,

> a remarkable consensus concerning the legitimacy of liberal democracy as a system of government had emerged throughout the world over the past few years, as it conquered rival ideologies like hereditary monarchy, fascism, and most recently communism. … It is possible that if events continue to unfold as they have done over the past few decades, that the idea of a universal and directional history leading up to liberal democracy may become more plausible to people, and that the relativist impasse of modern thought will in a sense solve itself. That is, cultural relativism (a European invention) has seemed plausible to our century because for the first time Europe found itself forced to confront non-European cultures in a serious way through the experience of colonialism and de-colonization. Many of the developments of the past century – the decline of the moral self-confidence of European civilization, the rise of the Third World, and the emergence of new ideologies – tended to reinforce belief in relativism. But if, over time, more and more societies with diverse cultures and histories exhibit similar long-term patterns of development; if there is a continuing convergence in the types of institutions governing most advanced societies; and if the homogenization of mankind continues as a result of economic development, then the idea of relativism may seem much stranger than it does now. … Rather than a thousand shoots blossoming into as many different flowering plants, mankind will come to seem like a long wagon train strung out along a road. Some wagons will be pulling into town sharply and crisply, while others will be bivouacked back in the desert, or else stuck in ruts in the final pass over the mountains. Several wagons, attacked by Indians, will have been set aflame and abandoned along the way. There will be a few wagoneers who, stunned by the battle, will have lost their sense of direction and are temporarily heading in the wrong direction, while one or two wagons will get tired of the

> journey and decide to set up permanent camps at particular points back along the road. Others will have found alternative routes to the main road, though they will discover that to get through the final mountain range they all must use the same pass. But the great majority of wagons will be making the slow journey into town, and most will eventually arrive there. (Francis Fukuyama, *The End of History and the Last Man*, London: Hamish Hamilton, 1992, pp. xi, 338–9.)

Fukuyama's image conjures up the western film genre, and is somewhat less than politically correct and multicultural in its slighting reference to Indians holding up the supposed onward march of Western civilisation. One could hardly be further away from postmodern ideals than here, given the author's insistence that there is only one point upon which all cultures should be converging. That is a totalitarian conclusion to a postmodernist, since it refuses to countenance difference.

Fukuyama's ideas were attacked vigorously by the left, most notably perhaps by Jacques Derrida, whose *Specters of Marx* took Fukuyama's claims of liberal democracy's cultural supremacy as its starting point to reach an accommodation between Marx and deconstruction (see Chapter two). More criticism of Fukuyama's theory of the end of history was to come after the events of 11 September 2001, when the World Trade Center Towers in New York were destroyed by terrorist attacks. The ensuing collision between the West and the Islamic world was felt by some to demolish Fukuyama's thesis of the triumph of liberal democracy. However, he was quick to reassert its validity against those critics:

> This view has been challenged by many people, and perhaps most articulately by Samuel Huntington.[26] He argued that rather than progressing towards a single global system, the world remained mired in a 'clash of civilisations' in which six or seven major cultural groups would co-exist without converging and constitute the new fracture lines of global conflict. Since the successful attack on the centre of global capitalism was evidently perpetrated by Islamic extremists unhappy with the very existence of western civilisation, observers have been handicapping the Huntington 'clash' view over my own 'end of history' hypothesis.
>
> I believe that in the end I remain right: modernity is a very powerful freight train that will not be derailed by recent events. Democracy and free markets will continue to expand as the dominant organising

> principles for much of the world. … But rather than psychologise the Muslim world, it makes more sense to ask whether radical Islam constitutes a serious alternative to western liberal democracy. (Radical Islam has virtually no appeal in the contemporary world apart from those who are culturally Islamic to begin with.) For Muslims themselves, political Islam has proved much more appealing in the abstract than in reality. After 23 years of rule by fundamentalist clerics, most Iranians, especially the young, would like to live in a far more liberal society. Afghans who have experienced Taliban rule feel much the same. Anti-American hatred does not translate into a viable political program for Muslim societies to follow.
>
> We remain at the end of history because there is only one system that will continue to dominate world politics, that of the liberal-democratic west. This does not imply a world free from conflict, nor the disappearance of culture. But the struggle we face is not the clash of several distinct and equal cultures fighting amongst one another like the great powers of 19th-century Europe. The clash consists of a series of rearguard actions from societies whose traditional existence is indeed threatened by modernisation. The strength of the backlash reflects the severity of the threat. But time is on the side of modernity, and I see no lack of US will to prevail. (Francis Fukuyama, 'The West Has Won', *The Guardian*, 11 October 2001, p. 21.)

Despite their differences, both Fukuyama and the Huntington camp are still viewing geopolitics through grand narrative glasses. The West may or may not have won the clash of civilisations, but this is an argument that simply disregards the postmodern ethos altogether. Grand narratives manifestly have not lost their power to attract the population as far as these thinkers are concerned, and incredulity does not feature large in the current geopolitical situation. Leaving aside the virtues of either argument, it has to be said that the revival of religious fundamentalism around the globe in recent decades (and it is a phenomenon not just confined to the Islamic world) does raise serious questions about the validity of postmodern theory. Metanarrative authority remains a potent feature of our world, whatever the postmodern movement may claim – or wish – to be the case.

The Islamic world has its internal critics of the fundamentalist metanarrative, who, interestingly, can regard postmodernism as a barrier to the development and promotion of incredulity. In a wide-ranging attack on the culture of Islamic fundamentalism, Ibn Warraq even includes

Edward Said and his theory of orientalism as part of the problem that Islamic reformers have to face:

> Said not only taught an entire generation of Arabs the wonderful art of self-pity … but intimidated feeble western academics, and even weaker, invariably leftish, intellectuals into accepting that any criticism of Islam was to be dismissed as orientalism, and hence invalid.
>
> But the first duty of the intellectual is to tell the truth. Truth is not much in fashion in this postmodern age when continental charlatans have infected Anglo-American intellectuals with the thought that objective knowledge is not only undesirable but unobtainable. I believe that to abandon the idea of truth not only leads to political fascism, but stops dead all intellectual inquiry. To give up the notion of truth means forsaking the goal of acquiring knowledge. But man, as Aristotle put it, by nature strives to know. Truth, science, intellectual inquiry and rationality are inextricably bound together. Relativism, and its illegitimate offspring, multiculturalism, are not conducive to the critical examination of Islam.
>
> Said wrote a polemical book, *Orientalism* (1978), whose pernicious influence is still felt in all departments of Islamic studies, where any critical discussion of Islam is ruled out *a priori*. For Said, orientalists are involved in an evil conspiracy to denigrate Islam, to maintain its people in a state of permanent subjugation and are a threat to Islam's future. These orientalists are seeking knowledge of oriental peoples only in order to dominate them; most are in the service of imperialism.
>
> Said's thesis was swallowed whole by western intellectuals, since it accords well with the deep anti-westernism of many of them. This anti-westernism resurfaces regularly in Said's prose, as it did in his comments in the *Guardian* after September 11.[27] The studied moral evasiveness, callousness and plain nastiness of Said's article, with its refusal to condemn outright the attacks on America or show any sympathy for the victims or Americans, leave an unpleasant taste in the mouth of anyone whose moral sensibilities have not been blunted by political and Islamic correctness. …
>
> The unfortunate result is that academics can no longer do their work honestly. A scholar working on recently discovered Koranic manuscripts showed some of his startling conclusions to a distinguished colleague, a world expert on the Koran. The latter did not ask, 'What is the evidence, what are your arguments, is it true?' The

> colleague simply warned him that his thesis was unacceptable because it would upset Muslims. (Ibn Warraq, 'Islam – the Final Taboo: Honest Intellectuals Must Shed their Spiritual Turbans', *The Guardian*, 'Saturday Review', 10 November 2001, p. 12.)

It is a familiar list of complaints about the impact of postmodernism, the conclusion being that it amounts to a form of intellectual betrayal. Since Islamic fundamentalism is, in effect, a pre-Enlightenment cultural phenomenon, postmodernism has nothing to contribute to its internal debate. Yet again, we find postmodernism's global relevance being questioned. It appears here, as it does in so many accounts across the intellectual spectrum, as an essentially Western, essentially élitist, phenomenon that signals cultural decline rather than cultural renewal. If it is a new paradigm to thinkers like Warraq, then it is a paradigm vigorously to be contested on the grounds of its negative impact. We are back with that central issue to the debate over postmodernism – radicalism or reaction? Given the spectrum of responses we have considered earlier, the jury still appears to be out on this. But, at the very least, it would seem to be the case that postmodernism is still news.

Another general area of discourse in which postmodernism is still very much news is that of recent science and technology. Indeed, the interaction of socio-political theory and scientific theory has led to some of the most exciting developments in postmodern thought, as we will move on to consider.

CHAPTER FOUR

The Science and Technology of the Postmodern

Science and technology are no less important to the postmodern era than they were to the modern, although it is fair to say that postmodern science and technology generally have a less imperialistic air about them than their modern counterparts. Certainly, they inspire different attitudes among cultural commentators, and perhaps we could say that postmodernity is less in awe of science and technology than modernity was – that is, less prone to turn it into something like a secular religion with scientists as its high priests. We move on to consider how science and technology have figured in debates over the postmodern.

It should be pointed out that not everyone agrees there *is* such a thing as 'postmodern' science, although since Lyotard's comments in *The Postmodern Condition* the term has passed into general usage within the critical disciplines. It is generally taken to revolve around such phenomena as catastrophe theory, chaos theory, complexity theory and the anthropic principle, and there is certainly a considerable literature on these topics to draw on. In the case of commentators such as James Gleick, Paul Davies and Roger Lewin, the material is relatively accessible to the general public. John D. Barrow and R.C. Lewontin also have interesting things to say about the limits of science and the limits of our knowledge, and heated debates have grown up around these topics. Debates in philosophy of science from Thomas Kuhn onwards have also helped to establish a specifically postmodern discourse on science. We will consider Kuhn's contribution first of all, given that he has had such a dramatic impact on debates about the nature of science and scientific practice over the last few decades.

Kuhn's Philosophy of Science

It is Kuhn's concepts of paradigm and scientific revolution that are felt to prefigure postmodern philosophy of science. For Kuhn, science is less a steady accumulation of knowledge than a periodic series of revolutions in which competing paradigms (that is, agreed bodies of knowledge, methods and world-views) clash. Paradigms are taken to be incommensurable with each other to the extent that they cannot co-exist; scientists have to believe one or the other. What tends to happen is that one paradigm supersedes another when it comes to display a greater predictive capability (as Einsteinian relativity did over previous Newtonian-based physical theories, or Copernican astronomy over Ptolemaic). However, this generally requires an older generation of scientists to die out before the new paradigm can be said definitively to control the field. It is extremely difficult to give up a paradigm that may well have been the basis for one's entire professional career. This is particularly the case when the new paradigm seems to deny the validity of your painstakingly accumulated store of specialist knowledge.

A scientific paradigm might be thought of as something like a grand narrative, and the radical part of Kuhn's thesis is that there is no overall grand scientific narrative holding over time. The situation is much more fluid than that, with paradigms always eventually coming under threat from rivals:

> Normal science, the activity in which most scientists inevitably spend almost all their time, is predicated on the assumption that the scientific community knows what the world is like. Much of the success of the enterprise derives from the community's willingness to defend that assumption, if necessary at considerable cost. Normal science, for example, often suppresses fundamental novelties because they are necessarily subversive of its basic commitments. Nevertheless, so long as those commitments retain an element of the arbitrary, the very nature of normal research ensures that novelty shall not be suppressed for very long. Sometimes a normal problem, one that ought to be solvable by known rules and procedures, resists the reiterated onslaught of the ablest members of the group within whose competence it falls. On other occasions a piece of equipment designed and constructed for the purpose of normal research fails to perform in the anticipated manner, revealing an anomaly that cannot, despite repeated effort, be aligned with professional expectation. In these and other ways besides, normal science repeatedly goes astray. And when it does – when, that is, the profession can no longer evade anomalies that subvert the existing tradition of scientific practice – then begin the extraordinary investigations that lead the profession at last to a

> new set of commitments, a new basis for the practice of science. The extraordinary episodes in which that shift of professional commitments occurs are the ones known in this essay as scientific revolutions. They are the tradition-shattering complements to the tradition-bound activity of normal science. …
>
> To be accepted as a paradigm, a theory must seem better than its competitors, but it need not, and in fact never does, explain all the facts with which it can be confronted. (Thomas Kuhn, *The Structure of Scientific Revolutions*, 2nd edn, Chicago and London: University of Chicago Press, 1970, pp. 5–6, 17–18.)

Scientific revolution is the normal state of affairs (more so over the last hundred years or so, with physics, for example, changing with bewildering regularity), and the scientific 'truths' of one generation can rapidly disappear after the triumph of a new paradigm. One can understand why the older generation of scientists would resist in the way it usually does. To put it in postmodern terms, science is a discourse rather than a body of revealed truth – which is to say that science is whatever the majority of the profession agrees it is at any given point (one critic has even complained that science is reduced to 'mob psychology' in Kuhn).[1] Strictly speaking, it is a narrative rather than a metanarrative. Kuhn also prefigures postmodern theory (his earliest writings on the history of science dating back to the 1950s) in that notion of there being a surplus to any paradigm. Our knowledge is always incomplete, a point subsequently to be made even more forcefully by John D. Barrow (see pages 163–5), and science always offers us something less than the total picture. This view certainly fits in with the postmodern suspicion of the validity of all totalising theories.

Lyotard's concept of the differend is another way of describing the condition of incommensurability that arises between competing paradigms. A differend results when competing parties in a dispute are using 'phrase regimes' (world-views or ideologies, for example) that exclude each other. Lyotard cites the example of an employer and an employee in dispute before an industrial relations tribunal, who cannot remotely be said to have commensurable objectives. One wants to cease being exploited; the other exploits as a way of life (and a way of life that is accepted as legitimate both by the tribunal and those who determine its remit). What usually happens when a differend occurs is that one side imposes its will on the other – as in Kuhn, in which one paradigm strives to exclude the other from positions of power (in teaching institutions, learned bodies and so on).

For Lyotard, this is politically unacceptable behaviour in that it suppresses difference, the feature of existence that postmodernists want, above all, to protect. But even in Kuhn we note that there is no sense of the winner in any given paradigm clash being an ultimate authority. Paradigms have authority only while their adherents believe they do (as Žižek is later to note, this is also the case with ideologies),[2] and incredulity towards the current metanarrative-paradigm can easily set in. What Kuhn tells us is that the scientific metanarrative is always provisional – a position that has been attacked as relativist by some critics. Relativism is, as we have come to realise over the course of our study, one of the main accusations levelled against postmodernist thought, and Kuhn helps to provide the basis for a postmodern philosophy of science with his relativist orientation.

Chaos Theory and Complexity Theory

The sense of entering into a new scientific paradigm comes through particularly strongly when we consider developments in chaos theory and complexity theory (the latter being a more advanced version of the former). Ilya Prigogine and Isabelle Stengers emphasise both the radical change in world-view that these theories require of us, and their all-embracing nature:

> Our vision of nature is undergoing a radical change toward the multiple, the temporal, and the complex. For a long time a mechanistic world view dominated Western science. In this view the world appeared as a vast automaton. We now understand that we live in a pluralistic world. It is true that there are phenomena that appear to us as deterministic and reversible, such as the motion of a frictionless pendulum or the motion of the earth around the sun. Reversible processes do not know any privileged direction of time. But there are also irreversible processes that involve an arrow of time. If you bring together two liquids such as water and alcohol, they tend to mix in the forward direction of time as we experience it. We never observe the reverse process, the spontaneous separation of the mixture into pure water and pure alcohol. This is therefore an irreversible process. All of chemistry involves such irreversible processes.
>
> Obviously, in addition to deterministic processes, there must be an element of probability involved in some basic processes, such as, for example, biological evolution or the evolution of human cultures.

> Even the scientist who is convinced of the validity of deterministic descriptions would probably hesitate to imply that at the very moment of the Big Bang, the moment of creation of the universe as we know it, the date of the publication of this book was already inscribed in the laws of nature. In the classical view the basic processes of nature were considered to be deterministic and reversible. Processes involving randomness or irreversibility were considered only exceptions. Today we see everywhere the role of irreversible processes, of fluctuations.
>
> Although Western science has stimulated an extremely fruitful dialogue between man and nature, some of its cultural consequences have been disastrous. The dichotomy between the 'two cultures' is to a large extent due to the conflict between the atemporal view of classical science and the time-oriented view that prevails in a large part of the social sciences and humanities. But in the past few decades, something very dramatic has been happening in science ... We are becoming more and more conscious of the fact that on all levels, from elementary particles to cosmology, randomness and irreversibility play an ever-increasing role. *Science is rediscovering time.* (Ilya Prigogine and Isabelle Stengers, *Order Out of Chaos: Man's New Dialogue with Nature*, London: Heinemann, 1984, pp. xxvii–xxviii.)

The 'reconceptualization of physics' to which Prigogine and Stengers draw our attention has ramifications, therefore, for all areas of our lives (Ibid., p. xxviii). Certainly, philosophers and social scientists have been quick to adapt the notions of pluralism and randomness to their own concerns.

James Gleick's work brings out the all-pervasive aspect of chaos theory in our daily existence, with systems often appearing to feature a high degree of disorder and randomness:

> Where chaos begins, classical science stops. For as long as the world has had physicists inquiring into the laws of nature, it has suffered a special ignorance about disorder in the atmosphere, in the turbulent sea, in the fluctuations of wildlife populations, in the oscillations of the heart and brain. The irregular side of nature, the discontinuous and erratic side – these have been puzzles to science, or worse, monstrosities.
>
> But in the 1970s a few scientists in the United States and Europe began to find a way through disorder. They were mathematicians,

> physicists, biologists, chemists, all seeking connections between different kinds of irregularity. Physiologists found a surprising order in the chaos that develops in the human heart, the prime cause of sudden, unexplained death. Ecologists explored the rise and fall of gypsy moth populations. Economists dug out old stock price data and tried a new kind of analysis. The insights that emerged led directly into the natural world – the shapes of clouds, the paths of lightning, the microscopic intertwining of blood vessels, the galactic clustering of stars. ...
>
> Now that science is looking, chaos seems to be everywhere. A rising column of cigarette smoke breaks into wild swirls. A flag snaps back and forth in the wind. A dripping faucet goes from a steady pattern to a random one. Chaos appears in the behavior of the weather, the behavior of an airplane in flight, the behavior of cars clustering on an expressway, the behavior of oil flowing in underground pipes. No matter what the medium, the behavior obeys the same newly discovered laws. That realization has begun to change the way business executives make decisions about insurance, the way astronomers look at the solar system, the way political theorists talk about the stresses leading to armed conflict.
>
> Chaos breaks across the lines that separate scientific disciplines. Because it is a science of the global nature of systems, it has brought together thinkers from fields that had been widely separated. (James Gleick, *Chaos: Making a New Science*, London: Sphere Books, 1988, pp. 3–4, 5.)

In other words, chaos is all around us. It is not just an esoteric scientific problem, it affects all of us down to the level of the most mundane aspects of our existence. It is also, in the best tradition of postmodern intellectual enquiry, intrinsically interdisciplinary, or 'intertextual' in nature, forcing continual reconsideration of intellectual boundaries – scientists from more or less any discipline may contribute. Postmodernists may prize this quality, but traditionalists will find it deeply threatening to their world-view. At the very least it challenges their power base, which largely depends on being arbiters of all that goes on within their own particular specialism.

Complexity represents a further degree of sophistication to chaos, the emphasis this time being on the factor of self-organisation within systems that are seen to have the capacity to evolve creatively:

> Within science, complexity is a watchword for a new way of thinking about the *collective* behavior of many basic but interacting units, be they atoms, molecules, neurons, or bits within a computer. To be more precise, our definition is that *complexity is the study of the behavior of macroscopic collections of such units that are endowed with the potential to evolve in time.* Their interactions lead to coherent collective phenomena, so-called emergent properties that can be described only at higher levels than those of the individual units. In this sense, the whole is more than the sum of its components, just as a van Gogh painting is so much more than a collection of bold brushstrokes. This is as true for a human society as it is for a raging sea or the electrochemical firing patterns of neurons in a human brain. A swirling vortex in a turbulent ocean cannot be expressed in terms of individual water molecules any more than a happy thought can be depicted in terms of events within a single brain cell. …
>
> For complexity to emerge, two ingredients are necessary. The first, and foremost, is an irreversible medium in which things can happen: this medium is time, flowing from the past that lies closed behind us toward a future that is open. … The second ingredient is *nonlinearity*. We are all familiar with linear systems that have been the mainstay of science for more than three hundred years: because one plus one equals two, we can predict that the volume of water flowing down a drain is doubled when a tap drips twice as long. Nonlinear systems do not obey the simple rules of addition. Compare the simple flow of water down a drain with the complex nonlinear phenomena that regulate the quantity of water in the human body, or the movement of water vapor in the clouds overhead. Nonlinearity causes small changes on one level of organization to produce large effects at the same or different levels. This is familiar to most of us through the example of positive feedback, which turns amplified music into a deafening howl, but the same effect is present in the propensity of plutonium atoms to fall apart during an explosive nuclear chain reaction. In general, nonlinearity produces complex and frequently unexpected results. (Peter Coveney and Roger Highfield, *Frontiers of Complexity: The Search for Order in a Chaotic World*, London: Faber and Faber, 1995, pp. 7, 9.)

Given irreversibility and nonlinearity, complexity can arise in systems that can then evolve to higher levels of operational sophistication. Self-organisation occurs within the system, but neither its exact nature nor its trajectory can be predicted with scientific accuracy. More than somewhat counter-intuitively, order and randomness co-exist. As one complexity theorist, Stuart Kaufmann, has described it in conversation with the science writer Roger Lewin, 'There is "order for free" out there, a spontaneous crystallisation of order out of complex systems, with no need for natural selection or any other external force' (Roger Lewin, *Complexity: Life on the Edge of Chaos*, London: Phoenix, 1993, p. 25). In other words, the future is open – a conclusion eagerly pounced on by postmodernists anxious to refute the claims of deterministic theories in the socio-political realm, Marxism being an outstanding example. Openness and unpredictability indicate limitations to human control, which is precisely what theorists of the postmodern, concerned as they are to undermine all totalising projects, want to hear about. Without such control, the authority assumed by political metanarratives simply seeps away. When the unexpected occurs, totalising theories are either thrown into confusion or are forced, as Marxism was with hegemony, into *ad hoc* alterations that become less and less plausible over time. In the scientific domain, one of the most famous examples of the latter response was the embarrassing number of adjustments that had to be built into Ptolemaic astronomy in order to explain the movement of the stars. Copernican astronomy, with its very different (sun-centred) view of the universe, did away with the need for these.[3]

A key aspect of complexity theory, and one of its most resonant for socio-political theory, is the concept of 'the edge of chaos'. It is in this state that systems are at their most sensitive to their conditions – and most creative. Interviewing another complexity theorist, Chris Langton, Lewin elicits the following assessment of what existence at the edge of chaos involves:

> 'I'm saying that the edge of chaos is where information gets its foot in the door in the physical world, where it gets the upper hand over energy. Being at the transition point between order and chaos not only buys you exquisite control – small input/big change – but it also buys you the possibility that information processing can become an important part of the dynamics of the system.' (Lewin, *Complexity*, p. 51.)

For systems, the edge of chaos is the most desirable condition to achieve, therefore, and that would apply to systems such as species, too:

> Can you test your model ecosystems to see what happens when you

> perturb them? I asked Stu [Kaufmann]. 'It was easy to do,' he said. 'We just made the external world ... another random connection'. If the fitness landscape of one species is deformed by such external perturbation, the species is likely to become less fit. Through mutation and selection it will then reclimb the peak, or a new peak, a change that in all probability will deform the fitness landscape of one or more species with which it interacts. If connectedness among species within the system is low, then the effects of the initial perturbation will soon peter out. This is when the system is near the frozen state. With high connectedness, any single change is likely to propagate hectically throughout the system, with many large avalanches. This is the chaotic state. At the intermediate state, the edge of chaos – with internal and between-species interactions carefully tuned – some perturbations provoke small cascades of change, others trigger complete avalanches, equivalent to mass extinctions. (Lewin, *Complexity*, pp. 61–2.)

Lewin lists several cases where such 'avalanches' have occurred, both in terms of the animal kingdom and human societies (possibly the most spectacular example of the former being the 'Permian extinction' of 250 million years ago, which accounted for around 96 per cent of species then existing).

It is easy to see why postmodern theorists would be attracted to ideas such as these, with their sense of a world far less predictable and controllable than traditional science had tended to picture for us. The notion of deterministic metanarratives such as Marxism claiming the ability to order the future seems untenable once we take these kinds of ideas on board. Not only can unexpected events occur, but also they are part of the natural order of things. The edge of chaos presents the postmodernist with just the kind of world she wants – one in which inputs by little narratives can have a critical impact and where there is always the potential for radical, to the extent of system-disorienting, change. As long as that potential continues to exist, metanarratives cannot succeed in their bid to exert total control. The unexpected lies in wait to catch them out.

One of the most intriguing aspects of complexity theory is its deployment of the anthropic principle. This principle certainly fits in well with the postmodern world-view in the way that it posits an open universe in which radical change is always possible. An open universe whose future is not predetermined cuts against the grand narrative of Marxism, as well as of most religions and, intriguingly enough, it also challenges the current scientific paradigm that predicts the heat death of our solar system in around 4.5 billion years (the earth's biosphere having dissipated within about a billion years). The 'strong' anthropic principle, in particular, enables scientists to postulate the existence of a degree of self-organisation that, just conceivably, could carry us past such apocalyptic events:

> [T]here is still a sense in which human mind and society may represent only an intermediate stage on the ladder of organizational progress in the cosmos. To borrow a phrase from Louise Young, the universe is as yet 'unfinished'.[4] We find ourselves living in an epoch only a few billion years after the creation. From what can be deduced about astronomical processes, the universe could remain fit for habitation for trillions of years, possibly for ever. The heat death of the cosmos, a concept that has dogged us throughout, poses no threat in the imaginable future, and by the time scale of human standards it is an eternity away.
>
> As our World 3 products [the collective achievements of human society as a whole] become ever more elaborate and complex (one need only think of computing systems) so the possibility arises that a new threshold of complexity may be crossed, unleashing a still higher organizational level, with new qualities and laws of its own. There may emerge collective activity of an abstract nature that we can scarcely imagine, and may even be beyond our ability to conceptualize. It might even be that this threshold has been crossed elsewhere in the universe already, and that we do not recognize it for what it is. (Paul Davies, *The Cosmic Blueprint: Order and Complexity at the Edge of Chaos*, Harmondsworth: Penguin, 1995, p. 196.)

The argument is that far from being a phenomenon to fear (as it is for Lyotard in *The Inhuman*), the development of ever-more sophisticated computer systems might even be our salvation in the longer term.

Some might find the concept of self-organization quite threatening, since it implies control of the human by some outside force working through it without the former's knowledge. However, Davies sees the process in a much more optimistic light than that:

> I have been at pains to argue that the organizational principles needed to supplement the laws of physics are likely to be forthcoming as a result of new approaches to research and new ways of looking at complexity in nature. I believe that science is in principle able

> to explain the existence of complexity and organization at all levels, including human consciousness, though only by embracing the 'higher-level' laws. Such a belief might be regarded as denying a god, or a purpose in this wonderful creative universe we inhabit.
>
> I do not see it that way. The very fact that the universe is creative, and that the laws have permitted complex structures to emerge and develop to the point of consciousness – in other words, that the universe has organized its own self-awareness – is for me powerful evidence that there is 'something going on' behind it all. The impression of design is overwhelming. Science may explain all the processes whereby the universe evolves its own destiny, but that still leaves room for there to be a meaning behind existence. (Davies, *The Cosmic Blueprint*, p. 203.)

Physics is transformed into metaphysics at such points, and we seem to be on the verge of a new narrative based on that old favourite, the 'argument from design'.[5] We may not know all the details, but the process does seem to be heading in a certain direction.

On the basis of complexity theory, Charles Jencks also speculates on the possible emergence of a new metanarrative for the postmodern age:

> The universe is a single, creative, unfolding event whose most salient feature is sudden emergence – creativity. … The lesson of emergence is that surprise, novelty, sudden jumps are always deeper than consciousness, and one step ahead of science. Nevertheless, knowledge is one-way and has deep implications. No one is going to refute gravity (in its entirety); we are not going to go back to the Ptolemaic system, or even the modern one. We cannot unlearn what we know about the universe, and this is the story of cosmogenesis: the generative nature of nature.
>
> So the post-modern age unfolds with the post-modern sciences of complexity as a guide, setting some of the limits and possibilities for thought and action. It would be wrong, however, to say that they set the entire agenda for culture, since they leave so much undecided, so much open to interpretation and creative design. We can rethink the metaphors, reinterpret the universe story and its meanings in different ways. We can get rid of the 'Big Bang' and other nasty, brutal and short appellations. We can even, when modernity is over, get rid of the label Post-Modernism – and that will be a relief. But as long as the

> juggernaut of modernisation asset-strips the world, the post-modern agenda will continue to flourish. ... [I]t is a view of the universe as the measure of all things; a single, creative unfolding event that is always trying to reach higher levels of organisation; its metanarrative the story that can orient a global civilisation. (Jencks, *What is Post-Modernism?*, pp. 76, 77.)

While we seem here to be moving away from the view of postmodern science as the realm of the unexpected, it has to be said that Jencks's is a fairly loose version of metanarrative as it is traditionally understood – more of a rolling process than a set body of doctrine to be obeyed as such. And since we can never tell before the event what emergence will produce, perhaps the unknown is still the dominating factor. Yet, as in the case of Davies, there is at least a hint of the argument from design to be noted in this further example of physics being translated into metaphysics.

Postmodern Science: Limits and the Unknown

Some writers on postmodern science may be willing to flirt with the argument from design, but Lyotard is not one of them. For this thinker, postmodern science is as much about uncertainty as certainty, and that is a quality to be prized in our intellectual enquiries:

> Postmodern science – by concerning itself with such things as undecidables, the limits of precise control, conflicts characterized by incomplete information, '*fracta*', catastrophes, and pragmatic paradoxes – is theorizing its own evolution as discontinuous, catastrophic, nonrectifiable, and paradoxical. It is changing the meaning of the word *knowledge*, while expressing how such a change can take place. It is producing not the known but the unknown. And it suggests a model of legitimation that has nothing to do with maximized performance, but has as its basis difference understood by paralogy [reasoning that seeks out paradox].
>
> ... [I]t is now dissension that must be emphasized. Consensus is a horizon that is never reached. Research that takes place under the aegis of a paradigm tends to stabilize it; it is like the exploitation of a technological, economic, or artistic 'idea'. It cannot be discounted. But what is striking is that someone always comes along to disturb the order of 'reason'. It is necessary to posit the existence of a power

> that destabilizes the capacity for explanation, manifested in the promulgation of new norms of understanding or, if one prefers, in a proposal to establish new rules circumscribing a new field of research for the language of science. This, in the context of scientific discussion, is the same process [René] Thom calls morphogenesis.[6] It is not without rules (there are classes of catastrophes), but it is always locally determined. Applied to scientific discussion and placed in a temporal framework, this property implies that 'discoveries' are unpredictable. In terms of the idea of transparency, it is a factor that generates blind spots and defers consensus.
>
> This summary makes it easy to see that systems theory and the kind of legitimation it proposes have no scientific basis whatsoever; science itself does not function according to this theory's paradigm of the system, and contemporary science excludes the possibility of using such a paradigm to describe society. (Jean-François Lyotard, *The Postmodern Condition: A Report on Knowledge*, trans. Geoff Bennington and Brian Massumi, Manchester: Manchester University Press, 1984, pp. 60, 61.)

This has been a contentious view of the scientific enterprise, particularly the notion that science produces the 'unknown' as opposed to pushing back its boundaries; but it receives support from hard scientific circles, as in the case of the astronomer John D. Barrow's theories on the limits of science – and by extension, human knowledge. For Barrow, science will always be confronted not just by the unknown, but by the unknowable:

> The idea that some things may be unachievable or unimaginable tends to produce an explosion of knee-jerk reactions amongst scientific (and not so scientific) commentators. Some see it as an affront to the spirit of human inquiry; raising the white flag to the forces of ignorance. Others fear that talk of the impossible plays into the hands of the anti-scientists, airing doubts that should be left unsaid lest they undermine the public perception of science as a never-ending success story. Finally, there are those who seize upon any talk of impossibility as an endorsement of their scepticism about unbridled technological progress, tramping roughshod over the environment and human dignity: the unstoppable in pursuit of the unsustainable.
>
> If this book [*Impossibility: The Limits of Science and the Science of Limits*] has taught the reader anything, I hope it is that the notion of impossibility is far subtler than naive assumptions about the endless

> horizons of science, or pious hopes that boffins will be baffled, would lead you to believe. Limits are ubiquitous. Science only exists because there are limits to what Nature permits. The laws of Nature and the unchanging 'constants' of Nature define the borders that distinguish our Universe from a host of other conceivable worlds where all things are possible. In those imaginary worlds of unlimited possibility there can exist neither complexity nor life. They contain no imaginations. The fact that we can conceive of logical and practical impossibilities is a reflection of a self-reflective consciousness that is so far unique among the fellow creatures with whom we share our planet. Impossibilities allow those conscious complexities to exist. ...
>
> Limits to what is impossible may turn out to define the Universe more powerfully than the list of possibilities. On a variety of fronts we have found that growing complexity ultimately leads to a situation that is not only limited, but self-limiting. Time and again, the development of our most powerful theories has followed this path: they are so successful that it is believed that they can explain everything. Commentators begin to look forward to the solution of all the problems that the theory can encompass. The concept of a 'theory of everything' occasionally rears its head. But then something unexpected happens. The theory predicts that it cannot predict: it tells us that there are things that it cannot tell us. (John D. Barrow, *Impossibility: The Limits of Science and the Science of Limits*, London: Vintage, 1999, pp. 248, 249.)

Barrow gives several examples of the unknowable. For instance, we can never have knowledge of the universe as a whole since some areas are simply too far away from our planet ever to manage to transmit light to us. There are also limits on what can be measured at the sub-atomic level, and without measurement, in science there is no knowledge. Then, too, the future states of non-linear dynamic systems in which chaos and complexity apply cannot be predicted because of their acute sensitivity to even very small alterations in their initial conditions – the beating of the butterfly's wings that is eventually transformed into a hurricane several thousand miles away, in the classic example of 'small input/ big change'.

Overall, Barrow's views on science fit in with the pattern of postmodern thinking. Modern science's claim to be a grand narrative on the verge of explaining everything to us, by means of a 'Grand Unified Theory', is undermined by Barrow's insistence on limits and impossibilities – and not just limits and impossibilities, but *necessary* limits and impossibilities. The Grand Unified Theory itself is an impossibility. Yet he seems to find the pervasiveness of the unknowable a liberating rather than a constricting state of affairs – a way of gaining a sense of proportion about our place in the universe. The unknowable might be regarded as a scientific version of the sublime, and it will only bother us if we believe (as Einstein did) that it is science's destiny to uncover the Grand Unified Theory that holds the universe together.[7]

R. C. Lewontin has been similarly concerned to challenge the notion of a 'theory of everything' with respect to DNA. In this instance it is the Human Genome Project that is striving to achieve grand narrative status, with Lewontin declaring himself deeply sceptical of both its claims and its methods. As far as Lewontin is concerned, the Human Genome Project is a case of 'science as ideology' – in his eyes a phenomenon to be treated with deep suspicion:

> [T]he ideology of modern science, including modern biology, makes the atom or individual the causal source of all the properties of larger collections. It prescribes a way of studying the world, which is to cut it up into the individual bits that cause it and to study the properties of these isolated bits. It breaks the world down into independent autonomous domains, the internal and the external. Causes are either internal or external, and there is no mutual dependency between them.
>
> For biology, this world view has resulted in a particular picture of organisms and their total life activity. Living beings are seen as being determined by internal factors, the genes. Our genes and the DNA molecules that make them up are the modern form of grace, and in this view we will understand what we are when we know what our genes are made of. The world outside us poses certain problems … [T]o find a mate, to find food, to win out in competition over others, to acquire a large part of the world resources as our own, and if we have the right kind of genes we will be able to solve the problems and leave more offspring. So in this view, it is really our genes that are propagating themselves through us. We are only their instruments, their temporary vehicles through which the self-replicating molecules that make us up either succeed or fail to spread through the world. … Genes make individuals, individuals have particular preferences and behaviors, the collection of preferences and behaviors makes a

> culture, and so genes make culture. That is why molecular biologists urge us to spend as much money as necessary to discover the sequence of the DNA of a human being. They say that when we know the sequence of the molecule that makes up all our genes, we will know what it is to be human. When we know what our DNA looks like, we will know why some of us are rich and some poor, some healthy and some sick, some powerful and some weak. We will also know why some societies are powerful and rich and others are weak and poor, why one nation, one sex, one race dominates another. (R. C. Lewontin, *The Doctrine of DNA: Biology as Ideology*, Harmondsworth: Penguin, 1993, pp. 12–13, 14.)

Mapping that sequence in its entirety is the objective that the Human Genome Project has set itself, and as stated here by Lewontin, it sounds like a textbook example of modernity in action. There is the characteristic belief that the application of rational principles will yield total understanding of a natural process, plus the desire to exert control over every aspect of the natural world, that mark out modernity from the Enlightenment onwards. Lewontin maintains an attitude of scepticism towards that ethos in general, with its mechanistic approach to such a complex system as the human. The spectre of genetic engineering is raised by the Human Genome Project, and that would represent modernity taken to its logical conclusion.

It has been argued that the move away from a mechanistic conception of science reintroduces a human dimension to scientific enquiry. For Stephen Toulmin this is a welcome development that opens up the possibility of a rapprochement between science and religion:

> The 'modern' world is now a thing of the past. Our own natural science today is no longer 'modern' science. Instead … it is rapidly engaged in becoming 'postmodern' science: the science of the 'postmodern' world, of 'postnationalist' politics and 'postindustrial' society – the world that has not yet discovered how to define itself in terms of what it is, but only in terms of what has *just-now-ceased-to-be*. …
>
> Science and natural religion parted company (I have argued) for reasons that operated powerfully in the nineteenth and twentieth centuries, but that no longer have the same power today. As a result of professionalization, the work of science was divided up between independent specialized disciplines, so that the broader concerns of

> traditional cosmology and natural theology ceased to be any scientists' professional business. Meanwhile, the role of the scientist came to be seen as that of a pure spectator whose task was simply to report 'objectively' on the workings of nature: this perception carried with it a belief in the 'value neutrality' of science, so that the moral, practical, and religious significance of our world view ceased to be a question on which science itself could throw any light.
>
> All that has gone by the board during the present century. Within our own 'postmodern' world, the pure scientist's traditional posture as *theoros*, or spectator, can no longer be maintained: we are always – and inescapably – participants or agents as well. Meanwhile, the expansion of scientific enquiry into the human realm is compelling us to abandon the Cartesian dichotomies and look for ways of 'reinserting' humanity into the world of nature.[8] Instead of viewing the world of nature as onlookers from outside, we now have to understand how our own human life and activities operate as elements within the world of nature. So we must develop a more coordinated view of the world, embracing both the world of nature and the world of humanity – a view capable of integrating, not merely aggregating our scientific understanding, and capable of doing so *with practice in view*. Only a broader, more coordinated view of the world of this kind can pick up once again the legitimate tasks undertaken by the traditional cosmology before the 'new philosophers' of the seventeenth century led to its dismantlement. (Stephen Toulmin, *The Return to Cosmology: Postmodern Science and the Theology of Nature*, Berkeley, Los Angeles, CA and London: University of California Press, 1982, pp. 254, 255–6.)

In this reading, postmodern science offers the opportunity of a more holistic world-view than was possible under a modern dispensation. Modern science is seen to be built on the illusion that we can step outside nature and observe its workings, but we now have to understand that we are caught up in the very processes we are trying to observe. Science-as-metanarrative is undermined by such a realisation, which for Toulmin is as much of a paradigm shift as that which instituted modern science in the first place. Yet another source of unquestioned authority is consigned to history: as far as Toulmin is concerned, we are now in uncharted territory.

Postmodern Science and Technology

For certain thinkers, postmodernism is inextricably bound up with the development of technology. Arthur Kroker is one such example:

> Contemporary French thought consists of a creative, dynamic and highly original account of technological society. Refusing the pragmatic account of technology as freedom and eschewing a tragic description of technology as degeneration, an arc of twentieth-century French thinkers, from Jean Baudrillard and Roland Barthes to Paul Virilio, Jean-François Lyotard, Deleuze and Guattari and Foucault have presented a description of technology as cynical power. Indeed, what might be called the key impulse of French 'bimodernism' has been to explore the mutation of technology within a series of critical discourses: technology as pure speed (Virilio), technology as simulation (Baudrillard), the rhetoric of technology (Barthes), technology as desiring-machine (Deleuze and Guattari), technology as aesthetics (Lyotard) and technologies of subjectivity (Foucault). Here, technological society is described under the sign of possessed individualism: an invasive power where life is enfolded within the dynamic technological language of virtual reality. Virtual reality? That is the recoding of human experience by the algorithmic codes of computer wetware. No longer alienation, reification or simulation as stages in the technological dialectic of social emancipation and human domination, but virtuality now as the dominant sign of contemporary technological society. Indeed, virtual reality – the world of digital dreams come alive – is what the possessed individual is possessed by.
>
> What emerges from the French mind, then, is an account of technological society that can be immediately and massively influential because it is a mirror of technology in the postmodern scene. This means that the reception of French thought in the outmoded form of post-structuralism has always been a trompe l'oeil deflecting attention from the key contribution of French thinkers as theorists of technology par excellence; that is, as brilliant interpreters of the virtual phase of technological society. Thus, for example, while American thought is trapped in a pragmatic description of technology as liberation, the French discourse on technology begins with the violent exteriorization of the self, actually producing an eerie and disturbing account of cynical technology. Of technology, that is, in its fully aestheticized phase where speaking means the rhetoric machine,

> where living means simulation, where the self *is* a desiring-machine, and where feeling is a rhizomatic network. To enter into the French mind ... is really to enter into the deepest recesses of postmodern subjectivity. (Arthur Kroker, *The Possessed Individual: Technology and Postmodernity*, Basingstoke and London: Macmillan, 1992, pp. 2–3.)

Kroker's distinction between French and American attitudes to technology charts the gulf between modernity and postmodernity. In an American context technology is essentially orientated towards the public good – that is, towards progress. But in postmodern French thought, technology is co-opted into a radical programme designed to bring about the end of the self as we know it. We might widen that notion of French thought to include all those inspired by French thought – in which case someone like Donna Haraway and her 'cyborgs' (see pages 172–4) become part of this radical programme. What Kroker describes is a move from technology as benign, to technology as ideologically subversive. The virtual world, after all, is one in which metanarrative's sway does not hold. It is also one in which little narratives are free to operate without interference from either authority or convention.

For all his support of postmodern science, Lyotard has reservations about the implications of technological change. Those doubts are expressed most forcefully in his late work *The Inhuman*, in which he accuses 'techno-science' of marginalising the human at the expense of computer technology. He speculates as to whether this may even include a programme to extend computer technology past the forecast heat death of the universe. The villain here is what Lyotard calls 'development' – in other words, the forces of advanced capitalism, which invariably lose sight of the human dimension in their desire to expand their empire ever further:

> The striking thing about this metaphysics of development is that it needs no finality. Development is not attached to an Idea, like that of the emancipation of reason and of human freedoms. It is reproduced by accelerating and extending itself according to its internal dynamic. It assimilates risks, memorizes their informational value and uses this as a new mediation necessary to its functioning. It has no necessity itself other than a cosmological chance.
>
> It has thus no end, but it does have a limit, the expectation of the life of the sun. The anticipated explosion of this star is the only

> challenge objectively posed to development. The natural selection of systems is thus no longer of a biological, but of a cosmic order. It is to take up this challenge that all research, whatever its sector of application, is being set up already in the so-called developed countries. The interest of humans is subordinate in this to that of the survival of complexity. (Jean-François Lyotard, *The Inhuman: Reflections on Time*, trans. Geoffrey Bennington and Rachel Bowlby, Cambridge and Oxford: Polity Press and Blackwell, 1991, p. 7.)

Lyotard goes on to construct a dialogue between two characters ('He' and 'She'), who debate the ethics of this supposed project within 'development':

> While we talk, the sun is getting older. It will explode in 4.5 billion years. … That, in my view, is the sole serious question to face humanity today. In comparison everything else seems insignificant. Wars, conflicts, political tension, shifts in opinion, philosophical debates, even passions – everything's dead already if this infinite reserve from which you now draw energy to defer answers, if in short thought as quest, dies out with the sun. … The body might be considered the hardware of the complex technical device that is human thought. … So the problem of the technological sciences can be stated as: how to provide this software [language] with a hardware that is independent of the conditions of life on earth.
>
> That is: how to make thought without a body possible. A thought that continues to exist after the death of the human body. …
>
> So theoretically the solution is very simple: manufacture hardware capable of 'nurturing' software at least as complex (or replex) as the present-day human brain, but in non-terrestrial conditions. … It's clear even to a lay person like myself that the combined forces of nuclear physics, electronics, photonics[9] and information science open up a possibility of constructing technical objects, with a capacity that's not just physical but also cognitive, which 'extract' (that is, select, process and distribute) energies these objects need in order to function from forms generally found everywhere in the cosmos. (Lyotard, *The Inhuman*, pp. 8, 9, 13–14.)

Lyotard concludes that it would not be thought (therefore not life either) as we know it that survived, but an example of the 'inhuman' instead. And the drift towards the inhuman is something he feels we should resist as strongly as we can. Development constitutes another grand narrative, and, as with grand narratives in general, it subordinates individuals to its objectives: in this case, the entire human race to the more malleable world of technology. The advantages of postmodern science, as Lyotard conceives of it anyway, become clear when compared to the imperialistic imperatives lying behind techno-science and development – which is more like modernity writ very large, modernity without unpredictable human beings to hinder its progress.

Lyotard's gloomy predictions can be countered, however, by developments in other areas of contemporary science. Proponents of the anthropic principle, that key aspect of complexity theory we considered earlier (pages 159–61), have questioned the inevitability of the heat death of the universe. If they are right, then the techno-science 'conspiracy' loses its rationale.

Lyotard's sceptical attitude towards unfettered technological development has its forerunners in French intellectual life in thinkers such as Jacques Ellul. Writing in the 1950s, Ellul strikes a postmodern note in his view of technology's impact on social consciousness and our political systems:

> Whenever we see the word *technology* or *technique*, we automatically think of machines. Indeed, we commonly think of our world as machines. This notion … arises from the fact that the machine is the most obvious, massive, and impressive example of technique, and historically the first. … Technique certainly began with the machine. It is quite true that all the rest developed out of mechanics; it is quite true also that without the machine the world of technique would not exist. But to explain the situation in this way does not legitimatize it. It is a mistake to continue with this confusion of terms, the more so because it leads to the idea that, because the machine is at the origin and center of the technical problem, one is dealing with the whole problem when one deals with the machine. And that is a greater mistake still. Technique has now become almost completely independent of the machine, which has lagged far behind its offspring.
>
> It must be emphasized that, at present, technique is applied outside industrial life. The growth of its power today has no relation to the growing use of the machine. The balance seems rather to have shifted to the other side. It is the machine which is now entirely dependent upon technique, and the machine represents only a small

> part of technique. If we were to characterize the relations between technique and the machine today, we could say not only that the machine is the result of a certain technique, but also that its social and economic applications are made possible by other technical advances. The machine is now not even the most important aspect of technique (though it is perhaps the most spectacular); technique has taken over all of man's activities, not just his productive activity.
>
> From another point of view, however, the machine is deeply symptomatic: it represents the ideal toward which technique strives. The machine is solely, exclusively, technique; it is pure technique, one might say. For, wherever a technical factor exists, it results, almost inevitably, in mechanization: technique transforms everything it touches into a machine.
>
> Another relationship exists between technique and the machine, and this relationship penetrates to the very core of the problem of our civilization. It is said (and everyone agrees) that the machine has created an inhuman atmosphere. (Jacques Ellul, *The Technological Society*, trans. John Wilkinson, New York: Alfred A. Knopf, 1964, pp. 3–4.)

What Ellul is describing is the process whereby technology comes to be an end in itself, projecting a deterministic image as it does so. 'Technique' is to be regarded as an earlier version of techno-science, defined by Ellul as 'the *totality of methods rationally arrived at*' to achieve consistent results 'in *every* field of human activity' (Ibid., p. xxv). This is the other side to the liberationist ideals of the Enlightenment project: the side that subjects us to goals that restrict our freedom, that are 'inhuman' in their effects. The pessimistic tone is very similar to that which we find later in Lyotard's *The Inhuman*, and there is clearly a similar unease about the implications for humanity of endless 'progress' based on technological innovation. Modernity has become a mixed blessing in this reading of our recent cultural history; enslaving us as much as liberating us. It is Adorno's vision of the 'administered' society reached by another route (see pages 37–8).

It is when we come to thinkers such as Sadie Plant and Donna Haraway that the postmodern enthusiasm for technology is seen to its fullest advantage. Haraway embraces the new technology to the extent of envisaging a re-engineering of the human body and concept of self through her work on the cyborg notion. There is a specifically feminist bias to Haraway's theories, although their implications extend wider than that to the more general relationship between humanity and technology. Lyotard may have been deeply worried about this relationship, but where he sees only problems, Haraway identifies exciting opportunities instead – particularly for women in their battle against the forces of patriarchy. In the forefront of that battle will be the cyborg, whose virtues are enumerated in what Haraway dubs 'A Cyborg Manifesto':

> A cyborg is a cybernetic organism, a hybrid of machine and organism, a creature of social reality as well as a creature of science fiction. Social reality is lived social relations, our most important political construction, a world-changing fiction. The international women's movements have constructed 'women's experience', as well as uncovered or discovered this crucial collective object. This experience is a fiction and fact of the most crucial, political kind. Liberation rests on the construction of the consciousness, the imaginative apprehension, of oppression, and so of possibility. The cyborg is a matter of fiction and lived experience that changes what counts as women's experience in the late twentieth century. This is a struggle over life and death, but the boundary between science fiction and social reality is an optical illusion.
>
> Contemporary science fiction is full of cyborgs – creatures simultaneously animal and machine, who populate worlds ambiguously natural and crafted. Modern medicine is also full of cyborgs, of couplings between organism and machine, each conceived as coded devices, in an intimacy and with a power that was not generated in the history of sexuality. Cyborg 'sex' restores some of the lovely replicative baroque of ferns and invertebrates (such nice organic prophylactics against heterosexism). Cyborg replication is uncoupled from organic reproduction. Modern production seems like a dream of cyborg colonization work, a dream that makes the nightmare of Taylorism seem idyllic.[10] And modern war is a cyborg orgy, coded by C^3I, command-control-communication-intelligence, an $84 billion item in 1984's US defence budget. I am making an argument for the cyborg as a fiction mapping our social and bodily reality and as an imaginative resource suggesting some very fruitful couplings. Michel Foucault's biopolitics is a flaccid premonition of cyborg politics, a very open field.
>
> By the late twentieth century, our time, a mythic time, we are all chimeras, theorized and fabricated hybrids of machine and organism; in short we are cyborgs. The cyborg is our ontology; it gives us our

> politics. The cyborg is a condensed image of both imagination and material reality, the two joined centres structuring any possibility of historical transformation. ... ['A Cyborg Manifesto'] is also an effort to contribute to socialist-feminist culture and theory in a post-modernist, non-naturalist mode and in the utopian tradition of imagining a world without gender, which is perhaps a world without genesis, but maybe also a world without end. (Donna J. Haraway, *Simians, Cyborgs, and Women: The Reinvention of Nature*, New York: Routledge, 1991, pp. 149–50.)

Gender, the basis of the grand narrative of patriarchy, is theorised out of existence here in one of the author's most striking 'reinventions' of nature. For this kind of postmodernist thinker, no assumption about our world lies beyond challenge; *any* possibility of historical transformation is now on the agenda. The conjunction of feminism, science and post-modern theory holds out the promise of a completely new form of politics, more radical than any yet seen in our cultural history. The cyborg is our destiny, as far as Haraway is concerned. But, as we will discover in the section entitled 'Film' in Chapter five, not everyone is as sanguine about our cyborg prospects.

Sadie Plant's studies of the relationship between women and technology also have an explicit feminist agenda, although, again, the implications go wider to suggest that the engagement with new technology may lead to the development of a new kind of self:

> There is always a point at which technologies geared towards regulation, containment, command, and control, can turn out to be feeding into the collapse of everything they once supported. All individuated notions of organized selves and unified lives are thrown into question on a Net whose connectivities do not merely extend between people as subjects with individual faces, names, and identities. The terminology of computer-mediated communication implies an increasing sense of distance and alienating isolation, and the corporate hype enthuses about a new sense of interpersonal interaction. But the keystrokes of users on the Net connect them to a vast distributed plane composed not merely of computers, users, and telephone lines, but all the zeros and ones of machine code, the switches of electronic circuitry, fluctuating waves of neurochemical activity, hormonal energy, thoughts, desires ...

> In spite or perhaps even because of the impersonality of the screen, the digital zone facilitates unprecedented levels of spontaneous affection, intimacy, and informality, exposing the extent to which older media, especially what continues to be called 'real life,' come complete with a welter of inhibitions, barriers, and obstacles sidestepped by the packet-switching systems of the Net. Face-to-face communication – the missionary position so beloved of Western man – is not at all the most direct of all possible ways to communicate.
>
> All new media, as Marshall McLuhan pointed out in the 1960s, have an extraordinary ability to rewire the people who are using them and the cultures in which they circulate.[11] The telephone, intended simply as a means of conversing at a distance, and not designed to redesign talk itself, is an obvious case of a new means of communication which had an enormous effect on the possibilities of communication both on and off the end of the line. What was supposed to be a simple device for the improvement of commercial interaction has become an intimate chat line for both women and the men who once despised such talk. And as means of communication continue to converge, the Net takes these tendencies to new extremes. Its monitors and ports do not simply connect people who are left unchanged by their microprocesses. The roundabout, circuitous connections with which women have always been associated and the informal networking at which they have excelled now become protocols for everyone. (Sadie Plant, *Zeros + Ones: Digital Women + The New Technoculture*, London: Fourth Estate, 1998, pp. 143–4.)

The Net registers as a quintessentially postmodern phenomenon in this reading, its ability to bypass older power structures and create a proliferation of new networks constituting a radical challenge to the cultural and political *status quo*. Like Deleuze and Guattari's rhizomatic structures (already discussed in Chapter two), the Net resists centralised control and offers endless opportunities for individuals to circumvent authority. Plant contends that the Net's absence of hierarchy has a natural appeal for women, given that patriarchal hierarchies traditionally have excluded them. In consequence, women have had to develop more personal ways of networking outside the hierarchy, a talent ideally suited to the ethos of the Net. At least in principle, the Net holds out the possibility of a feminisation of our culture that would benefit men no less than it would women.

Between them, Haraway and Plant map out a programme for the transformation of both our bodies and our minds by technology. No area of contemporary life has a keener interest in such processes than medicine, simultaneously one of our most developed sciences and one of the major users of, as well as believers in, advanced technology. Postmodernism's influence is beginning to make itself felt within this field, leading to questions about how that technology is currently deployed, and to what ends. An editorial in the *British Medical Journal* brings out the issues involved when medicine, a prototypically modernist enterprise as most of us would probably perceive it, confronts the postmodern:

> I came across a curious word the other day – credicide. The death of belief. Not this or that one but all and every. Strictly speaking, of course, it means the active killing of belief rather than just its simple demise. …
>
> What is dying … is not just Progress, Education, Science, Justice, or God – though all these do look anaemic shadows of their former selves. What is dying is the House of Belief itself. …
>
> Medicine alone seems to remain curiously immune to these epidemic uncertainties. Health is one of few remaining social values that garners unambiguous support. This is largely due to our continuing and communal belief that there is one truth 'out there' which can be known, understood, and controlled by anyone who is rational and competent. The faith that we can accumulate an objective understanding of reality which is true for all times and all places underlies our treatments and our clinical trials. Stating this may seem unexceptional to doctors, yet this 'modernist' view is in fact rather unusual. Great swathes of the world increasingly act according to the rather different set of assumptions of postmodernism.
>
> In a postmodern world, anything goes. There are no overarching frameworks to steer by. Instead, everything is relative, fashion and ironic detachment flourish, and yesterday's dogma becomes tomorrow's quaint curiosity. To the postmodern eye truth is not 'out there' waiting to be revealed but is something which is constructed by people, always provisional and contingent on context and power.
>
> Within medicine one response to the relativism and uncertainty created by postmodernism has been to emphasise the evidence on which medicine is based. After all, if there are knowable medical truths 'out there' then we should get our act together and apply them. Evidence[-]based medicine promises certainty – do enough MED-

> LINE searches and you will find the answer to your prayers. Read in this way, evidence[-]based medicine is a reaction to the multiple, fragmented versions of the 'truth' which the postmodern world offers. It is also a serious attempt to invent a new language that might reunite the Babel of doctors and patients, managers and consumers. However, an evidence[-]based approach will only work for as long as we all view medicine as 'modern' – that is, as making statements about an objective, verifiable external reality. To the postmodernist the question is whose 'evidence' is this anyway and whose interests does it promote? (Paul Hodgkin, 'Medicine, Postmodernism, and the End of Certainty', *British Medical Journal*, 313, 21 December 1996, pp. 1568–9.)

Evidence-based medicine has been a particularly strong trend in recent years, and can claim a sizeable body of adherents. Hodgkin goes on to make a case for the adoption of some postmodern attitudes by the medical profession, however, arguing that the 'end of certainty' is by no means incompatible with medical practice. Doctors cannot remain immune to the changing nature, both sociological and physical, of our world in which old certainties – down to the level of our belief in a stable climate – are disappearing in front of our eyes.

Predictably enough, some respondents to Hodgkin's editorial *did* see an incompatibility between postmodern theory and medical practice:

> As certainties pass away, competing ideologies and treatments step into the health supermarket. In this brave new world who needs licences and mandates to practise? ... All providers are welcome to bid, and the consumer decides. ...
>
> Such deregulation shatters the hierarchical division between scientific and alternative medicine. The traditional autonomy of the medical profession collapses as corporations and competing therapists invade the newly created health market. Indeed, this is already beginning to happen. Here the consumer picks and mixes medical care options from the shelves of enticing therapies. This is where McDonalds meets Mrs Thatcher.
>
> The beauty of traditional general practice has been its ability to be both patient advocate and health service gatekeeper. This potentially compromised dual role has survived intact to date. Such a possibility reflects a meta-narrative that speaks of licensed doctors who act with integrity, seeking to balance patient need, service capability, and

> scientific evidence. Such doctors continue their privileged role by consensus and through agreements over what is true and trustworthy.
>
> Although the postmodern world will persist in challenging all our assumptions and practices, we have a duty to remain true patient advocates, not least as robust defenders of the scientific medical heritage. We must firmly resist the idea that nothing can be known, that truth is what you make it. That way leads to superstition and a new dark age. (James Harrison, 'Doctors Have a Duty to Remain True Patient Advocates', *British Medical Journal*, 314, 5 April 1997, p. 1044.)

For such a practitioner, relativism has no place in the context of a science, and our 'scientific medical heritage' is justifiably to be considered a reliable source of authority when it comes to patient treatment. The metanarrative of Enlightenment modernity is well worth defending against such a competitor as postmodernist irrationalism. However, what is missed out of such an account is the unequal nature of the relationship between general practitioner and patient. That is a political issue worth addressing, especially if medicine is taken to be an art as well as a science, since no art can offer the kind of guarantee that a science feels it can.

The commitment to the metanarrative of Enlightenment modernity in the context of medicine raises questions for some feminist theorists, who see its assumptions about the nature of the human body as having a detrimental effect on the treatment of women. When it comes to biomedicine – 'the interactive field of science, medicine and health care', as it has been described (Margrit Shildrick, *Leaky Bodies and Boundaries: Feminism, Postmodernism and (Bio)Ethics*, London and New York: Routledge, 1997, p. 7) – some critical ethical problems come to the fore. Shildrick points out that the existing model of medical practice tends to treat the body as a machine (the complaint made by Lewontin about the Human Genome Project). This conception assumes an ability to correct any malfunctions it may have or, at the very least, the duty to intervene in those malfunctions in an attempt to restore normal working. For Shildrick, this is a reductive conception that postmodern theory, with its radical notion of the self, helps to undermine:

> In the late twentieth century, the rapid development of an array of high-tech medical interventions, particularly in the area of procreation, has brought into crisis the purpose of health care. The possibilities are no longer simply those of corporeal normalisation, but,

> on the contrary, of the transgressive interchangeability of body parts; the blurring of distinctions between life and death; the bypassing of generations in reproduction; the creation of genetically transformed individuals; and much else besides. But it is not that medical science has become detached from solid foundations and is now out of control, both materially and morally. Rather, it is that the relative technical sophistication of a postmodern age starkly underlines the *illusion* of control that has sustained medical knowledge from the start. The 'theory' of deconstruction and the practices of postmodern bioscience mesh together to dis-integrate the unified self, the gender binary, the normal body, and the ethics of sameness and difference. I am not suggesting that there is no place for the paradigms of the post-Enlightenment ['post' here refers to post-eighteenth-century culture running through to the twentieth century; that is, to modernity], but that they are no more than necessary fictions to be negotiated with caution and scepticism. A science and culture of boundaries generates an ethics of autonomy, of the proper, of rights and interests, and of contracts; an ethics of fixed limits rather than an ethics of the lived and changing body. It is moreover an ethics in which sexual difference is reduced to the binary exclusivity of the male/not-male pair. (Shildrick, *Leaky Bodies and Boundaries*, p. 215.)

Women suffer most under the paradigm just mentioned, which tends to entrench an essentially modernist world-view rather than the more fluid, postmodern one that enables authority – such as medical authority – to be challenged. When doctors treat women as mere machines with various malfunctions requiring treatment (no matter how sincere they may be in their role as patient advocates), they reinforce a passivity on the woman's part that has long since been sanctioned by patriarchal societies. From that standpoint, medicine, for all its good intentions on behalf of the patient (disinterested advocacy and so on), becomes yet another mechanism of social control by which the *status quo* is preserved. Feminism can only resist this particular discourse. The good side of postmodern bioscience is that it demonstrates just how little basis there is for that mechanical model of the body. Postmodern bioscience rapidly translates into politics when it comes to women. And it is not all that large a step from there into the world of Haraway's cyborgs. At that point, women have wrested control away from doctors, and are viewing them as little more than technicians working to order, rather than authorities to whom they should defer.

Clearly, medicine is an area in which postmodernism has the capability to prompt radical reassessment of a whole range of traditional practices. The gap between those who regard themselves as patient advocates, and those for whom postmodern theory and postmodern technology fundamentally, and irreversibly, alter the nature of the doctor–patient relationship, is only likely to widen even further in the near future. Given that we all have regular contact with the area of health care throughout our lives, the debate over postmodernism in medicine takes on considerable significance. With one side claiming the advent of a brave new world and the other a return to the dark ages (a case of incommensurability if ever there was one), it is hard not to become involved. It will be a debate to be followed with interest, and it is convincing evidence of just how deeply postmodernism has infiltrated our daily existence. Even a visit to your local surgery to check on a minor ailment is not immune from the reach of the postmodern.

The Critique of Postmodern Science

For all the efforts of the enthusiasts, the debate within medicine indicates the depth of unease that many feel at the introduction of postmodern notions into scientific practice. Even more vocal opposition can be found concerning the general appropriation of science by postmodern theorists. Perhaps most notable is the critique offered by Alan Sokal and Jean Bricmont, whose book *Intellectual Impostures* created a storm of controversy in French intellectual circles in its original French edition. The fact that the book was preceded by a hoax article by Sokal, published in a highly respected American academic journal, merely added to the sense of outrage.[12] Sokal and Bricmont were almost totally dismissive of the scientific understanding of the leading postmodern philosophers, claiming extensive misuse of concepts from chaos theory and quantum mechanics in particular in the work of these thinkers. The authors' confrontational manner is made plain from the start:

> The goal of this book is to make a limited but original contribution to the critique of the admittedly nebulous *Zeitgeist* that we have called 'postmodernism'. We make no claim to analyze postmodernist thought in general; rather, our aim is to draw attention to a relatively little-known aspect, namely the repeated abuse of concepts and terminology coming from mathematics and physics. We shall also analyze certain confusions of thought that are frequent in postmodernist

writings and that bear on either the content or the philosophy of the natural sciences.

The word 'abuse' here denotes one or more of the following characteristics:

1 Holding forth at length on scientific theories about which one has, at best, an exceedingly hazy idea. The most common tactic is to use scientific (or pseudo-scientific) terminology without bothering much about what the words actually *mean*.

2 Importing concepts from the natural sciences into the humanities or social sciences without giving the slightest conceptual or empirical justification. If a biologist wanted to apply, in her research, elementary notions of mathematical topology, set theory or differential geometry, she would be asked to give some explanation. A vague analogy would not be taken very seriously by her colleagues. Here, by contrast, we learn from Lacan that the structure of the neurotic subject is exactly the torus (it is no less than reality itself ...), from Kristeva that poetic language can be theorized in terms of the cardinality of the continuum ... and from Baudrillard that modern war takes place in a non-Euclidean space ... all without explanation.

3 Displaying a superficial erudition by shamelessly throwing around technical terms in a context where they are completely irrelevant. The goal is, no doubt, to impress and, above all, to intimidate the non-scientist reader. Even some academic and media commentators fall into the trap: Roland Barthes is impressed by the precision of Julia Kristeva's work ... and *Le Monde* admires the erudition of Paul Virilio ...

4 Manipulating phrases and sentences that are, in fact, meaningless. Some of these authors exhibit a veritable intoxication with words, combined with superb indifference to their meaning.

These authors speak with a self-assurance that far outstrips their scientific competence ... And they seem confident that no one will notice their misuse of scientific concepts. No one is going to cry out that the king is naked.

Our goal is precisely to say that the king is naked. (Alan Sokal and Jean Bricmont, *Intellectual Impostures: Postmodern Philosophers' Abuse of Science*, London: Profile Books, 1998, pp. 3–5.)

Lyotard is one of the main targets of Sokal and Bricmont's attack, and they clearly reject the notion of there being such a thing as a specifically postmodern science: for Sokal and Bricmont this is a term to be placed between quotation marks or prefaced by the phrase 'so-called'. As to the various misuses of scientific terminology in postmodern philosophy, Sokal and Bricmont point out, quite reasonably, that concepts like chaos, linearity and non-linearity mean something quite different to a scientist than to a cultural theorist. These are commentators for whom the transformation of physics into metaphysics is at best a dubious exercise and at worst outright charlatanism that deserves all the opprobrium they proceed to heap upon it.

Other concerns about the relationship between science and postmodernism have been voiced by feminist critics, particularly those defending the notion of a specifically feminist science. Sandra Harding is a case in point:

> However a specifically feminist alternative to Enlightenment projects may develop, it is not clear how it could completely take leave of Enlightenment assumptions and still remain feminist. The critics are right that feminism (also) stands on Enlightenment ground. … I think *feminist postmodernism* has important contributions to make to feminist theory and politics. But here I want to note two ways in which it appears to subscribe to too many Enlightenment assumptions. Paradoxically, feminist postmodernists adhere to some powerful Enlightenment assumptions that even the feminist empiricists do not.
>
> For one thing, in criticizing the very goal of an improved, specifically feminist science and epistemology, they appear to agree with Enlightenment tendencies that all possible science and epistemology – anything deserving these names – must be containable within modern, androcentric, Western, bourgeois forms. However, we are certainly entitled to skepticism about this assumption. It is virtually impossible to specify significant commonalities between the industrialized production of knowledge that characterizes research in the natural sciences and much of the social sciences today and the craft tinkering that produced Galileo's astronomy and Newton's physics. Obviously, science has changed immensely even during modernity … Why can't it continue to change in the future? Why aren't scientific projects formulated for specifically feminist ends an important part of such change? …

> Additionally, the postmodernist critics of feminist science, like the most positivist of Enlightenment thinkers, appear to assume that if one gives up the goal of telling one true story about reality, one must also give up trying to tell less false stories. They assume a symmetry between truth and falsity. Yet even Thomas Kuhn argued that it would be better to understand the history of science in terms of increasing distance from falsity rather than closeness to truth. … If even such relatively traditional thinking about science can propose that truth and falsity need not always be regarded as symmetrical, as opposite poles of the same continuum, this certainly should be a real option within feminist thought. Feminist inquiry can aim to produce less partial and perverse representations without having to assert the absolute, complete, universal, or eternal adequacy of these representations. Isn't that how we should take the feminist Enlightenment critics' own analyses? (Sandra Harding, 'Feminism, Science, and the Anti-Enlightenment Critiques', in Linda J. Nicholson, ed., *Feminism/ Postmodernism*, London and New York: Routledge, 1990, pp. 83–106 (pp. 99–100).)

Science is pictured as an essentially Enlightenment activity, and Harding concedes that traditionally it has been male-dominated. However, she sees no necessity for it to continue to be so into the future. The feminist empiricists whom she mentions argue that scientific practice is riddled with prejudices (sexism and racism, for example), but that, when done correctly, science disproves these. The means to dispel prejudice lie within scientific method itself for such thinkers. That is one way of attacking the masculinist bias in science, but Harding is calling for a much more fundamental shift in perspective with regard to the Enlightenment and modernity. Her argument is that we have an over-rigid conception of these phenomena, and that change is possible without it having to take on a postmodernist, anti-Enlightenment form. Modernity, that is, can be reformed from within, and made to serve our changing ideological needs. Postmodernism can help feminists to attain such a goal, but they are not bound to accept its extreme relativism or cultural pessimism as well. Contrary to many of the pronouncements made about postmodern science, scientific enquiry will continue to have a progressive and liberating quality for feminists, even in the absence of any overarching metanarrative. In other words, there is room for a feminist scientific paradigm within the general scientific enterprise – no matter how this may be conceived in a postmodern world. Postmodern relativism is being countered not by absolutism but by a commitment to finding 'less false' explanations than the ones the scientific heritage has bequeathed us. Less false need not mean that absolute truth is an objective possibility, and perhaps there is room for accommodation here with the less iconoclastic elements of postmodern thought.

Postmodern theory certainly succeeds in shaking up thinking in science and technology, therefore, inducing much talk of both crisis and new opportunities as cherished assumptions are challenged. It has been no less successful in the realm of aesthetics in which, as we now go on to observe, irony comes into its own as a distinctive feature of the postmodern project.

CHAPTER FIVE

The Aesthetics of the Postmodern: Postmodern Culture, the Arts, and the Critical Disciplines

Postmodernism is now well established as an aesthetic theory, and has had a very considerable impact on both creative and critical practice. In this chapter we will look at the nature of that impact in terms of the following arts and their accompanying critical disciplines:

- Architecture – pp. 187–201
- Literature – pp. 201–16
- Visual Arts – pp. 216–26
- Film – pp. 226–34
- Media – pp. 235–43, and
- Music – pp. 243–9.

First, however, some general remarks from the film critic Gilbert Adair about the way in which the line between 'high' art and 'low' art has been systematically blurred in recent cultural history. For Adair, the critical distinguishing feature of postmodern artistic activity is its obsessive self-referentiality, particularly with regard to the past:

> In the haemorrhage of images typical of contemporary culture the past (mostly the recent past) has been transformed into a mammoth lucky dip. All you have to do, if you are a maker of TV commercials or pop promos, a designer of shop windows or record sleeves, the editor of *The Face* or *GQ*, an architect, a painter, even a marketing entrepreneur, is plunge in and scoop out whatever happens to address your particular need. With the decades mingling indiscriminately (the 'recent past' is that which is divisible by decades, not centuries), nothing, *absolutely nothing* ... need seem dated or outmoded. Rare is the artistic expression of the earlier years of this century that has not

> been artificially regilded or pulverised into a thousand glinting particles by the inflationary, insatiable image-spinning of the present. … From those dreamy Edward Hopperesque bistros, neither wholly American nor wholly 'Continental', neither wholly of the past nor wholly of the present, which play so predominant a role in the advertising of soft drinks and alcohol-free lagers, to the enduring taste for a 'Laura Ashley' school of fabrics and furnishings which, not content simply to mass-market a style whose very cachet was once that it could not be industrialised, also contrives to effect an instantaneously faded quality that further serves to camouflage the manufacturing process, from the sudden fad for Forster adaptations in the cinema to the endless musical comedy revivals that have come to monopolise the stages of the West End, from the tabloid depiction of the Royal Family's quotidian round as just another soap opera (or, to be more precise, Ivor Novello-ish soap operetta) to the ruthlessly systematic appropriation by book jacket designers of a pallidly Impressionist school of British painters (in the Tate Gallery I once heard a woman remark to her companion, as they squinted at a murkily gaslit Sickert: 'That would make an awfully nice Virago cover, don't you think?'), the postmodern phenomenon has gradually infiltrated every vacant pocket of our lives and lifestyles. (Gilbert Adair, *The Postmodernist Always Rings Twice*, London: Fourth Estate, 1992, pp. 17, 18–19.)

Adair can also identify some positive aspects in this new, highly self-conscious relationship being constructed with the past. It has, for example, encouraged revivals of little-known musical works and fostered a greater interest in the details of period performance. However, his comments also indicate the dangers of the phenomenon: the sheer glibness and superficiality to which double coding can descend in a society so saturated with images as our own. As he goes on to say, 'at this juncture of our cultural history, assailed as we are by a blitz of often conflicting and contradictory signals from the communications media, we find ourselves at the centre of what Baudrillard has termed a "universe of persuasion"'(Ibid., p. 19). All the more need for critics, one might think, to guide us through the cultural maze of references and cross-references that such a universe involves.

Another example of the high/low culture conflation on which postmodernism thrives, and one to which Adair refers in passing, is Umberto Eco's now-famous 'appropriation' of Barbara Cartland in *Reflections on 'The Name of the Rose'*:

> I think of the postmodern attitude as that of a man who loves a very cultivated woman and knows he cannot say to her 'I love you madly', because he knows that she knows (and that she knows that he knows) that these words have already been written by Barbara Cartland. Still, there is a solution. He can say, 'As Barbara Cartland would put it, I love you madly'. At this point, having avoided false innocence, having said clearly that it is no longer possible to speak innocently, he will nevertheless have said what he wanted to say to the woman: that he loves her, but he loves her in an age of lost innocence. If the woman goes along with this, she will have received a declaration of love all the same. Neither of the two speakers will feel innocent, both will have accepted the challenge of the past, of the already said, which cannot be eliminated; both will consciously and with pleasure play the game of irony. (Umberto Eco, *Reflections on 'The Name of the Rose'*, trans. William Weaver, London: Secker and Warburg, 1984, pp. 67–8.)

Eco's scene perfectly conveys the infiltration of popular culture into 'every vacant pocket of our lives and lifestyles', as Adair put it, as well as the ironic manner that invariably accompanies the practice of cultural referencing in a postmodern age. Irony is a figure with which we will all become familiar as we work our way through the artistic and critical disciplines below, although we might just wonder if Eco has caught its somewhat arch and glib quality, too. As we saw in Hebdige's critique of Biff cartoons in Chapter three, there are those who consider irony to be too knowing for its own good, as well as a figure subject to the law of diminishing returns. Just how many declarations of love, after all, could be framed in Eco's terms of reference and still retain the ironic edge he appreciates? The anti-irony brigade will be well represented in the pages that follow.

Architecture

In the introduction to this critical history, we have already seen how Jencks provocatively dates the 'death of Modern Architecture' from the demolition of the Pruitt–Igoe housing estate in St Louis in 1972, and it is worth considering the reasons he advances for the estate's failure to fulfil its architect's vision:

> Pruitt–Igoe was constructed according to the most progressive ideals of CIAM (the Congress of International Modern Architects)[1] and it

> won an award from the American Institute of Architects when it was designed in 1951. It consisted of elegant slab blocks fourteen storeys high with rational 'streets in the air' (which were safe from cars, but as it turned out, not safe from crime): 'sun, space and greenery', which Le Corbusier called the 'three essential joys of urbanism' (instead of conventional streets, gardens and semi-private space, which he banished). It had a separation of pedestrian and vehicular traffic, the provision of play space, and local amenities such as laundries, crèches and gossip centres – all rational substitutes for traditional patterns. Moreover, its Purist style, its clean, salubrious hospital metaphor, was meant to instil, by good example, corresponding virtues in the inhabitants. Good form was to lead to good content, or at least good conduct; the intelligent planning of abstract space was to promote healthy behaviour. Alas, such simplistic ideas, taken over from the philosophies of Rationalism, Behaviourism and Pragmatism proved as irrational as the philosophies themselves. Modern Architecture, as the son of the Enlightenment, was an heir to its congenital naiveties. (Jencks, *The Language of Post-Modern Architecture*, pp. 23–4.)

Modern Architecture is seen to be a 'grand narrative' trading on Enlightenment ideals of progress. However, it is a progress imposed on a largely uncomprehending, and ultimately also largely hostile, populace. As Oscar Newman pointed out, once vandalism became the norm in projects like Pruitt–Igoe, residents simply voted with their feet:

> Our research indicates that even the most disadvantaged will not tolerate for very long extreme negativism in their living environment. Pruitt–Igoe and other public housing monstrosities, while created accidentally, did for a while succeed in creating a subculture victimized by criminals and the deranged preying on each other. But, in a short time, most residents rebelled and simply moved out; the remaining few got together to insist on administrative and physical changes. With a 65 percent vacancy rate, in a city where housing for welfare recipients is in very short supply, there appears to be little future in negative planning to achieve negative results.
>
> The past few years have witnessed efforts by the Federal Government, in partnership with large corporations, to apply large-scale technological and financial methods to the mass production of housing (as in Project Breakthrough). One danger is all too clear: in

> our concern for coming to grips with the problem of providing mass housing, we may be moving into that period where technological and economic acumen in the provision and construction of buildings have become ends in themselves. A parallel empirical and theoretical breakthrough is necessary in defining the social and psychological constraints with which these new forms will have to reckon. (Oscar Newman, *Defensible Space: People and Design in the Violent City*, London: Architectural Press, 1973, p. 207.)

Newman's point about the dominance of 'technological and economic acumen' is a telling one: this is Enlightenment ultra-rationalism in full flow, with individuals being ruthlessly subordinated to the grand narrative of modernity and its ruling aesthetic. That aesthetic, rather than any human considerations, is what drives the architectural planning:

> The design approach which produces projects in the Pruitt–Igoe mold has its roots in a 'compositional' commitment and orientation: the architect was concerned with each building as a complete, separate, and formal entity, exclusive of any consideration of the functional use of grounds or the relationship of a building to the ground area it might share with other buildings. It is almost as if the architect assumed the role of a sculptor and saw the grounds of the project as nothing more than a surface on which he was endeavoring to arrange a series of vertical elements into a compositionally pleasing whole. Little effort was expended in developing relationships between buildings and ground activities; in fact, separation was most desired. Success in building disposition was thought to be achieved through strict adherence to compositional dictates; therefore concern with function on the part of the designer would only serve to muddy this design approach. Only when the composition of buildings was completed were access paths, play equipment, and seating areas located to serve the buildings. (Newman, *Defensible Space*, p. 59.)

Clearly, the aesthetic is in control here to the exclusion of the human dimension. Humans must adapt to the grand narrative rather than the other way round. It has become a quasi-scientific experiment in social engineering. Pruitt–Igoe's failure thus becomes symbolic of the flaws of an entire world-view, and the rejection of the building by the majority of its tenants within a relatively short period of time provides a grass-roots example of incredulity towards metanarratives. The solution to such failures, in Jencks's eyes, will be the 'radical eclecticism' of the postmodern manner – a deliberate rejection of the new brutalism, with the mix of old and new styles offering a less aesthetically alienating experience to the general public. Modernism had involved almost no concession to popular taste; radical eclecticism starts from the premise that this is an integral part of the architectural process. Architecture is to be conceived of as a partnership between architects and their public.

Paolo Portoghesi has emphasised the historical aspect of postmodern architecture, and was responsible for organising the important 1980 Venice Biennale exhibition 'The Presence of the Past', which mounted a strong defence of postmodern architectural practices. Portoghesi treats postmodern architecture as an opportunity to reconstruct a meaningful relationship with our past – a relationship that had been lost in the modern movement:

> It is worth our while today to reflect upon the unforeseeable fortune of this word [postmodern] in architecture, in order to try to clear up many misunderstandings, and to establish just how useful it can be in relating parallel phenomena taking place in very different areas. In the field of architecture, the term has been used to designate a plurality of tendencies directed toward an escape from the crisis of the Modern Movement with a radical refusal of its logic of development. In the last several decades, this development has led to a chaotic labyrinth, or to the anachronistic attempt to restore the orthodoxy of the golden age of functionalism; the age, of course, of the Bauhaus and C.I.A.M.[2]
>
> The Postmodern has signalled, therefore, the way out of a movement that had for some time stopped 'moving ahead', that had transformed itself into a gaudy bazaar of inventions motivated only by personal ambition and by the alibi of technological experimentation. ... And since modernity coincides in Western architectural culture with the progressive rigorous detachment from everything traditional, it should be pointed out that, in the field of architecture, the postmodern means that explicit, conscious abolition of the dam carefully built around the pure language elaborated *in vitro* [in laboratory, that is closed, conditions] on the basis of the rationalist statute. This language is put into contact again with the universe of the architectural debate, with the entire historical series of its past experiences, with no more distinctions between the periods before or after the first indus-

trial revolution. With the barrier torn down, old and new waters have mixed together. The resulting product is before our eyes, paradoxical and ambiguous but vital, a preparatory moment of something different that can only be imagined: reintegration in architecture of a vast quantity of values, layers, semitones, which the homologisation of the International Style had unpardonably dispersed.

The return of architecture to the womb of its history has just begun, but the proportions of this operation are quite different from those which orthodox critics suppose. This reversion to history would always be a laboratory experiment if it were not also the most convincing answer given thus far by architectural culture to the profound transformations of society and culture, to the growth of a 'postmodern condition' following from the development of post-industrial society. (Paolo Portoghesi, *Postmodern: The Architecture of the Post-industrial Society*, trans. Ellen Shapiro, New York: Rizzoli International, 1983, pp. 10–11.)

Portoghesi's argument is that this re-emergence of historical consciousness is not really captured by the work of other postmodern architectural theorists like Jencks. Jencks's theory of double coding posited the necessity of a relationship between past and present in contemporary buildings, in order to provide the public with familiar, comforting reference points. Yet, as Portoghesi contends, such an approach with its concentration on the stylistic aspects of the postmodern, 'risks confining the phenomenon to an area within the private realm of the architect' (Ibid., p. 10). For Portoghesi, postmodern architecture is a response to deep-lying cultural trends – for example, of the type outlined by Lyotard – rather than a response to modern architecture as such. This is a useful point to make, although it is perhaps a bit unfair to Jencks, who, throughout the course of his extensive writings on the postmodern, shows himself to be very aware of the wider socio-political implications of architectural style. Pruitt–Igoe is a *social* disaster, and not just an aesthetic one.

Scott Lash is far less persuaded by postmodernist architecture's claims to have achieved a successful appropriation of the past – or to have detached itself from the modernist paradigm:

As regards *humanism*, the attempt of postmodern architects at reconstituting the anthropometric and anthropocentric scale and fabric of our cities has turned into the highly individualistic and atomized isolation of the buildings of the 1980s financial districts. This has

> been only a radicalization of modernism's loss of foundations. Modernist architecture came under the spell of industrial society's polarization of manufacturing capital and labour. Industrial capital in the initial tertialization [the transition from the industrial to the service sectors] – the proliferation of high rise buildings for white collar employees of manufacturing firms – of our city centres. And industrial labour in the modernist public housing blocks of first Germany and then Britain, the US and elsewhere. In contradistinction, postmodernist architecture has been subjected to the imperatives of a *post*-industrial economy, of the internationalization of fictive commodities, of financial, business and culture services, of the property developers.
>
> As regards historicity, one must be suspicious of the authenticity of engagement of postmodern architects such as [Charles] Moore and [Michael] Graves with historical universals. Their more populist counterparts, such as Helmut Jahn, Robert Stirling, [Robert] Venturi and Philip Johnson are quite openly 'playful' with historical elements. They operate with historical signifiers only for 'effect' or 'impact' on the public. Their focus surely is not on meaning. Theirs is a desemanticized historicity. (Scott Lash, 'Postmodernism as Humanism?: Urban Space and Social Theory', in Turner, ed., *Theories of Modernity and Postmodernity*, pp. 62–74 (pp. 71–2).)

The playful quality of postmodernism continues to provoke a mixed response from commentators. Some enthuse over it, while others feel that it casts the entire postmodern project of establishing a new cultural paradigm into doubt. Lash, for one, is unimpressed by a theory that has such frequent recourse to playfulness, deciding that 'postmodernism *fails* in its humanist, historical, conventional and other referential undertakings' (Ibid., p. 62). Perhaps there is a slightly puritanical quality about such a response, with its implication that the arts ought to be marked above all by moral seriousness – as if playfulness compromised artistic integrity.

More questions arise about that element of playfulness, especially when it comes to the postmodern recourse to irony:

> Buildings that play ironic games lead a risky life. Suppose that a building has been carefully designed with ironic references to past styles. As time goes on and the building is used, do the ironic references and undertones survive? Or are they smoothed out as the building takes on its own immediate identity? ...

> Some who talk about postmodern architecture speak as if with the modernist barriers down we can roam freely through the past, taking historical allusions and forms from where we will for our double coding or ironic enjoyment. The fall of the modernist prohibition against historical reference coincides with a new world where history is available but we are not restricted by the premodern tradition. We, in our self-consciousness, can use all of history as our material. ... We recognize here the Nietzschean will to power that appropriates the already formed and revalues it into a new meaning. This attitude gets results: Venturi puts a temple in the garden; [Arata] Isozaki puts the Campidoglio at Tsukuba; [Leon] Krier wants to put a ziggurat at La Villette. The architects seem to roam freely. And they are creatively changing their historical originals for the new context: the temple is a decorated shed; the Japanese Campidoglio conspicuously lacks a heroic central focus; the ziggurat would be a hotel.
>
> We are told we can do this because we hold historical content within a new self-consciousness. Unlike our literal-minded ancestors and eclectic nineteenth-century grandparents (not to mention our narrow modern parents), we understand the nature of coding and the semiotics of architecture and, in that awareness, can use all of history as material for play. Our eclecticism is different ...
>
> All this sounds suspiciously similar to ... Gropius implying that the modern style was not a style at all but a free creation based on logic and technology, which one arrived at by abandoning styles and following the strict logic of function.[3] For the postmodern theorists quoted above, history provides a space for free movement. Of course they are not saying that we should follow a strict logic of function. What they are saying is that the postmodern architect stands toward history differently because of a special self-consciousness. But that is what the modern movement claimed. Moderns and postmoderns disagree about historical reference, but is that significant? No style, all styles, what's the difference? (David Kolb, *Postmodern Sophistications: Philosophy, Architecture, and Tradition*, Chicago and London: University of Chicago Press, 1990, pp. 102, 103–4.)

This argument against double coding is well worth pondering. What *will* today's postmodern buildings look like to the next generation? Or even to this same generation just a few years down the line? Postmodernism does tend to act as if it has found a solution to the problems, cultural as well as aesthetic, of modernism. But that solution might soon seem misguided, or just plain *passé*. Fashion can be very fickle in that respect. Then, too, as Kolb points out, it is a very superior attitude on our part to assume that we can raid the past at will for our own purposes. The past, he is suggesting, has its own integrity that should be respected. When analysed in this manner, double coding can appear very facile. And it is always worth remembering that Nietzsche was an inspiration to the modernists as well as to the postmodernists (and not always the happiest of inspirations either, if we take fascism as the dark side of modernity).

Perhaps it is not so much the act of raiding the past that is the problem – this has been done often enough before in architectural history, as in the phenomenon of Victorian Gothic – as the spirit in which it is being conducted. Critics like Kolb are objecting to what they consider to be a patronising air on the part of postmodern architects in their dealings with the past. Irony is, in effect, taken to be disrespectful.

Following on from Jencks, Kenneth Frampton characterises postmodernism as a 'Populist' form of architecture. But, unlike Jencks, he has considerable reservations about the intellectual pretensions of the style:

> [M]any so-called Populist works have nothing more to convey than a gratifying cosiness or an ironic comment on the absurdity of suburban kitsch. More often than not Post-Modernist architects use the private house as an occasion for indulging in idiosyncratic obsessions, as is all too evident from the triviality of Stanley Tigerman's Hot Dog and Daisy Houses of the mid-1970s.
>
> Each year American Populism seems to grow increasingly diffuse in its eclectic parodies from the Art Deco conceits of[,] say[,] Venturi's Brant House at Greenwich, Connecticut (1971) and [Robert] Stern's closely related Ehrman House at Armonk, New York (1975) to the self-styled 'Popular Machinism' (in effect, neo-Art Deco) of Helmut Jahn's typical crystal skyscraper, the high-rise, curtain-walled structure rendered as a giant Wurlitzer organ. ... By scenographically simulating the profiles of classical and vernacular and thereby reducing the architectonics of construction to pure parody, Populism tends to undermine the society's capacity for continuing with a significant culture of built form. The consequence of this for the field as a whole has been a seductive but decisive drift towards a kind of 'tawdry pathos', to use Jencks's felicitous yet ambivalent assessment of the theatrical effects created by [Charles] Moore and

> [William] Turnbull in their designs for Kresge College on the University of California's Santa Cruz campus (1974). The cynicism which ultimately motivates such scenographic operations has since been openly conceded by Moore. (Kenneth Frampton, *Modern Architecture: A Critical History*, 3rd edn, London: Thames and Hudson, 1992, pp. 292–3.)

Moral seriousness is once again conspicuous by its absence, as if the Populists had simply given up on the idea of architecture as an art form. This is a damning indictment of the postmodern architectural project, which Frampton proceeds to castigate in the most uncompromising terms:

> If there is a general principle that can be said to characterize Post-Modern architecture, it is the conscious ruination of style and the cannibalization of architectural form, as though no value either traditional or otherwise can withstand for long the tendency of the production/consumption cycle to reduce every civic institution to some kind of consumerism and to undermine every traditional quality. Today the division of labour and the imperatives of 'monopolized' economy are such as to reduce the practice of architecture to large-scale packaging; and at least one Post-Modern architect, Helmut Jahn, has frankly acknowledged that this is how he sees his role. At its most predetermined, Post-Modernism reduces architecture to a condition in which the 'package deal' arranged by the builder/developer determines the carcass and the essential substance of the work, while the architect is reduced to contributing a suitably seductive mask. This is the predominant situation in city centre development in America today. (Frampton, *Modern Architecture*, pp. 306–7.)

Postmodernism in architecture is, therefore, simply the recycling of older forms, lacking any real creative dynamic of its own. For Frampton, it is an intellectually lazy response, architecture by numbers as it were, and his contempt for it shows quite clearly. Architecture has declined from art to mere 'packaging' – a wounding assessment of the efforts of an entire generation of practitioners.

Instead of postmodernism, Frampton recommends 'critical regionalism', which, as he points out, is more of an attitude of mind than a specific programme:

> [B]y critical regionalism I do not mean any kind of specific style, nor of course do I have in mind any form of hypothetical vernacular revival, nor any kind of unreflected [*sic*] so-called spontaneous grass roots culture. Instead, I wish to employ this term in order to evoke a real and hypothetical condition in which a critical culture of architecture is consciously cultivated in a particular place, in express opposition to the cultural domination of hegemonic power. It is, in theory at least, the critical culture, which, while it does not reject the thrust of modernisation, nonetheless resists being totally absorbed and consumed by it. (Kenneth Frampton, 'Some Reflections on Postmodernism and Architecture', in Lisa Appignanesi, ed., *Postmodernism: ICA Documents 4 and 5*, London: Free Association Books, 1989, pp. 75–87 (p. 78).)

Frampton is reacting against the 'International Style' that came to dominate in modern architecture, in which the same kind of buildings (geometric tower-blocks and so on) could be found in every part of the globe regardless of local vernacular styles. Postmodernism is also reacting against this, of course (hence the criticism of Pruitt–Igoe and its ilk), but Frampton is unwilling to go down that route; he wants to reform, rather than reject, modernism.

Peter Eisenman is also critical of postmodern architecture's obsession with the past, which for him is a commentary on the philosophical failings of architectural modernism:

> In other disciplines, particularly in science and philosophy, there have been extreme changes in the substantive form, the method for producing meaning, since the mid-19th century. Today, the cosmology that articulates the relationships among Man, God and Nature has moved far from the strictures of the Hegelian dialectic. Nietzsche, Freud, Heidegger, and more recently Jacques Derrida, have contributed to the dramatic transformation of thought and the conceptualisation of man and his world. However, very little impact of this transformation has found its way into contemporary architecture. While science and philosophy were critically questioning their own foundations, architecture did not. Architecture remained secure in those very foundations derived from philosophy and science that were themselves being rendered untenable by the internal questioning which characterised those disciplines. Today, the foundations of

> those disciplines remain essentially uncertain. Therefore it is possible to question whether architecture's foundations are also in a state of uncertainty. In architecture this question has never been articulated, its answer is left unformulated.
>
> This is because architecture has never had an appropriate theory of Modernism understood to be a set of ideas which deals with the intrinsic uncertainty and alienation of the modern condition. Architecture always believed that the foundations for its Modernism lay in the certainty and Utopian vision of 19th-century science and philosophy. Today, that vision cannot be sustained. All of the speculative and artistic disciplines – theology, literature, painting, film, and music – have in one way or another come to terms with this dissolution of foundations. Each has reconceptualised the world in its own way in what might be called post-Hegelian terms. What has been called Post-Modernism in architecture, a blatant nostalgia for the lost aura of the authentic, the true and the original, has specifically avoided this most important task.
>
> It can be seen that today the last bastion of individual design is in the commitment to this aura of the authentic, the original and the true. The result of architectural Post-Modernism, however, has been the mass-production of objects which attempt to appear as though they were not mass-produced. In this way, Post-Modernism destroys its own essence, its own *raison d'être*, by becoming a vehicle for the aestheticisation of the banal. (Peter Eisenman, 'Blue Line Text', *Architectural Design*, 58, 1988, pp. 6–9 (pp. 6–7).)

Like Frampton, Eisenman finds postmodern architecture unchallenging; going on to ask, 'What is there of real value in the recreation of an 18th-century village today in Los Angeles or Houston?' (Ibid., p. 9.) To turn to the past, even in the self-conscious mode of pastiche and double coding, is to avoid the present as far as this critic is concerned. It is interesting to note, however, that where Kolb sees a lack of respect for the past in postmodern architectural practice, Eisenman sees almost too much. Postmodernists look back not in irony but in nostalgia, which for Eisenman is just as suspect an attitude to adopt. Nostalgia solves no problems.

While recognising the ambivalent character of postmodern architecture's appropriation of the past, other theorists are more willing to give it the benefit of the doubt. Drawing on the work of the German architectural historian Heinrich Klotz, who praises the wit and humour of postmodern architecture, Donald Kuspit argues that pastiche and double coding can in fact bring a human touch back into the discipline:

> It is appropriate that architecture, the most public of arts, once again openly serve human needs – the need of being human – and that it resist the tendencies of modernist architecture to annihilate all traces of humanness. Clearly, for Klotz, postmodernist architecture at its best is an attempt to counteract the annihilative anxiety that haunts contemporary bourgeois society. Where the modernist building was a metaphor for the modern ideal of robotic man, the postmodernist building is an attempt to make buildings once again like essentially organic human beings, however integrated with the machine. Freud has remarked on the uncanny effect of certain automata that seem human, suggesting that certain human beings operate automatically.[4] While not denying the machine presence in contemporary life, postmodernist architecture is an attempt to restore the human to predominance. The compromises and reconciliations it proposes, from the return to decoration (inseparable from the notion of improving decor or environment) and ornament (once thought of as a 'necessary accident' of human existence), to the symbolizing and signing of historical human presence, are all indications of the postmodernist path to integrity of self.
>
> The fact that an irreversible intersubjectivity is suggested by the 'theatrical' turn to history, in the form of remembered architectural styles, is perhaps the most dynamic part of postmodernism. Postmodernist architecture suggests that it is never possible to be an integral subject without remembering the intersubjectivity of the past. In this sense, it is a kind of healing of the wound modernist architecture gave to the human beings who inhabited it by asking them to forget everything but the present. Modernist architecture functioned like the commissar of a brave new world ruthlessly liquidating all traces of the old worlds that once existed. Now this mechanistic inhumanity is itself eliminated as criminal by postmodernist architecture. This is correlate with the assimilation of the technological revolution that inspired modernist architecture. In however strange a way – and that it is often an apparently comic way suggests that there was a tragic aspect to the old modernist architecture – postmodernist architecture struggles to articulate a sense of human self that, while appropriate to the present, takes its cues from older

> statements of humanness which it struggles to remember. These become its sources. In its encyclopaedic, quasi-museumlike character, postmodernist architecture shows a hunger for old ideas of authenticity. (Donald Kuspit, 'The Contradictory Character of Postmodernism', in Hugh J. Silverman, ed., *Postmodernism – Philosophy and the Arts*, New York and London: Routledge, 1990, pp. 53–68 (pp. 67–8).)

In its contradictory character, postmodernism is both cultural 'ailment' and 'cure' for Kuspit, and he methodically itemises its good and bad points. Kuspit complains that, all too often, postmodern theory lacks a real critical edge and has been absorbed into bourgeois culture anyway, thus dissipating its radical potential. Yet postmodern architecture, in its ability to link back to human history, offers the possibility of a cure for our theoretical ailments. That link to history is taken to be vital, and is something our culture loses at its peril. There *is* moral seriousness in postmodern architecture, therefore, and even wit, humour and playfulness can be deployed in its cause. Modernism's tendency to cut itself off from the past is seen to constitute a grave error of judgement on its part.

For an unashamed celebration of the vernacular in architecture, we can turn to *Learning from Las Vegas*, which attacks modern architecture for having lost sight of the use-value of buildings and public spaces in its narrow-minded concern with formal qualities:

> Learning from the existing landscape is a way of being revolutionary for an architect. Not the obvious way, which is to tear down Paris and begin again, as Le Corbusier suggested in the 1920s, but another, more tolerant way; that is, to question how we look at things.
>
> The commercial strip, the Las Vegas Strip in particular … challenges the architect to take a positive, non-chip-on-the-shoulder view. Architects are out of the habit of looking non-judgmentally at the environment, because orthodox Modern architecture is progressive, if not revolutionary, utopian, and puristic; it is dissatisfied with *existing* conditions. Modern architecture has been anything but permissive: Architects have preferred to change the existing environment rather than enhance what is there. …
>
> Las Vegas is analyzed here only as a phenomenon of architectural communication. Just as an analysis of the structure of a Gothic cathedral need not include a debate on the morality of medieval religion, so Las Vegas's values are not questioned here. … Analysis of existing

> American urbanism is a socially desirable activity to the extent that it teaches us architects to be more understanding and less authoritarian in the plans we make for both inner-city renewal and new development. In addition, there is no reason why the methods of commercial persuasion and the skyline of signs analyzed here should not serve the purpose of civic and cultural enhancement. But this is not entirely up to the architect. ...
>
> Architects who can accept the lessons of primitive vernacular architecture, ... and of industrial, vernacular architecture, ... do not easily acknowledge the validity of the commercial vernacular. For the artist, creating the new may mean choosing the old or the existing. Pop artists have relearned this. Our acknowledgement of existing, commercial architecture at the scale of the highway is within this tradition.
>
> Modern architecture has not so much excluded the commercial vernacular as it has tried to take it over by inventing and enforcing a vernacular of its own, improved and universal. (Robert Venturi, Denise Scott Brown and Steven Izenour, *Learning from Las Vegas*, 2nd edn, Cambridge, MA and London: MIT Press, 1977, pp. 3–6.)

This extract exemplifies a consistent postmodernist criticism of the modernist architectural tradition – that is, in its obsession with originality it has lost touch with the human dimension. Form becomes an end in itself, with the geometrical and the abstract dominating the architectural vision to the exclusion of all other considerations – including, crucially, function and sense of place. The alternative that *Learning from Las Vegas* suggests is to move from 'high art' to popular culture for inspiration. That way, we can regain the human scale that should be present in all architecture, but that the modernist movement had so ruthlessly expunged from the architectural vocabulary for most of the twentieth century. What is being called for is a new relationship with both the general public and the past, even if this means surrendering architecture's commitment to aesthetic purity – as exemplified in the universally applied International Style. What is also being called for is a new sense of humility among the architectural profession. Postmodernism's suspicion of hierarchies of authority comes through very strongly in this study. The argument is that architects have no *right* to dictate the nature of our environment; this has to be a matter of negotiation. As in Jencks, Le Corbusier becomes the symbol of the sheer intolerance to be found in modernist architecture, an authoritarian figure whose unfortunate legacy has to be overcome if architecture is ever to get back in touch with the general public. For Venturi and his associates, the architect as visionary is a concept to be laid to rest.

Literature

Defining what can count as postmodern literature has taxed the critical community quite considerably. One of the key commentators in this field has been Brian McHale, whose formalistic approach to the postmodern novel in the study *Postmodernist Fiction*, although rather restrictive, has been very influential. McHale's concern is to establish common attitudes and narrative strategies running throughout postmodernist fiction:

> [T]he dominant of modernist fiction is *epistemological*. That is, modernist fiction deploys strategies which engage and foreground questions such as … 'How can I interpret this world of which I am a part? And what am I in it?' Other typical modernist questions might be added: What is there to be known?; Who knows it?; How do they know it, and with what degree of certainty?; How is knowledge transmitted from one knower to another, and with what degree of reliability?; How does the object of knowledge change as it passes from knower to knower?; What are the limits of the knowable? … [T]he dominant of postmodernist fiction is *ontological*. That is, postmodernist fiction deploys strategies which engage and foreground questions like the ones Dick Higgins calls 'post-cognitive': 'Which world is this? What is to be done in it? Which of my selves is to do it?'[5] Other typical postmodernist questions bear either on the ontology of the literary text itself or on the ontology of the world which it projects, for instance: What is a world?; What kinds of worlds are there, how are they constituted, and how do they differ?; What happens when different kinds of worlds are placed in confrontation, or when boundaries between worlds are violated?; What is the mode of existence of a text, and what is the mode of existence of the world (or worlds) it projects?; How is a projected world structured? … [O]nce we have identified the respective dominants of the modernist and postmodernist systems, we are in a good position to begin describing the dynamics of change by which one system emerges from and supplants the other. There is a kind of inner logic or inner dynamics … governing the change of dominant from modernist to postmodernist fiction. Intractable epistemological uncertainty becomes at a certain point

> ontological plurality or instability: push epistemological questions far enough and they 'tip over' into ontological questions. By the same token, push ontological questions far enough and they tip over into epistemological questions – the sequence is not linear and unidirectional, but bidirectional and reversible. … [H]owever we characterize the ontology of postmodernism, whether in terms of acceptance of the world or in terms of ontological indeterminacy, we are not characterizing postmodernist poetics as such but only that *part* of its poetics that we might call postmodernist *thematics*. Clearly, a wide range of ontological themes or attitudes is available to postmodernist writers, and it is important to specify which writers display which attitudes. But it is equally important to recognize that these attitudes, whatever they may be, come to our attention only through the foregrounding of ontological concerns which is common to all postmodernist writers, and that to accomplish this foregrounding all postmodernists draw on the same repertoire of strategies. (Brian McHale, *Postmodernist Fiction*, New York and London: Methuen, 1987, pp. 9, 10–11, 26–7.)

The validity of that division between the epistemological and the ontological has been the subject of much debate. However, it does provide a useful approach to the work of such otherwise difficult-to-categorise writers as Kurt Vonnegut, Robert Coover and Raymond Federman.

McHale himself has since come to regard the ultra-formalist approach of *Postmodernist Fiction* as too narrow, and in *Constructing Postmodernism* tries to develop a more sophisticated model that steers away from defining postmodernism quite as tightly as he had done before:

> *Postmodernist Fiction* perhaps seemed to propose a single, all-inclusive inventory of features or characteristics of postmodernist writing, and a single corpus of texts, and seemed to aspire (however inadequately) to encyclopedic exhaustiveness. By contrast, *Constructing Postmodernism* proposes multiple, overlapping and intersecting inventories and multiple corpora [collections of writings; plural of 'corpus', above]; not *a* construction of postmodernism, but a plurality of constructions; constructions that, while not necessarily mutually contradictory, are not fully integrated, or perhaps even integrable, either. In other words, the present book, much more so than its predecessor, tries to acknowledge (however feebly) what Robert Venturi … has called 'the obligation towards the difficult whole'.

> I choose to regard the 'imperfect' integration of these essays as illustration and corroboration of the point I have tried to make throughout this book about the plurality of possible constructions in literary history (and cultural studies generally) and the strategic nature of construction. I wish I could pretend that I set out programmatically to produce a plurality of constructions; unfortunately, it was not as deliberate as that. However, having recognized *post factum* that these essays *do* possess this kind of plurality, I have not sought to reduce multiplicity by imposing on it some (arbitrary) uniformity of model: rather, I have let the multiplicity stand, as appropriate to the book's thesis. (Brian McHale, *Constructing Postmodernism*, London and New York: Routledge, 1992, p. 3.)

The plural aspect of postmodern fiction is what McHale chooses to emphasise this time around, although there is still a clear sense of what differentiates that plurality from other styles of literature.

Linda Hutcheon has also put forward a poetics of postmodernism, in which she focuses on the kind of novel she defines as 'historiographic metafiction':[6]

> Because it is contradictory and works within the very systems it attempts to subvert, postmodernism can probably not be considered a new paradigm (even in some extension of the Kuhnian sense of the term). It has not replaced liberal humanism, even if it has seriously challenged it. It may mark, however, the site of the struggle of the emergence of something new. ... While all forms of contemporary art and thought offer examples of ... postmodernist contradiction, this book (like most others on the subject) will be privileging the novel genre, and one form in particular, a form that I want to call 'historiographic metafiction.' By this I mean those well-known and popular novels which are both intensely self-reflexive and yet paradoxically also lay claim to historical events and personages: *The French Lieutenant's Woman*, *Midnight's Children*, *Ragtime*, *Legs*, *G.*, *Famous Last Words*. In most of the critical work on postmodernism, it is narrative – be it in literature, history, or theory – that has usually been the major focus of attention. Historio*graphic meta*fiction incorporates all three of these domains: that is, its theoretical self-awareness of history and fiction as human constructs (historiographic metafiction) is made the grounds for its rethinking and reworking of the forms and contents of the past. This kind of fiction has often been noticed by

> critics, but its paradigmatic quality has been passed by: it is commonly labelled in terms of something else – for example as 'midfiction' (A. Wilde, 1981)[7] or 'paramodernist' (Malmgren, 1985).[8] Such labelling is another mark of the inherent contradictoriness of historiographic metafiction, for it always works *within* conventions in order to subvert them. It is not just metafictional; nor is it just another version of the historical novel or the non-fictional novel. Gabriel García Márquez's *One Hundred Years of Solitude* has often been discussed in exactly the contradictory terms that I think define postmodernism. For example, Larry McCaffery sees it as both metafictionally self-reflexive and yet speaking to us powerfully about real political and historical realities: 'It has thus become a kind of model for the contemporary writer, being self-conscious about its literary heritage and about the limits of mimesis … but yet managing to reconnect its readers to the world outside the page' (1982).[9] What McCaffery here adds as almost an afterthought at the end of his book … is in many ways my starting point. (Linda Hutcheon, *A Poetics of Postmodernism: History, Theory, Fiction*, New York and London: Routledge, 1988, pp. 4, 5–6.)

Hutcheon's conception of the postmodern is notably low-key, and she chooses to explore it largely through artefacts, taking much of her inspiration from postmodern architectural theory. Historiographic metafiction is held to work in a similar fashion to the kind of architecture lauded by theorists such as Jencks, where the audience is given something familiar with which to identify in order to minimise the possibility of alienation. Concessions are made to the public of a kind that modernism would never countenance.

Critics have even taken to periodizing postmodern literature, as in the case of Barry Lewis, who, writing in the late 1990s, felt he could already look back on it as a historical phenomenon:

> The dominant mode of literature between 1960 and 1990 was postmodernist writing. A few inaugural and closing events can be aligned with these dates (give or take a year or two either way).
>
> > The assassination of John F. Kennedy and the *fatwa* decree against Salman Rushdie.
> >
> > The erection and demolition of the Berlin Wall.

> Philip Roth's essay 'Writing American Fiction' (1961) and Tom Wolfe's 'Stalking the Billion-Footed Beast: A Literary Manifesto for the New Social Novel' (1989).
>
> The killing of Kennedy, and the death threat against Rushdie for writing *The Satanic Verses* (1989) provided two sinister book-ends for a period of history that was rife with terrorism and doubt. The Berlin Wall was the most potent symbol of the Cold War and its accompanying suspicion. This was a world uneasy with rapid technological change and ideological uncertainties.
>
> The essays by Roth and Wolfe indicate how literature responded to this climate. Roth's piece declared that the daily news was more absurd than anything fiction could render. This gave hundreds of novelists the go-ahead to experiment with fantasy and self-consciousness. Wolfe's manifesto, on the other hand, was a rallying-cry for a return to realism. He claimed that postmodernist novelists had neglected the task of representing the complex life of the city. His own work *The Bonfire of the Vanities* (1988) was an attempt to redress the balance by applying the journalistic methods of Balzac and Thackeray to the urban New York jungle.
>
> Another plausible set of benchmarks for this postmodern period involves *Naked Lunch* (1962) by William Burroughs, a novel that challenged every norm of narrative unity and decorum upon its original French publication in 1959. The Boston Superior Court created a sensation when it concluded that the book's portrayal of the hallucinations of a drug addict was nasty and brutish (and not particularly short). Few eyelids were batted, however, in 1992 at the release of the feature film *Naked Lunch* (directed by David Cronenberg). Despite its lurid depiction of talking anuses and virulent cockroaches, the movie met with apathy and not apoplexy, disdain and not disgust. This suggests not only a rise in schlock-tolerance levels, but also a change in attitudes towards transgressive fictional forms. (Barry Lewis, 'Postmodernism and Literature (or: Word Salad Days, 1960–90)', in Stuart Sim, ed., *The Routledge Companion to Postmodernism*, London and New York: Routledge, 2001, pp. 121–33 (pp. 121–2); originally published as *The Icon Critical Dictionary of Postmodern Thought*, Cambridge: Icon Books, 1998.)

As Lewis points out, this particular periodisation can be found even earlier in critical history as, for example, in the work of Richard Ruland

and Malcolm Bradbury, who in 1991 are already consigning postmodern literature (in America at least) to the past:

> It may well be that, as the century ends, postmodernism is on the wane. If so it will undoubtedly remain an influential and revealing phase not just in the history of American literature but of twentieth-century writing generally – a deep-rooted search for a late modern form and style in an age of cultural glut that has been called an age of no style. ... What it most sharply represents is the feeling that, still under the complex shadow of modernism, the aesthetic and intellectual importance of which we have more and more grown to understand, we have both a stylistic situation all our own and a peculiar vacancy of meaning. History has upset the coherence of any single vision – we are after the modern; we are no longer content with an innocent and confident realism. Nor do we still share the modernist crisis, which was related to the historical and political anxieties of the first half of a century whose fundamental direction has changed. Capitalism and radicalism have both had to reconstruct themselves, thereby changing our progressive expectations. The avant-garde is no longer *avant*, but our political, technological, social and artistic philosophies remain as perplexed as ever by the ironies, paradoxes and indeterminacies of a universe science has opened to much vaster exploration. We are abundant in commodities, clever in the creation of systems; we multiply the technologies of information, the powers of artificial intelligence, the channels of global interaction. All our stories have changed, but the fundamental task of stories – to discover for us the meanings we need and the tracks of the imagination down which we might reach them – remains, but anxiously, the same. Now we are no longer in the postwar world but near the close of a century that will give way to a new one with a yet more extensive conception of our modernity. By then it may well seem that our critical philosophies of structuralism and deconstruction were not just explorations but revelations of our awareness both of philosophical and historical indeterminacy – ambiguous, half-destructing products of an age that needed to replenish itself by turning toward the future while recreating what was salvageable from the past.
>
> Postmodernism now looks like a stylistic phase that ran from the 1960s to the 1980s and left the intellectual landscape looking very different – partly reshaped in the anxious, self-doubting liberalism of the 1950s, partly by the indeterminate, radical spirit of the 1960s

> which encouraged expressionist art, aleatory music [based on chance principles], performance theater, the happening, the random street event. Today more conservative styles return to fashion, intellectually and experimentally. (Richard Ruland and Malcolm Bradbury, *From Puritanism to Postmodernism: A History of American Literature*, London and New York: Routledge, 1991, pp. 324–5.)

There is something of a nod here towards the Lyotardean notion of postmodernism and modernism as cyclical phenomena alternating with each other over time, with another episode of modernity being forecast for the new century (although it has to be said that Lyotard himself refuses to periodise postmodernism).[10] Nevertheless, now that we are in that new century, postmodernism is still very much with us in terms of cultural discourse (in literary studies and elsewhere), and it is a moot point whether it can be so neatly periodised as it is by Ruland and Bradbury, and Lewis. Certainly, for commentators like Jencks, and Lyotard too in terms of his broader vision, postmodernism is more than just a temporary cultural phase.

Another way of looking at the transition from modernism to postmodernism is to treat it as the consequence of modernism having exhausted its possibilities as a literary style. One of the major proponents of this notion is the novelist John Barth, whose essay 'The Literature of Exhaustion' puts forward some provocative views on the current state of literature in 1967:

> By 'exhaustion' I don't mean anything so tired as the subject of physical, moral, or intellectual decadence, only the used-upness of certain forms or exhaustion of certain possibilities – by no means necessarily a cause for despair. ... One of the modern things about these two [Samuel Beckett and Jorge Luis Borges] is that in an age of ultimacies and 'final solutions' – at least *felt* ultimacies, in everything from weaponry to theology, the celebrated dehumanization of society, and the history of the novel – their work in separate ways reflects and deals with ultimacy, both technically and thematically, as, for example, *Finnegans Wake* does in its different manner. One notices, by the way, for whatever its symptomatic worth, that Joyce was virtually blind at the end, Borges is literally so, and Beckett has become virtually mute, musewise, having progressed from marvellously constructed English sentences through terser and terser French ones to the unsyntactical, unpunctuated prose of *Comment C'est* and 'ultimately' to wordless

mimes. One might extrapolate a theoretical course for Beckett: language, after all, consists of silence as well as sound, and the mime is still communication ... but by the language of action. But the language of action consists of rest as well as movement, and so in the context of Beckett's progress, immobile, silent figures still aren't altogether ultimate. How about an empty, silent stage, then, or blank pages (an ultimacy already attained in the nineteenth century by that *avant-gardiste* of East Aurora, New York, Elbert Hubbard, in his *Essay on Silence*) – a 'happening' where nothing happens, like [John] Cage's *4'33"* performed in an empty hall?[11] But dramatic communication consists of the absence as well as the presence of the actors; 'we have our exits and our entrances'; and so even that would be imperfectly ultimate in Beckett's case. Nothing at all then, I suppose: but Nothingness is necessarily and inextricably the background against which Being et cetera; for Beckett, at this point in his career, to cease to create altogether would be fairly meaningful: his crowning work, his 'last word'. What a convenient corner to paint yourself into! ...

After which, I add on behalf of the rest of us, it might be conceivable to rediscover validly the artifices of language and literature – such far-out notions as grammar, punctuation ... even characterization! Even *plot*! – if one goes about it the right way, aware of what one's predecessors have been up to. (John Barth, 'The Literature of Exhaustion', in Malcolm Bradbury, ed., *The Novel Today: Contemporary Writers on Modern Fiction*, Manchester: Manchester University Press, 1977, pp. 70–83 (pp. 70, 73–4).)

Postmodernism is that act of rediscovery in which we break with a mode of writing that has 'painted itself into a corner' and has no place else to go. When that happens, it is entirely legitimate for literature to begin all over again – if with a different attitude to the past than had marked out its modernist practitioners. A break with modernism becomes a condition for literature's survival, with Barth in a later essay referring to postmodern fiction as a 'literature of replenishment'.[12] Postmodernism becomes a rediscovery of the act of artistic creation; a brave new world to replace a 'used-up' one that has nothing left to say to us.

Against the confident assertion of postmodernism as a clear break with a modernist past, we have the views of a critic like Gerald Graff, for whom postmodernism is far more rooted in literary tradition than it would like to admit – and for that reason, is to be considered ideologically suspect:

> The postmodernist tendency in literature and literary criticism has been characterized as a 'breakthrough', a significant reversal of the dominant literary and sociocultural directions of the last two centuries. Literary critics such as Leslie Fiedler, Susan Sontag, George Steiner, Richard Poirier, and Ihab Hassan have written about this breakthrough, differing in their assessments of its merits and dangers but generally agreeing in their descriptions of what is taking place. What these critics see happening is the death of our traditional Western concept of art and literature, a concept which defined 'high culture' as our most valuable repository of moral and spiritual wisdom. ... [T]wo strains can be discerned within the general complex of attitudes which have become associated with postmodernism: the apocalyptic and the visionary. These two strains may operate separately or in conjunction ... The first strain is dominated by the sense of the death of literature and criticism; literary culture assumes a posture acknowledging its own futility. The second strain, involving the resurrection of the new sensibility out of the ruins of the old civilization, expresses hopefulness for revolutionary changes in society through radical transformations in human consciousness. ... I want here to raise some critical questions about the postmodernist breakthrough in the arts and about the larger implications claimed for it in culture and society. I want in particular to challenge the standard description of postmodernism as representing a sharp break with romantic-modernist traditions. To characterize postmodernism as a 'breakthrough' – a cant term of our day – is to place a greater distance between current writers and their predecessors earlier in the century than is, I think, justified. ... [P]ostmodernism should be seen not as breaking with romantic and modernist assumptions but rather as a logical culmination of the premises of these earlier movements, premises which are not always clearly defined in discussions of these issues. ... I want to argue that the revolutionary claims which have been widely made for the postmodernist new sensibility are overrated, and that when we view it in the context of the current social and cultural situation, postmodernism shows itself to be a reactionary tendency, one which reinforces the effects of technocratic, bureaucratic society. (Gerald Graff, 'The Myth of the Postmodernist Breakthrough', *TriQuarterly*, 26, 1973, pp. 383–417 (pp. 383–4).)

For Graff, postmodernism is the latest form of anti-rationalism, and as such it is to be resisted: 'In a society increasingly irrational and barbaric, to regard the attack on reason and objectivity as the basis of our radicalism is to perpetuate the nightmare we want to escape.' (Ibid., p. 417.) Rejecting postmodern scepticism as a revolutionary tactic, Graff joins the chorus of voices for whom postmodernism represents an accentuation of all that is most problematical in our culture (although it is fair to say that he has since modified his position on this somewhat).[13] From this perspective, postmodernism is a movement that we follow at our peril.

Despite such reservations, academic literary criticism has developed a strong fascination with the postmodern, with Steven Connor arguing that, breakthrough or not, it has led to modernism taking on a more precise character as a literary phenomenon than might otherwise have happened:

> [T]he contours of the postmodern paradigm are much less clear in literary studies than elsewhere. For one thing, the idea of modernism (though powerful) has never taken hold quite so strongly in literary studies as in, say, art history. Modernism in art and architecture represented itself and was represented as the avant-garde pitting itself remorselessly against the ingrained repressions of the past, and heroically transforming human destiny. Although literary studies depend upon this notion of the shock of the new – every student knows Ezra Pound's battle-cry of 'Make it new'[14] – it is also strangely the case that the ugly duckling of the avant-garde in literature was always quickly transformed into a sleek canonical swan. ... It has been correctly observed that the New Criticism, the critical practice which was so influential in the US and Britain in the middle years of the century, with its fierce emphasis on the play of irony, tension and resolution within a text which is considered as an autonomous artefact, provides an ideal way of reading a body of modernist texts which seemed more and more to deny their readers the pleasures of immediate comprehension, and indeed to demand a highly self-conscious attention to verbal or poetic substance over and above its meaning.
>
> But it is also true that academic literary criticism, especially in Britain, turned away from the modernist writing which its theory seemed to foster. F.R. Leavis and the *Scrutiny* group were much less concerned to act as public relations agents for modernist writing than to assimilate, where it seemed appropriate, the forms and energies of modernism to the native (that is, 'English') traditions of literature. So when Charles Newman speaks of the academic legitimating and con-

taining of the dangerous energies of modernism as a 'second revolution', there is a dangerous simplification: first of all, literary modernism was never exactly the 'revolution' which it might have been elsewhere, and secondly, the literary academy has accommodated and identified itself with modernism in a much less extensive way than Newman believes.[15]

> Nevertheless, the idea of the *post*modern has taken root very firmly in literary studies. It even seems that the urge to identify and celebrate the category of the postmodern has been so strong as to produce by back-formation a collective agreement about what modernism was, in order to have something to react against. (Steven Connor, *Postmodernist Culture: An Introduction to Theories of the Contemporary*, Oxford and Cambridge, MA: Blackwell, 1989, pp. 104–5.)

In other words, postmodernism has been instrumental in defining modernism in the literary academy, perhaps even making the latter seem more important and programmatic than in reality it ever was.

Ihab Hassan argues that we may need to rewrite literary history in order to understand how the postmodern developed out of certain aspects of the modern:

> [I]t is time, perhaps, to make a new construction of literary history. A different line has emerged *within* the tradition of the modern. It leads more directly, through the present, to a literature to come. Its authors sing on a lyre without strings. ... The Avant-Gardists at the turn of the century and the Absurdists of the sixties place these authors within a shadowy frame. Across that frame pass reflections of a changed consciousness, a radical crisis of art, language, and culture. ... The negative, then, informs silence; and silence is my metaphor of a language that expresses, with harsh and subtle cadences, the stress in art, culture, and consciousness. The crisis is modern and postmodern, current and continuous, though discontinuity and apocalypse are also images of it. Thus the language of silence conjoins the need both of autodestruction and self-transcendence. (Ihab Hassan, *The Dismemberment of Orpheus: Toward a Postmodern Literature*, New York: Oxford University Press, 1971, pp. 4, 12.)

In this rewriting of literary history from the modern into the postmodern age, it is this negative quality that is taken to be the dominant characteristic:

> Doubtless the evidence of postmodern literature is quarrelsome, abundant, various. The trends change rapidly and change again from place to place. Yet the two accents of silence, heard throughout this study, persist in postmodern literature: (a) the negative echo of language, autodestructive, demonic, nihilist; (b) its positive stillness, self-transcendent, sacramental, plenary. Sometimes, these accents appear rhythmically, contrapuntally, in an author's work. More often, they sound a distinct keynote of his sensibility. It is impossible to survey the postmodern scene – from Artaud, Brecht, and Ionesco, to Harold Pinter, Peter Weiss, Edward Albee, and Fernando Arrabal (or Jerzy Grotowski and Julian Beck, for that matter); from the last Joyce, Broch, and Céline to Iris Murdoch and Rayner Heppenstall, Günter Grass and Uwe Johnson, Philippe Sollers and Claude Ollier – without assaying a new work full of elaborations and qualifications. … We are compelled at last to discover in the tradition of silence, in some imaginary realm where Sade, Jarry, Tzara, Breton, Hemingway, Kafka, Sartre, Camus, Sarraute, Robbe-Grillet, Genet, and Beckett meet in common awe of human destiny, a meaning larger than criticism can yield. A part of us – at least a part – wants to join them in anticipating a reality which may become all together ours. (Hassan, *The Dismemberment of Orpheus*, pp. 248–50, 257.)

The postmodern in this reading is a literature of cultural crisis, a crisis that is inherited from the modern period. Hassan's canon of postmodern literature ranges particularly widely in this respect, with each author's attitude towards silence being the determining criterion for inclusion. John Barth for one would not approve, most likely seeing this as an attempt to extend the 'literature of exhaustion' past its natural limit.

Postmodernism is not just a phenomenon informing contemporary writing practice, however; it can also be backdated on to literary history to generate new readings of classic texts. In this context we can cite my own and David Walker's work on John Bunyan. This study, *Bunyan and Authority*, explores both Bunyan's fiction and non-fiction in terms of their role in the seventeenth century's well-attested 'crisis of sovereignty' (which gave rise to a civil war in the 1640s and a revolution in 1688–9). The little narrative of Bunyan's nonconformist outlook is caught up in a struggle against the grand narrative of the Restoration monarchy, as well as all the various other little narratives of the period's deeply divided nonconformist movement. The study concludes from this that the mid-to later-seventeenth-century period in English history can be regarded as proto-postmodern, with the various competing little narratives preventing a new grand narrative from successfully forming:

> The explosive growth of religious sectarianism in the seventeenth century certainly argues a situation analogous to the postmodern, in that the more sectarianism proliferates – as it does so spectacularly in the sympathetic climate of the 1640s and 50s, for example – the less chance there is of any grand religious narrative surviving intact; rather, in the desperate search for legitimation procedures undertaken by each new sect, we have the constant production of what Lyotard calls 'differends', irresolvable disputes between discrete phrase regimes which call for the development of ever more elaborate rhetorical skills in the defence of one's position.[16] As a highly vocal proponent of the nonconformist cause, Bunyan can be considered a major figure in this process, whereby, paradoxically enough, it is the very fact of nonconformism's success that serves to entrench religious division within English culture for the foreseeable future. ... [I]f we backdate such a theory as Lyotard's onto seventeenth-century England, what we find is a cultural context where several kinds of grand narrative are unmistakably breaking down (the grand narrative of monarchy, of Anglicanism, of social hierarchy on the feudal model, of religious absolutism and religious authority in general) and where the problem of legitimacy, or more precisely how you *secure* legitimacy, is becoming acute. What do you do when the grand narrative that guarantees the authority of your discourse starts to erode? The very existence of sectaranism is itself symptomatic of a collapse of grand narrative authority. Bunyan's writings exist within, and are responses to, a breakdown of grand narrative and the crisis of legitimacy that it leaves in its wake: Bunyan, we might say, is trying to grapple with the conflict of incommensurable cultural narratives – searching for modern solutions within a postmodernist cultural framework, where the postmodern continually frustrates the modern. (Stuart Sim and David Walker, *Bunyan and Authority: The Rhetoric of Dissent and the Legitimation Crisis in Seventeenth-century England*, Bern and New York: Peter Lang, 2000, pp. 13, 15–16.)

Through postmodern theory we gain a new perspective on the cultural conflicts of an earlier period and how these were being negotiated in the literary domain.

Other critics have pointed to interesting correspondences between eighteenth-century fiction and postmodernism, with Laurence Sterne's *Tristram Shandy* (1759–67) becoming a favoured text for exploration. The hero's search in this narrative for a coherent sense of personal identity, and thus a more stable conception of the self, is consistently frustrated by the jumble of ideas passing through his mind ('association of ideas' in the terminology of the philosopher John Locke).[17] As a result of the constant deflections these cause from the matter in hand, Tristram is unable to identify any pattern in his life, a situation that, to many commentators, prefigures postmodern notions of the self as a fragmented entity:

> Tristram wants to reach a shared awareness of his identity ... [T]he self will emerge from a process to which the reader is invited to contribute: he has to participate in Tristram's creation of himself and his world, otherwise Tristram's attempt at acquiring an identity fails. This makes him entirely dependent upon the reader and his acquiescence in playing the role of an accomplice; in fact, it brings Tristram dangerously near to becoming a postmodern construct ...
>
> Tristram could therefore be thought to be a precursor of postmodern identity, which is also characterised by 'difference' and does not exist on its own, but only in contradistinction to other identities within a web of relationships. The self is defined – and defines itself – only through these external relationships, and since they are continuously changing, so is the self. The same applies to the world in which the self exists, which is also only one of many possible worlds with no particular claim to be considered of any special value. There can be no question of 'gaining an understanding' of this world (or the self, for that matter), since it does not exist apart from the self's particular vision of it. This view of identity in the postmodern world seems to be a fair description of the subject in the world of the postmodern novel. (Herbert Klein, 'The Art of Being Tristram', in David Pierce and Peter de Voogd, eds, *Laurence Sterne in Modernism and Postmodernism*, Amsterdam and Atlanta, GA: Editions Rodopi, 1996, pp. 123–32 (pp. 128, 129).)

As several critics have suggested, such a view of personal identity as a continuously unfolding, and often bewildering, process turns Sterne into a postmodernist *avant la lettre*. Despite repeated researches into his own, and family circle's, past, Tristram fails to find an essential self that would define his character, but that is precisely what postmodern theorists consistently deny exists. The self has no unity. Sterne's hero is left bemused by this state of affairs; but for the postmodernist it is a liberating experience that means we can respond creatively to events as they occur.

Ralph Cohen argues that it is a trait shared by postmodernist and eighteenth-century authors to combine several genres (fictional and non-fictional) within the novel format. Although many critics have claimed that postmodern fiction is concerned to subvert rather than deploy genres, Cohen argues that the novel has a long tradition of being a site of 'multiple discourses', and that this links postmodern novelists with their eighteenth-century predecessors:

> The combinatory nature of genres moves in our time to mixtures of media and to mixtures resulting from the electronic world in which we live. Films, TV genres, university educational programs, our very explanations of identity and discourses all indicate combinations of one kind or another. The precise nature of these combinations differs, but what genre critics and theorists can now study are the interactions within combinations and how these differ from earlier combinations, whether in epic, tragedy, novel, lyric, etc.
>
> This generic procedure, this combinatory genre theory no less than that of the postmodern 'novel' or surfiction,[18] has significant antecedents in the writings of the early eighteenth century. …
>
> To pursue one example of this that is pertinent to postmodern genres, I wish to consider some of the innovative genres that occur at the beginning of the eighteenth century. One of the characteristic features of that species of writing which came to be called the novel reveals a narrator who quite consciously addresses the reader and suggests how the text should be read. The obvious example, *Tristram Shandy*, resists narrative closure, linear narration, includes genres such as the sermon, letter, and story, produces interventions of musical and other non-verbal genres. Certainly with regard to the postmodern … assumption that each new text is written over an older one, one need only consult a satire like Swift's *A Tale of a Tub* [1710]. And Henry Fielding's *Joseph Andrews* [1742] announces itself as 'Written in Imitation of Cervantes, Author Don Quixote'.[19] I am not suggesting that … 'imitation' as used in the eighteenth century is anything but resisted and discarded by postmodern critics. What I am arguing is that Fielding's self-conscious addresses to the reader, that his use of inset stories and thus of multiple narrators who result in

> making the primary characters become secondary while some of the trivial characters become, for the inset story, the primary narrators, that these practices are analogous to some in postmodern genres. When the inset story of Leonard and Paul is interrupted and left uncompleted in *Joseph Andrews* we have a further instance of the discontinuity characteristic of postmodern writing. A generic history will not merely point to these recurrences, but suggest that these are tied to social and cultural no less than literary phenomena. (Ralph Cohen, 'Do Postmodern Genres Exist?', *Genre*, 20, 1987, pp. 241–57 (pp. 241, 248–9).)

This is to argue for postmodern features in eighteenth-century culture generally, and not just in its literature. The formal devices represent a response to those aspects of the culture rather than just experimentation for its own sake. Postmodern theory, therefore, enables us to write a new history of our literary past.

Visual Arts

Surveying the art scene in America from the 1960s, Andreas Huyssen observes the emergence of two distinct forms of postmodernism:

> I will now suggest a historical distinction between the postmodernism of the 1960s and that of the 1970s and early 1980s. My argument will roughly be this: 1960s' and 1970s' postmodernism both rejected or criticized a certain version of modernism. Against the codified high modernism of the preceding decades, the postmodernism of the 1960s tried to revitalize the heritage of the European avantgarde and to give it an American form along what one could call in short-hand the Duchamp–Cage–Warhol axis. By the 1970s, that avantgardist postmodernism of the 1960s had in turn exhausted its potential, even though some of its manifestations continued well into the new decade. What was new in the 1970s was, on the one hand, the emergence of a culture of eclecticism, a largely affirmative postmodernism which had abandoned any claim to critique, transgression or negation; and, on the other hand, an alternative postmodernism in which resistance, critique and negation of the status quo were redefined in non-modernist and non-avantgardist terms, terms which match the political developments in contemporary culture more effectively than the older theories of modernism. ... While the 1960s could still be

> discussed in terms of a logical sequence of styles (Pop, Op, Kinetic, Minimal, Concept) or in equally modernist terms of art versus anti-art and non-art, such distinctions have increasingly lost ground in the 1970s.
>
> The situation in the 1970s seems to be characterized rather by an ever wider dispersal and dissemination of artistic practices all working out of the ruins of the modernist edifice, raiding it for ideas, plundering its vocabulary and supplementing it with randomly chosen images and motifs from pre-modern and non-modern cultures as well as from contemporary mass culture. … [T]he great divide that separated high modernism from mass culture and that was codified in the various classical accounts of modernism no longer seems relevant to postmodern artistic or critical sensibilities. (Andreas Huyssen, *After the Great Divide: Modernism, Mass Culture and Postmodernism*, Basingstoke and London: Macmillan, 1988, pp. 188, 196–7.)

For Huyssen, postmodernism's great virtue is that it enables artists to efface the boundary between aesthetics and politics, and that argues the case for

> a postmodernism of resistance, including resistance to that easy postmodernism of the 'anything goes' variety. … How such resistance can be articulated in art works that would satisfy the needs of the political and those of the aesthetic, of the producers *and* of the recipients, cannot be prescribed, and it will remain open to trial, error and debate. But it is time to abandon that dead-end dichotomy of politics and aesthetics which for too long has dominated accounts of modernism. (Huyssen, *After the Great Divide*, pp. 220–1.)

Too often, however, it has been the 'anything goes' variety of postmodernism that critics have concentrated on, thus missing the political potential that someone like Huyssen identifies in it. As we have seen, for many commentators 'anything goes' sums up postmodernism, confirming its essential triviality. However, for Huyssen it by no means exhausts the postmodern aesthetic.

Paul Crowther is another critic who has identified two main streams of postmodern art practice:

> [T]here are two fundamentally different aspects to Postmodernism in the visual arts. First, in the late 1960s and 1970s, there developed a

> kind of art which is sceptical about the legitimizing discourse of art as a vehicle of elevation and improvement. Now, whereas radical modern movements such as Cubism and Surrealism redeploy traditional genres such as still life, and fantasy, as a means of elevating subjectivity, artists such as [Malcolm] Morley and [Anselm] Kiefer radically question the affirmative discourse of high art, as such. They do so either by incorporating (in an *apparently* unmediated fashion) that which is most directly antithetical to high art – namely mechanically reproduced imagery; or by thematizing (within the particular work) the inadequacy of artistic categories, and, indeed, art's inability to express the complexities and catastrophes of concrete historical experience. We have, in other words, a new form of art whose very pictorial means embody a scepticism as to the possibility of high art. By internalizing this scepticism and making it thematic within art practice, *Critical* Super-Realism and *Critical* Neo-Expressionism give art a *deconstructive* dimension. Such work embodies the same kinds of strategy which inform contemporary poststructuralist approaches to discourse in general. They can, therefore, be defined as the definitive postmodern tendency. ... Now in the latter half of the 1980s the Critical aspect of postmodern art has reached a crisis point. ... Much art practice in the late 1980s involves a kind of ironic deconstruction that recognizes and internalizes its inevitable assimilation by the market. In the Neo-Geo abstractions of Phillip Taafe, for example, we find parodies and subversions of Modernist colour-field painting and 'Op' Art.[20] ... Now in all these Neo-Geo paintings and sculptures a dimension of deconstruction is present, in so far as art's pretensions to elevation or improvement are called into question or shifted to the level of the humorous. But the very good humour of this strategy and the ludicrousness of its means bespeaks an overtly self-ironical and self-negating level of insight. We can deconstruct, but the legitimizing discourse and the market will still have us – so let's have fun with the whole situation while we can. This comic fatalism is of some broader significance, in so far as it marks the point where Critical postmodernism recognizes its own limits. (Paul Crowther, *Critical Aesthetics and Postmodernism*, Oxford: Clarendon Press, 1993, pp. 190–2.)

Crowther is concerned to establish a sense of historical context for postmodernism, taking issue with the theories of Arthur Danto, who had come to the conclusion that postmodern art was post-historical. For Danto, modern art had exhausted itself (recalling Barth's views on modern literature), leaving art in general with nowhere specific to go. The end of modern art effectively signalled the end of art itself. Crowther emphatically disagrees with this assessment, regarding art as a constant process of negotiation between present practitioners and the history of art: 'The moral is clear. Art lives.' (*Critical Aesthetics*, p. 196.)

Danto saw the 1960s as the point when modern art reached its logical end:

> The history of Modernism, beginning in the late 1880s, is a history of the dismantling of a concept of art which had been evolving for over half a millennium. Art did not have to be beautiful; it need make no effort to furnish the eye with an array of sensations equivalent to what the real world would furnish it with; need not have a pictorial subject; need not deploy its forms in pictorial space; need not be the magical product of the artist's touch. All these substractions [*sic*] were achieved over the course of the decades, making it possible for something to be art which resembled as little as one pleased the great art of the past, and to open up space for a liberalized view of art-making which was in its way a model for the various modes of liberations aspired to in the 1960s. Warhol's thought that anything could be art was a model, in a way, for the hope that human beings could be anything they chose, once the divisions that had defined the culture were overthrown. ... What Warhol's dictum amounted to was that you cannot *tell* when something is a work of art just by looking at it, for there is no particular way that art has to look. ... I was immensely excited by what was taking place in those years in art, particularly so by the exhibition of Warhol's work which took place at the Stable Gallery on East Seventy-fourth Street in late spring of 1964, in which the artist showed various cartons of the kind one might see stacked up in the storerooms of supermarkets, packed with cans of Del Monte peach halves or Campbell's tomato juice or bottles of Heinz tomato ketchup, packages of Kellogg's corn flakes, boxes of Brillo pads. I was at the time less interested in what made them art than in the somewhat different question of how they could be seen as art and not as mere artifacts of commercial culture. ... Some years later, however, I began to attach a different philosophical significance to the exhibition. First of all, I came to feel that with the *Brillo Box*, the true character of the philosophical question of the nature of art had been attained. Closely connected with this, I began to believe, appropriating a famous thesis of Hegel's, that with the disclosure or

> discovery of its true philosophical nature, art attains the end of its history – that that exhibition in the Stable Gallery marked what I somewhat impishly called the End of Art.[21] ... For the *Brillo Box* really does look so like boxes of Brillo that the differences surely cannot constitute the difference between art and reality. ... I call this the Post-Historical Period of Art, and there is no reason for it ever to come to an end. Art can be externally dictated to, in terms either of fashion or of politics, but internal dictation by the pulse of its own history is now a thing of the past. ... [T]he Post-Historical Period is a post-narrative period of art. ... [W]e face the future without a narrative of the present. We live in the afterwash of a narrative which has come to its end, and though the memory of it continues in coloring the consciousness of the present, it is clearer and clearer from the way art has become pluralized after the *Brillo Box* that the master narrative of Western art is losing its grip and nothing has taken its place. My thought is that nothing can. (Arthur Danto, *Beyond the Brillo Box: The Visual Arts in Post-Historical Perspective*, Berkeley, Los Angeles, CA and London: University of California Press, 1992, pp. 4–7, 9–10.)

Another name for that age 'without a narrative of the present' is the postmodern. Danto can be quite scathing about this, referring to its double-coding strategies at one point as 'pathetic' (Ibid., p. 129). Nevertheless, he finds living in post-historical times to be 'as exciting as it is ill-defined', so to some extent he can be said to have embraced the postmodern (Ibid., p. 12).

Peter Halley is sceptical about the very conception of modernism in art, arguing that it is all too often reductive. He is also doubtful about the claims of postmodernists to have gone 'beyond' modern art in some way:

> In the last few years, there has been growing interest on the part of many critics in the idea of post-modernism. These writers define post-modernism in various ways, but they share in common the belief that the age of modernist art is over and that a new set of theories is needed to describe today.
>
> No writer, however, seems to have entertained the possibility that what is today thought of as modernism is not really outdated, but merely badly formulated in the first place. Critics today seem to universally equate modernism with the formalist ideas developed by Clement Greenberg in the 1950s.[22] But Greenberg's definition of modernism has never been adequate to define the full range of

twentieth-century modernist art. This formalist modernism was no better suited to define the past than it is the present. Another definition of modernism, outlined by the Spanish writer José Ortega y Gasset in his 1925 essay, '*The Dehumanization of Art*', is both possible and more useful.

Any attempt to define the extent and character of modernist art is both a descriptive and a prescriptive exercise, since no definition of the characteristics of a society's artistic production can be free of the author's aspirations for that society. Greenberg's modernism sought to provide an artistic equivalent for America's post-war aspirations to leadership of the western and developing nations. Today, with those aspirations in shambles, it is not surprising that the ideas behind the equivalent aesthetic movement seem irrelevant and distant. …

Like Greenberg, Ortega has a prescriptive role for modernist art. He sees modernism as the characteristic art of the twentieth century and of the liberal society, which he extols. For Ortega, the primary intellectual force in the twentieth century is relativism. This relativism is produced by individuals with a profound capacity for doubt, and necessitates the invention of a tolerant political system that can encompass such doubt. For Ortega, that political system is liberalism, 'the noblest cry that has ever resounded in this planet'. … Today, the post-modernist critics claim, younger artists are no longer working within the parameters of a modernism. This is true – and has been for a long time – if we define modernism as Greenbergian formalist modernism.

However, if we adopt the assumptions of Ortegan modernism, we find that a good many younger artists, especially among those supported by post-modernist critics, are working within the assumptions of this fifty year-old theory. R.M. Fischer, Steven Keister, Cindy Sherman, and Richard Prince come to mind as artists who aspire to the kind of modernism that Ortega advocates.

On the other hand, a variety of art being produced today truly is something other than modernist. However, to call this art post-modernist is probably a mistake, since it exhibits all the signs of being, in fact, pre-modernist. The return to perspective techniques, the unique art object, human expression, 'sensibility' – these are simply a retreat into nineteenth-century strategies by retrograde artists … There has always been retrogressive art in our culture, but the unusual phenomenon today is that such work has gained the status of major art. (Peter Halley, 'Against Post-modernism: Reconsidering Ortega', in

> *Collected Essays, 1981–1987*, Zurich and New York: Bruno Bischofberger Gallery and Sonnabend Gallery, 1988, pp. 26–46 (pp. 27–8, 29–30, 42–3).)

Halley goes on to insist that modernism is thriving in other areas such as popular music (citing groups like Talking Heads and the Clash as examples), and that 'This market-structure has allowed modernism to flourish today in music. It could provide the necessary impetus for a modernist resurgence in the visual arts.' (Ibid., p. 46.) This suggests that postmodernism amounts to little more than a temporary loss of inspiration or failure of nerve in the face of economic problems that have affected the art market in the 1970s and 80s. In other words, Halley's is another example of the argument that postmodernism is more symptom than cure of cultural crisis. To be postmodern is to be retrograde and reactionary, and if Halley considers your work *not* to be retrograde and reactionary (Fischer, Keister, Sherman, Prince and so on) then, by definition, you cannot be postmodern and can be accepted back into the 'serious' art community.

Craig Owens puts a feminist slant on postmodernist art by arguing that there is an affinity between postmodernism's 'critique of representation' and feminism's 'critique of patriarchy'. To exploit that affinity is to challenge repressive cultural norms:

> That the priority our culture grants to vision is a sensory impoverishment is hardly a new perception; the feminist critique, however, links the privileging of vision with sexual privilege. Freud identified the transition from a matriarchal to a patriarchal society with the simultaneous devaluation of an olfactory sexuality and promotion of a more mediated, sublimated visual sexuality. What is more, in the Freudian scenario it is by looking that the child discovers sexual difference, the presence or absence of the phallus according to which the child's sexual identity will be assumed. … However, it is not only the discovery of difference, but also its denial that hinges upon vision (although the reduction of difference to a common measure – woman judged according to the man's standard and found lacking – is already a denial). …
>
> What can be said about the visual arts in a patriarchal society that privileges vision over the other senses? Can we not expect them to be a domain of masculine privilege – as their histories indeed prove them to be – a means, perhaps, of mastering through representation

> the 'threat' posed by the female? In recent years there has emerged a visual arts practice informed by feminist theory and addressed, more or less explicitly, to the issue of representation and sexuality – both masculine and feminine. Male artists have tended to investigate the social construction of masculinity (Mike Glier, Eric Bogosian, the early work of Richard Prince); women have begun the long-overdue process of deconstructing femininity. Few have produced new, 'positive' images of a revised femininity; to do so would simply supply and thereby prolong the life of the existing representational apparatus. Some refuse to represent women at all, believing that no representation of the female body in our culture can be free from phallic prejudice. Most of these artists, however, work with the existing repertory of cultural imagery – not because they either lack originality or criticize it – but because their subject, feminine sexuality, is always constituted in and as representation, a representation of difference. It must be emphasized that these artists are not primarily interested in what representations say about women; rather, they investigate what representation *does* to women (for example, the way it invariably positions them as objects of the male gaze). (Craig Owens, 'The Discourse of Others: Feminists and Postmodernism', in Hal Foster, ed., *Postmodern Culture*, London and Concord, MA: Pluto Press, 1983, pp. 57–82 (pp. 59, 70–1).)

For Owens, the critique of representation inevitably raises gender issues, although he claims that the critical community generally has tended to miss – or even, perhaps, to avoid – these. The contention is that postmodern art practice is uniquely suited to support feminism's campaign to reveal patriarchy's mechanisms of control. Far from being retrograde and reactionary, therefore, postmodern art is for this commentator at the very forefront of cultural radicalism.

As we can see from Halley's comments, though, the character of postmodern art is a topic that has much exercised the critical fraternity – for example, in terms of whether or not it can be described as avant-garde. Thus we have Robert Dunn's reflections on the relationship between modernist and postmodernist art practice:

> In recent discussions perhaps the most promising approach has been the various attempts to redefine modernism, and specifically the contradictions and complexities of this movement. In this regard, the

> concept of the avant-garde has acquired special significance, raising a fundamental issue: are postmodern artists simply presiding over the close of an era, an 'intermezzo', a stagnant or dying culture; or, are they a new avant-garde, seeking to revitalize the connection between art and life while subverting dominant institutional patterns? Signs of both resistance and co-optation, of rebirth and degeneration, can easily be found in postmodern theories and practices. However, while the concept of postmodernism bears no simple relationship to political categories of 'left' and 'right', obvious continuities with the historical avant-garde suggest themselves.
>
> Whereas the historical avant-garde appealed to both elitism and populism in its attacks on established aesthetic and social conventions, my analysis sees postmodernism as constituting a new kind of cultural populism. Behind this populism lies the ascendancy of the mass media and consumer society on the one hand, and cultural pluralism on the other, contradictory tendencies which account for the ambiguous nature of postmodern culture. My argument sees an end to an *aesthetic* avant-garde, elements of which still could be found in the art movements of the 1960s, and a growth of *cultural* avant-gardes which function within a broad terrain of social and political relationships. Whereas the aesthetic avant-garde of the past attempted to subvert tradition and hegemonic structures on narrowly artistic grounds, cultural avant-gardes are defined by their functions in contesting and reconstructing meanings across a wide range of social and cultural issues. Whereas the former case assumed a public sphere, the latter does not.
>
> I see these avant-gardes operating in a highly fragmented and contradictory environment shaped by the opposition between commercialism (the forces of homogeneity, or 'domination') and cultural politics (the forces of heterogeneity, or 'pluralism'). Underlying and cutting across this distinction is a larger antagonism between the values of scientific and technological advancement and those of tradition and related anti-modernist tendencies (right-wing populism, communitarianism, mysticism, new agism, etc.). Postmodernism and cultural populism have arisen within this complex network of contending forces. (Robert Dunn, 'Postmodernism: Populism, Mass Culture, and Avant-garde', *Theory, Culture and Society*, 8, 1991, pp. 111–35 (pp. 111–12).)

As an example of how the respective avant-gardes operate, Dunn notes a 'shift in values from production to consumption ... as manifested in the break with abstract expressionism in painting and other developments concerned with effect rather than intention or meaning' (Ibid., p. 113).

Achille Bonito Oliva's position is that the avant-garde has now been replaced by a trans-avantgarde:

> The cultural area in which the art of the latest generation moves is that of the trans-avantgarde, which considers language a tool of change, a passage from one work to another, from one style to another. The avant-garde, in all its post-World War II variations, developed along the evolutionistic lines of a *linguistic Darwinism* rooted in the great movements of early twentieth-century art. The trans-avantgarde instead operates outside these confines, following a nomadic attitude which advocates the reversibility of all the languages of the past.
>
> The dematerialization of the work and the impersonality of execution which characterized the art of the seventies, along strictly Duchampian lines, are being overcome by the reestablishment of manual skill through a pleasure of execution which brings the tradition of painting back into art. The trans-avantgarde overturns the idea of progress in art, which was entirely geared toward conceptual abstraction. It introduces the possibility of previous art as only one of several possibilities, directing its attention even toward languages that have previously been abandoned.
>
> Such revival does not mean identification, but rather the capacity to cite the surface of the revived languages with the awareness that, in a changing society whose final form has yet to be defined, one has no choice but to adopt a nomadic and transitory outlook. If there is a crisis in philosophical positivism, which has permeated and determined the development of Western civilization, accelerating social and economic transformations in terms of technological experimentation, then there is also a crisis in the hysteria of the New typical of the traditional avant-garde, which is the cultural effect of this philosophy.
>
> This has caused the historical optimism of the avant-garde – the idea of progress inherent in its experimentation with new techniques and new materials – to collapse. The attention of the artists of the trans-avantgarde is thus polycentric and dispersed over a broad area. These artists no longer seek head-on confrontation. They engage instead in a continuous lateral movement whose path crosses every contradiction and every commonplace, including that of technical and operative originality. ... The trans-avantgarde ... advocates the

> recovery of an internal reason unbounded by the fetters of the art of the immediate past (the chief asset of which was the coherent development of the linguistic precedents of the major movements of the early twentieth century). (Achille Bonito Oliva, *Trans-avantgarde International*, trans. Dwight Gast and Gwen Jones, Milan: Giancarlo Politi Editore, 1982, pp. 6–7.)

Again, we have that insistence on the need to reconstruct a relationship with the past – a relationship that had been lost in the onward march of a purist-minded modernism. Neither is the past treated with disrespect, as critical voices were complaining was the case in postmodern architecture. Instead, there is a sense of recovering the best aspects of past artistic practice, much as John Barth had encouraged authors of fiction to do in order to overcome the 'literature of exhaustion'. To go back into the past is to widen the range of expression in art, which had become fixated on abstraction. The trans-avantgarde refuse to acknowledge the authority of the grand narrative of modernism, or the notion of any dominant style at all with its unwelcome overtones of teleology. Their approach, instead, is in the manner of most postmodern philosophy, intensely pragmatic. It is not so much a case of 'anything goes' as 'whatever works'.

One notes in Oliva, too, echoes of Deleuze and Guattari's theories of nomadism and rhizomatic structures. Artists are to be free to make whatever connections they see fit, without any reference to a central authority (such as the idea of progress that is embedded in modernism), and to drift nomadically across the various practices and styles of art and its history. Modernism is seen as a tyranny, from which the trans-avantgarde has had to free itself – to the immense benefit of the artistic imagination.

Film

Cinema is an area in which postmodernism has had a notable impact, and for some critics it is a medium with a unique capability to capture the postmodern moment:

> The postmodern terrain is defined almost exclusively in visual terms, including the display, the icon, the representations of the real seen through the camera's eye, captured on videotape, and given in the moving picture ... In these traces of the visible and the invisible the figures of postmodern man, woman, and child emerge, as if out of a misty fog. The search for the meaning of the postmodern moment is a study in looking. It can be no other way. This is a visual, cinematic

> age. The collage and the mixed-media-tele/audio text are the iconic markers of this moment. ... The postmodern is a cinematic age; it knows itself through the reflections that flow from the camera's eye. The voyeur is the iconic, postmodern self. Accordingly, a critical cultural studies must orient itself to the cinematic images and narratives that define this age. It respects those realist, and neo-realist narrative and cinematic forms, which, like their 'social consciousness' counterparts in the 1940s and 1950s ... awaken the social structure from its slumber, and force a recognition of social problems and social issues (e.g. *Long Time Companion* [1990]). At the same time it challenges those narratives which offer simplistic, ideological answers to complex questions (for example, *sex, lies and videotape* [1989], *Wall Street* [1987]). It negatively judges those texts which resolve their problems through recourse to the old Oedipal myths of the culture (*Blue Velvet* [1986], *Wild at Heart* [1990]). It promotes gay, lesbian, feminist, and African American, Indian, Spanish American, and Asian American films which illuminate the repressive dimensions of the Oedipal myth and its American dream. It values attempts to experiment with the cinematic apparatus in ways which expose the postmodern condition and all its contradictions (*Do the Right Thing* [1989], *Blade Runner* [1982]). It promotes discursive, figural, and transgressive postmodern films (*Brazil* [1985]), self-reflective cinema (*Speaking Parts* [1990]), postmodernist science fiction (*The Fly* [1986], *Videodrome* [1983]), and the morality tales of Woody Allen.
>
> Subversive texts which unravel the cinematic eye, showing its distortions[,] ... are central to a critical postmodernism. Those which mock and parody the 'astral'[23] and the cinematic apparatus (*Zelig* [1983]) are also needed, as are those films which judge and compare the real against its representations and reproductions (*Broadcast News* [1987]). (Norman K. Denzin, *Images of Postmodern Society: Social Theory and Contemporary Cinema*, London: Sage, 1991, pp. viii–ix, 155.)

The bold claim being put forward by this critic is that cinematic texts have an unrivalled ability to reveal the multiple contradictions of the postmodern age, and thus provide a way to a more profound understanding of contemporary culture. Denzin argues that cinema is the area where recent social theory most needs to test itself ('new ways of inscribing and reading the social must be found' (Ibid., p. ix)), given that the artefacts in question are so rich in capturing the widely varied aspects that go to make up the postmodern condition.

Fredric Jameson, on the other hand, has argued that postmodernism can have a detrimental effect on film-making, encouraging the production of such dubious artefacts as, in his slighting term, the 'nostalgia film':

> Nostalgia film, consistent with postmodernist tendencies generally, seeks to generate images and simulacra of the past, thereby – in a social situation in which genuine historicity or class traditions have become enfeebled – producing something like a pseudo-past for consumption as a compensation and a substitute for, but also a displacement of, that different kind of past which has (along with active visions of the future) been a necessary component for groups of people in other situations in the projection of their praxis and the energising of their collective project.
>
> ... [I]f the 'truth' sought by various kinds of left and radical cultural production in recent times has always turned around production, the dominant of nostalgia film is rather reception and consumption.
>
> What is received is however far from being straightforward: nostalgia film may for example – along with a number of other postmodernisms, such as what is variously called neo-expressionism or the new figuration – involve a return to storytelling, after what are sometimes inaccurately thought of as the 'abstractions' of the modern. As its name suggests, it also seems to involve a new kind of return to History, but then in that case its affinities are probably to be found in the various eclectic historicisms of the other postmodernisms, and not in some renewed or original historicity itself. (Fredric Jameson, *Signatures of the Visible*, New York and London: Routledge, 1990, pp. 137, 221.)

This is a variant of Jameson's 'postmodernism as the cultural logic of late capitalism' argument discussed in Chapter two of this critical history, with the nostalgia film being criticised for deflecting attention away from the genuine historical consciousness of the left. Nostalgia is no more acceptable to Jameson than it is to Eisenman, although for different reasons. The nostalgia film is the past as mere consumption, rather than the past as a source of knowledge, and even inspiration, for the construction of future political programmes to improve the lot of humanity. Double coding is reduced in this instance to the mere capturing of 'the surface sheen of a period fashion reality', so that it can be 'transformed into a visual commodity' (Ibid., p. 130). Both political content and political context, the integrity of the past as many commentators would have it, are effaced in the process. Once again the past is not being accorded the respect it deserves. Postmodern film, no less than postmodern theory in general, becomes a distraction from the political present. It is Habermas's 'neoconservative argument' revisited.

John Belton draws on Jameson's work to argue that postmodern films are marked by a sense of aesthetic exhaustion:

> In terms of stylistic practices, postmodern artists rely upon *pastiche* – a form of imitation of the unique style or content of earlier works that lacks any trace of the satire or parody that characterizes traditional forms of imitation. Pastiche is an entirely *neutral* practice; it conveys no perceptible attitude toward the original. The artist merely adopts a preexistent stylistic mask and speaks blankly (i.e., without expressing any perspective whatsoever toward the work imitated) in the voices of others. [Brian] De Palma's 360-degree tracking shots epitomize the concept of pastiche. They are expressionless imitations of shots that had been highly charged with romantic feeling in [Alfred] Hitchcock.
>
> Postmodern works also acknowledge the primary obstacle confronting contemporary artists – the inability to say anything that has not already been said, the inability to create or to express that which is unique or novel. It is no longer possible, as it was for D.W. Griffith, Hitchcock, [Orson] Welles, [John] Ford, and others, to 'invent' ways of 'writing the cinema'. Hollywood's postclassical filmmakers, like De Palma, could only draw upon a preexistent dictionary of shots, situations, themes, and meanings to express themselves. The authentic expression of ideas that took place in the past is today replaced by quotation and allusion to that authentic expression. (John Belton, *American Cinema/American Culture*, New York: McGraw-Hill, 1994, p. 308.)

Like Jameson, too, Belton notes a sense of *political* exhaustion about postmodern cinema, remarking of its products that, 'Unlike classical cinema, which gives a definite order to experience, these works capture the chaotic spirit of their times. As works that did not know what they wanted to say, they simply reflect the cultural conditions that produced them.' (Ibid., p. 309.) He is talking here of films such as *Taxi Driver* (1976) and *Looking for Mr Goodbar* (1977), the implication being that their makers have simply given up trying to make sense of their world. Postmodernism for this critic is an admission of defeat.

Capturing the chaotic spirit of the times can be seen as a positive characteristic, however, as in the films of Pedro Almodóvar, which for his supporters communicate the sheer exuberance of the postmodern world:

> At the time when Almodóvar was making his first films, the 'end of history' proclaimed by postmodernism had a special meaning in Spain; it signified the end of Francoism as well as the fratricidal legacy of the two Spains. Thus Spanish postmodernism took on an air of carnival, a *fiesta popular*, lived out, like the *Movida* [the youth culture movement], in the streets and public spaces.
>
> Almodóvar brings this festival to the film screen. …
>
> The eclecticism or hybridism so characteristic of the poetics of postmodernism achieves its cinematic hour of glory in Almodóvar's films. Consistent with their reflexive character, the films flaunt this dimension. Yolanda, the nightclub singer-protagonist of *Dark Habits* [1984], remarks that she specializes in cultivating hybrids, while the taxi driver husband and father of … *What Have I Done to Deserve This?* [1985] … brags of his skill as a forger, a talent inherited by his son. With total lack of inhibition and a properly postmodern sense of the ludic [playful], Almodóvar recycles styles and genres from different periods and directors. Parody, pastiche, *mise-en-abîme*, and intertextuality characterize all his films.[24] Together with the carnivalesque, the cannibalization of diverse subjects, styles, and modes of representation is a constant in his films. (Victor Fuentes, 'Almodóvar's Postmodern Cinema: A Work in Progress …', trans. Kathleen M. Vernon and Barbara Morris, in Kathleen M. Vernon and Barbara Morris, eds, *Post-Franco, Postmodern: The Films of Pedro Almodóvar*, Westport, CT and London: Greenwood Press, 1995, pp. 155–70 (pp. 157, 159).)

Anything but a sense of exhaustion or defeat is suggested here, with Almodóvar's films symbolising the creative burst of energy that occurred in Spanish culture on the collapse of a particularly repressive metanarrative (the Franco regime that emerged victorious from the civil war of the 1930s). Cinema in this case, in line with Denzin's dictum, does indeed seem to be 'defining' the age. Granted, the cultural contexts of post-Franco Spain and Reaganite America are very different, but there is no suggestion this time around that the postmodern inhibits the creative imagination – quite the opposite, in fact. Following on from Barth's remarks about a 'literature of replenishment', perhaps we can postulate a 'cinema of replenishment' to counter the Jameson–Belton line of a 'cinema of exhaustion'?

American film history is often divided into 'classical' and 'post-classical' periods, the 'Old' Hollywood and the 'New' Hollywood respectively – that is, the old studio system versus the looser model of production that came into being from the 1970s onwards, driven by certain key directors such as Steven Spielberg, George Lucas and Francis Ford Coppola. For some film historians, post-classical effectively equals postmodern:

> [I]f New Hollywood in the economic sense (the revival of the US film business ...) and the post-classical in the textual sense (a high-concept visual impact movie, preferably in the thriller mode) share the vigorous refiguring of the text and its limits, of the product and its market, we might define the new (postmodern) episteme as one which joins economic with textual excess. Consequently, a 1990s film about Dracula, figure of excess *par excellence*, as well as boundary-creature and boundary-crosser, invariably alerts one to the possibility of different forms of audience engagement, different ways of being inside and outside when it comes to identification and participation. Riding on the new audience demographics with their split mode of address is a 'post-classical' treatment of often very classical narratives, a new treatment of sound and of the image, or at any rate, of the hierarchies between them. My argument would be that Coppola's *Bram Stoker's Dracula* [1992] is symptomatic because in it the classical, the post-classical and the postmodern find distinct articulations. Indeed, part of the ambiguity of the response or irritation this has generated amongst the critics, seems negatively to confirm the slippery, self-referential and mocking pose the film strikes in respect to its own place in movie history. Yet this overdetermined hybridity evidently appealed to the volatile audiences Hollywood is chasing, perhaps not least because the film features an agelessly youthful hero who remembers a future, while living in a past which is yet to happen. What Pierre Sorlin has suggested about film history in general – namely that since there can be no history without singularity or absence, films do not have a history, given that they are fully 'present' every time they are screened – thus refers quite accurately not only to Count Dracula, but to our 'postmodern' position *vis-à-vis* classical cinema:[25] because of its undead nature, the cinema perhaps does not have a history (of periods, styles, modes). It can only have fans, clans

> and believers, forever gathering to revive a fantasm or a trauma, a memory and an anticipation. (Thomas Elsaesser, 'Specularity and Engulfment: Francis Ford Coppola's *Bram Stoker's Dracula*', in Steven Neale and Murray Smith, eds, *Contemporary Hollywood Cinema*, London and New York: Routledge, 1998, pp. 191–208 (pp. 196–7).)

Bram Stoker's Dracula, with its sense of double coding, dense intertextuality (Elsaesser noting citations to 60 other films in it), self-referentiality, cultivation of irony, and effacement of the boundary between high art and popular culture, comes to form almost a template for postmodern American film. It works on several levels, and moreover knows and exploits the fact that it works on several levels.

The extent to which postmodern cinema, even *European* postmodern cinema, can be said to be drawing consciously on postmodern philosophical theory has been a matter of some debate in the discipline:

> The links between the European 'postmodern' cinema of the 1980s and 1990s, and the poststructuralist and postmodernist theory of figures such as Derrida, Lyotard and Baudrillard, are far from transparent, and few, if any, of the European films commonly referred to as postmodern have been directly or substantively influenced by the ideas issuing from such theorists. On the contrary French film-makers, such as Luc Besson, Léos Carax and Jean-Jacques Beineix, were primarily influenced by stylistic developments which occurred within the American cinema, and it was films such as *Chinatown* ([Roman] Polanski, 1974), *American Graffiti* ([George] Lucas, 1973) and *Star Wars* (Lucas, 1977), rather than post-Saussurian theory, which were the inspiration for European 'postmodern' films such as Beineix's *Diva* (1982).
>
> Despite this, a number of clear conceptual correspondences can be traced between postmodern philosophy and postmodern cinema. Postmodern philosophy emphasises creativity, libertarianism, avoidance of value judgements, eschewal of analysis and a rejection of both authoritarianism and grand narratives. Similarly, postmodern cinema erases distinctions between high and low art, mixes styles and genres together in defiance of existing (authoritarian) rules of taste, and employs irony, pastiche and historical indeterminacy in place of directive conceptual analysis. It is the existence of such correspondences which has led some to link films such as *Diva* and Luc Besson's

> *Subway* (1985) to the tradition of Derridean, post-Saussurian philosophy, and to the deconstructionist values contained within that philosophy.
>
> Claims for the radical and progressive potential of postmodern cinema are often based on the perceived presence of these values. (Ian Aitken, *European Film Theory and Cinema: A Critical Introduction*, Edinburgh: Edinburgh University Press, 2001, p. 155.)

There is therefore a commonality of interests rather than any direct set of connections between European postmodern cinema and European postmodern philosophy. They can be said to inhabit, and to provide a commentary on, the same world. That would seem to be the kind of argument that was being made for Almodóvar. The films are both of their age, and help to define it.

There is no doubt that film *theory* has drawn extensively on postmodern philosophy, however, and that the influence of the latter has been to inspire several new approaches to the analysis of film:

> Postmodernism and its relation to film theory depends very much on whether we see it as (1) a *discursive/conceptual grid*; (2) a *corpus of texts* (both those which theorize postmodernism (e.g. Jameson, Lyotard, etc.) and those which are theorized by it (e.g. *Blade Runner*)); (3) a *style or aesthetic* (characterized by self-conscious allusiveness, narrational instability and nostalgic recycling and pastiche); (4) an *epoch* (roughly the post-industrial, transnational information age); (5) a *prevailing sensibility* (nomadic subjectivity, historical amnesia); or (6) a *paradigm shift*: the end of Enlightenment meta-narratives of Progress and Revolution. Some theorists, such as Fredric Jameson, take a multi-dimensional approach which sees postmodernism as *simultaneously* a style, a discourse, and an epoch. (Robert Stam, 'The Politics of Postmodernism: Introduction', in Robert Stam and Toby Miller, eds, *Film and Theory: An Anthology*, Malden, MA and Oxford: Blackwell, 2000, pp. 753–7 (p. 754).)

One of those multi-dimensional approaches can be seen in the following deconstructive reading of 'cyborg' films, in which most of the above categories are clearly in evidence:

> A deconstructive reading is itself an unstable but productive *activity*, one which forces us to confront the constructedness of certain

> concepts, such as the human, that we may have presumed to be stable essences and that we may have preferred not to look much into. The point is not, therefore, to 'deconstruct' movies 'from the outside' but to bring 'deconstructive' questions to bear upon them in order to understand how the films are *already* soliciting or working on the more significant oppositions. It is not, therefore, merely a matter of taking theory to the movies but of apprehending how movies project considerable theoretical light of their own on the screen of our concerns. It thus may be the case that when theory leaves the movie theater, it does not leave unchanged – particularly when that theory is called deconstruction.
>
> It is certainly the case that the issues raised by deconstruction regarding the instability of the concept of the human are evident in films such as *Blade Runner* and both *Terminators* [1984, 1991]; these films take the technological threat to the human as their narrative point of departure and make that threat into the occasion for a cinematic treatment and exploration of the status of the human. Each of the films takes up a consideration of the relationships between human and technology, moreover, not simply in the stories they tell but by their presentation of the spectacle of movies. ... And each of these films asks in its own way what happens when the status and fate of the human becomes intertwined with the technologically reproduced image of the cyborg. (Forest Pyle, 'Making Cyborgs, Making Humans: Of Terminators and Blade Runners', in Jim Collins, Hilary Radner, and Ava Preacher Collins, eds, *Film Theory Goes to the Movies*, New York and London: Routledge, 1993, pp. 227–41 (p. 231).)

Several themes of postmodern thought come together in this piece. First of all there is the rejection of any metanarrative, this time in the aesthetic sense. Neither the film nor the theory dominates in interpretative terms; both must work together interactively. Readings are constructed in that interaction, but they must be continually reconstructed against our current cultural preoccupations (the chaos and contradictions of the times, as it were). Then there is the vexed issue of the relationship between technology and the human, which can create such divergent responses in the postmodern camp – Lyotard on one side, Haraway on the other. In this case, the cinematic artefact invites us to explore that spectrum of response, since it is an issue that has by no means yet been resolved. Personal identity remains an area in which the politics of postmodernism are at their most radical – and their most contentious.

Media

E. Ann Kaplan's analysis of the rock-video channel MTV concludes that it is a quintessentially postmodern phenomenon, although she does not necessarily consider that to be an entirely positive point. Noting that some commentators criticise rock-videos as merely escapist or nihilistic, and thus as offering no real threat to American culture, she provides a more complex interpretation – but with some significant warnings attached:

> A more positive reading of MTV would involve linking it to a radical kind of postmodernism such as has emerged recently from theoretical developments in France. In its radical, Derridean form, postmodernism embodies an attack on bourgeois signifying practices. As a critical theory, postmodernism exposes how these practices, posing as speaking what is 'natural' and 'true', in fact set up a transcendental self as a point outside of articulation. But the practices contain this point of enunciation, which is that of bourgeois hegemony, so that the spectator is unaware of being addressed from a particular position. The postmodernist critic and artist use radically transgressive forms in an effort to avoid the false illusionist position of a speaker outside of articulation. The 'freeing' of the signifiers in this case is a kind of strategy – a way of preventing their usual linkage to mythic signifieds. The decentering of the spectator/reader then has a radical effect in releasing him/her from predictable, confining signifieds.
>
> From this perspective, one could see the effacing in MTV of old boundaries between high and low culture, between past, present, and future, and between previously distinct art forms and genres as an exhilarating move toward a heteroglossia that calls into question moribund pieties of a now archaic humanism.[26] The refusal of classical continuity editing, of the normal cause-effect narrative progression, of shot/counter-shot, of time-place unities makes new demands on the spectator, requiring a more active involvement; videos provide a whole variety of filmic worlds, as against the monolithic world of the classical realist Hollywood film. The creativity and energy of rock videos could represent a refusal to be co-opted into the liberalism that has brought America to its present crisis. …
>
> The very possibility of such contradictory readings of MTV is, again, part of what marks it as postmodernist. The institution is itself embedded in contradictions that are an inevitable part of its cultural

> context. There is some truth to the reading of MTV as a merely co-opted kind of postmodernism that utilizes adolescent desire for its own, commercial ends. The adoption of adolescent styles, images, and iconography by the adult fashion and advertising worlds, by TV shows like *Miami Vice* and by Hollywood films, does not necessarily signal a healthy acceptance of youth's subversive stances; it rather suggests the cynicism by which profit has become the only value. (E. Ann Kaplan, *Rocking Around the Clock: Music Television, Postmodernism, and Consumer Culture*, New York and London: Routledge, 1987, pp. 147–8.)

It is the worry we have found being expressed by several other commentators on the postmodern scene: that postmodernism might be absorbed by the dominant ideology, and end up being, in some sense, complicit with that ideology. Given that it rejects old categories of 'left' and 'right', postmodernism becomes difficult to place politically, and the debate as to whether it is radical or neoconservative goes unresolved. What Kaplan has noted, however, is how easily the surface gestures of postmodernism can be appropriated across the political spectrum. It is not all that difficult to strike a postmodernist pose, as MTV's rock-video culture consistently reveals, but that does not necessarily translate into radical subversion of the dominant ideology. Postmodernism just might turn out to be more style than substance – or at the very least to be interpreted that way by the general public.

Douglas Kellner argues that postmodern style can still conceal reactionary political messages, and needs to be analysed with that fact in mind. He finds most postmodern media criticism, however, far too superficial for the task in hand:

> While the postmodern intervention in the arts is often interpreted as a reaction against modernism, against the stifling elitist canonization of the works of high modernism, the postmodern intervention within television is a reaction against realism and the system of coded genres (sitcom, soaps, action/adventure, and so on) that define the system of commercial television in the United States. In this sense, postmodern interventions within television replicate the assault on realism and genre which modernism itself had earlier attacked. Modernism never took hold in television, especially in the commercial variety produced in the United States – which is culturally hegemonic in many sites throughout the world. Instead, commercial television is predomi-

> nantly governed by the aesthetic of representational realism, of images and stories which fabricate the real and attempt to produce a reality effect. Television's relentless representational realism has also been subordinated to narrative codes, to story-telling, and to the conventions of highly coded genres. …
>
> If for most of its history, narrative story-telling has been the name of the game, on a postmodern account of television image often decenters the importance of narrative. It is claimed that in those programs usually designated 'postmodern' – MTV music videos, *Miami Vice, Max Headroom*, high-tech ads, and so on – there is a new look and feel: the signifier has been liberated and image takes precedence over narrative, as compelling and highly artificial aesthetic images detach themselves from the television diegesis[27] and become the center of fascination, of a seductive pleasure, of an intense but fragmentary and transitory aesthetic experience. … [I]t follows that a postmodern cultural theory should rest content to describe the surface or forms of cultural texts, rather than seeking meanings or significance. Against such a formalist and anti-hermeneutic[28] postmodern type of analysis connected with the postulation of a flat, postmodern image culture, I would advocate a cultural studies which draws on both postmodern and other critical theories in order to analyze both image *and* meaning, surface *and* depth, as well as the politics *and* erotics of cultural artifacts. … [T]he images, fragments and narratives of media culture are saturated with ideology and polysemic [plural, multiple] meanings and … ideology critique continues to be an important and indispensable weapon in our critical arsenal. (Douglas Kellner, *Media Culture: Cultural Studies, Identity and Politics Between the Modern and the Postmodern*, London and New York: Routledge, 1995, pp. 235–6.)

Kellner goes on to demonstrate how *Miami Vice* (1984–9), far from being 'all surface without any depth or layered meanings', is in fact a 'text with a multiplicity of possible meanings which require multivalent readings that probe the various layers of the text' (Ibid., p. 239). Those layers are found to be full of ideological significance, particularly with regard to the overtly consumerist ethic of the 1980s. In effect, the programme's image was selling a lifestyle that glorified American capitalism in an era of right-wing politics – not so much a case of political exhaustion as political promotion for the value system of the Reagan presidency. To treat *Miami Vice* as pure surface, as some critics did, was to have been taken in by the dominant ideology of the time; to have failed to recognise what that surface might signify or who it might benefit. Kellner's point, as is usual in his work, is that we cannot escape politics: no theory can be value-free, no position ideologically neutral. Hence his refusal to give up the practice of ideology critique, the major task of which is to reveal who is controlling whom at each level of society – even that of entertainment.

Ien Ang worries, too, about who is controlling whom when it comes to the role of television in a postmodern world:

> The intellectual challenge posed by the postmodern, as I see it, consists of the need to come to grips with the emergence of a cultural space which is no longer circumscribed by fixed boundaries, hierarchies and identities and by universalist, modernist concepts of truth and knowledge. In this sense, what this book ... hopes to contribute to is a move away from various modernist ways of understanding television audiences, which I believe have dominated established traditions of communication research and which now have generally reached their point of exhaustion. Why? Because television itself has undergone massive postmodernization – manifested in a complex range of developments such as pluralization, diversification, commercialization, commodification, internationalization, decentralization – throwing established paradigms of understanding how it operates in culture and society into disarray. This transformation of television points to the central 'mover' of postmodern culture: an increasingly global, transnational, postindustrial, post-Fordist capitalism, with its voracious appetite to turn 'culture' into an endlessly multiplying occasion of capital accumulation. This has resulted in a seemingly unstoppable ballooning of the volume and reach of television and other media culture in the last few decades, which can therefore no longer be conceived as an easily researchable, contained and containable reality. The 'dominant paradigm' of mass communication research, firmly locating itself in modernist social science, has become obsolete because its scholarly apparatus was not able to grasp the new questions and issues which emerged out of the 'mess' created by the postmodernization of television. (Ien Ang, *Living Room Wars: Rethinking Media Audiences for a Postmodern World*, London and New York: Routledge, 1996, p. 3.)

For all the efforts of post-Fordist capitalism, however, there is still a ray of hope to be discerned from that 'mess'. Given that the postmodern world is governed more by uncertainty than certainty, this means that communication does not always work out as it is designed to by those who are controlling media output. Ang suggests it ought to be

> the *failure* of communication that we should emphasize if we are to understand contemporary (postmodern) culture. That is to say, what needs to be stressed is the fundamental *uncertainty* that necessarily goes with the process of constructing a meaningful order, the fact that communicative practices do not necessarily have to arrive at common meanings at all. This is to take seriously the radical implications of semiotics as a theoretical starting point: if meaning is never given and natural but always constructed and arbitrary, then it doesn't make sense to prioritize meaningfulness over meaninglessness. Or, to put it in the terminology of communication theory: a radically semiotic perspective ultimately subverts the concern with (successful) communication by foregrounding the idea of 'no necessary correspondence' between the Sender's and the Receiver's meanings. That is to say, not success, but failure to communicate should be considered 'normal' in a cultural universe where commonality of meaning cannot be taken for granted. (Ang, *Living Room Wars*, pp. 162, 167.)

Once again, it is an argument against any bid for total control. Both linguistic processes and the audience are too fragmented for such a bid to be successful past a certain point. The 'wars' of the study's title are most definitely political in nature, and the 'mess' is, for this critic, ideologically highly desirable in keeping the totalisers from reaching their desired objectives.

Angela McRobbie offers a particularly robust defence of postmodernism, arguing that its sheer breadth provides greater opportunity for scrutiny of contemporary media, and thus for the development of social and political dissent:

> Postmodernism allows what were respectable sociological issues to reappear on the intellectual agenda. It implicitly challenges the narrowness of structuralist vision, by taking the deep interrogation of every breathing aspect of lived experience by media imagery as a starting-point.
>
> … [T]he frenzied expansion of the mass media has political consequences which are not so wholly negative. This becomes most apparent when we look at representations of the Third World. No longer can this be confined to the realist documentary, or the exotic

> televisual voyage. The Third World refuses now to be reassuringly out of sight of 'us', in the West. It is as adept at using the global media as the old colonialist powers. Equally the 'we' of the British nation no longer possesses any reliable reality. That spurious unity has been decisively shattered. New alliances and solidarities emerge from within and alongside media imagery. A disenchanted black, inner city population in Britain, can watch in an 'ecstasy of communication' as black South Africans use every available resource at hand to put apartheid into crisis. Jokily, and within a kind of postmodern language, Dick Hebdige wrote, in *Subculture* [1979], that TV images of Soweto in 1976 taught British youth 'the Soweto dash'. Ten years later this connection has amplified. The image is the trigger and the mechanism for this new identification. (Angela McRobbie, *Postmodernism and Popular Culture*, London and New York: Routledge, 1994, pp. 14, 16.)

The medium is the message in a positive sense here, in that the ability to use the medium carries a definite political message. McRobbie goes on to argue that, although the 'frenzied expansion of the mass media' is in the first instance market-driven, that need not be taken to mean that the public are simply pawns of global capitalism. Postmodernism's interrogation of media imagery reveals how the process of manipulation works, one medium feeding off the other in an endless round of 'self-referentiality', and thus provides the basis for its subversion (McRobbie, *Postmodernism and Popular Culture*, p. 17):

> [W]hat is often forgotten is that the media also enter the classroom. This remains an undocumented site in the history of the image. But in seminar rooms across the country, slides are projected and students prise open new readings. The educational incorporation of contemporary mass media represents something other than the simple consumption of images, but it is also part of the widening-out process I mentioned earlier. People's usage of and experience of the media increases not just because there is more of it, but because it crops up in different places. Almost all the new disciplines in the arts and social sciences make use of pop imagery, whether in adult education, in degree courses, or on project work with unemployed young people. This gives rise to a rather more optimistic reading of the mass media than that offered by Baudrillard. The invasive impact of these new technologies, because they now occupy a place within these

> institutions, provides a basis for the production of new meanings, new cultural expressions. (McRobbie, *Postmodernism and Popular Culture*, pp. 18–19.)

Cultural studies and media studies act as facilitators of change and dissent, therefore, keeping the media under such close scrutiny that they are unable to dominate as ideally they would like to do, controlling the consumption inspired by their constantly accessible, remorselessly self-referential imagery. The medium is a message that can be turned against the medium.

John Fiske puts foward the thesis that the sheer saturation of our culture by media makes total control difficult. There is, as he puts it, a 'media spectrum', the sheer diversity of which defies attempts to stage-manage audience response:

> The 1992 presidential campaign was characterized by the way its politics leaked over the boundaries of the cultural categories that traditionally organized and controlled them: it spread across the whole media spectrum. Entertainment television – sitcoms, talk shows, and MTV – was as active a terrain of political contest as information television. Postmodernism often points to our technological saturation with images as both a cause and a symptom of this liquefying of structural categories: images are so promiscuous as to defy any attempt to control and organize them. The mediated world is not only the world that we in the West live in, it is a world that has overtaken one in which an unmediated experience seemed possible. It never was, of course, but the rapid growth of our technological media does make a world of oral language, print, live performances, and non-reproduced visuals appear unmediated by comparison.
>
> This technological growth is, if anything, accelerating, particularly with the development of computing. Our appetite for new media appears insatiable – we rarely discard the old to make room for new, but add the new to our existing media aggregate. Radio did not replace books, television did not smother the cinema, and recorded music killed neither the concert nor the radio. Electronic mail and bulletin boards will not replace the telephone, and probably even the old postal distribution of pieces of paper carrying handwritten messages will survive. New media technologies may modify the content, function, and use [of] earlier ones, but they rarely replace them altogether, unless, of course, they can perform the same function more

> efficiently. So the CD has (almost) replaced the LP, and the camcorder the 8mm home movie camera. But in general, the history of media technology is one of aggregation rather than replacement. (John Fiske, *Media Matters: Everyday Culture and Political Change*, 2nd edn, Minneapolis, MN and London: University of Minnesota Press, 1996, pp. 237–8.)

Since Fiske's study was published, text messaging has taken off as a new means of communication, and television delivered through the Internet (generally involving sporting or popular music events) is yet one more option to add to the list. The message is that proliferation of media forms works against the notion of ideological control. There is simply too much of it to monitor.

Fiske feels that the diversity of the 'media spectrum' can be turned to our political advantage, but only if we enter into an active relationship with it:

> A degree of cultural diversity is available to us if we have the will to look for it, and the more often we find it, and the more often we take advantage of it, then the more we will help it to secure its place. Similarly, by using the mainstream media less exclusively and less often, we will pressure them to diversify the voices they admit onto their airwaves and into their columns: they are market driven, and they do need readers, viewers, and listeners. (Fiske, *Media Matters*, p. 53.)

Fiske's is an optimistic outlook on the postmodern condition. Individuals are not to be considered as mere pawns in the service of media interests, to be manipulated as those interests see fit in the pursuit of profits. Rather, individuals can resist such pressure, and even campaign to exert influence over media content. The media need us even more than we need them. Postmodern technology can be enabling, especially as the media spectrum grows ever wider (as it is likely to continue to do); and the postmodern condition is not necessarily one of Baudrillardean post-political passivity, waiting aimlessly for just anything at all to come along. As Fiske insists, we must not 'displace the sins of ourselves onto our media' (Ibid., p. xxviii), but look instead to turn the media against themselves. If we revert to cynicism and nihilism with regard to the outcome of our society's 'living room wars', then, Fiske is contending, we have only ourselves to blame: to some extent, we get the media we deserve. Building on that point, we might say that we get the postmodern world we deserve, too. Perhaps in the end it is all a matter of attitude, and Fiske's line is 'be positive'.

Music

We have already considered in passing the impact of postmodernism on popular music in terms of MTV rock-videos, but there are those who disagree with Kaplan's thesis and, in particular, dispute that it tells us anything of note about the music behind the video. Andrew Goodwin, for example, calls attention to the lack of discussion of the music in such analyses, while also contending that there is little real basis in the music itself for claims of its postmodern status. Goodwin finds the application of postmodern theory to popular music to be somewhat facile – a case of following fashionable theoretical trends rather than identifying some paradigm shift in the material in question:

> Some writers argue that rock music is postmodern by virtue of its eclecticism, through its foundations in interracial, intercultural and intertextual practices ... Lipsitz (1986/7)[29] provides the most fully empirical version of this position. His argument is acute and important, although in my opinion its references to postmodernism are largely redundant. Empirically, Lipsitz cannot be faulted for his observation that rock music is characterized by extraordinary eclecticism and intertextuality: specifically, his argument relates postmodern concepts to Mexican-American musics developed by musicians in East Los Angeles, including the internationally popular band Los Lobos. But, like all accounts which use eclecticism as their founding postmodern motif, it is hard to see what is being *explained* here. The logic that one typically finds is this: postmodernism employs eclecticism and intertextuality; rock music is eclectic and intertextual; *ergo*, rock music is postmodern. But what does this tell us about rock music or postmodernism, other than that they might explain *each other*? (In other words, postmodernism might well be a parasite *description* of post-war pop, rather than an explanatory paradigm.)
>
> If the textual specifics of pop's genres are merely redundant (if, in fact, one believes that rock, pop, and contemporary music *tout court* are postmodern in some more general sense), then what is the point of analyzing them? There is an urgent need to clarify the terms of the debate. ...

> The confusion arises because postmodern theory has mixed up two different issues – the identification of eclecticism (which pervades rock and pop) and the collapse of distinctions based on cultural capital (which remain pervasive, especially *within* the field of rock music ...). When this mistake is laid over the misapprehension that modernism operates in the field of pop music just as it does in 'serious' modern music, the result is conceptual chaos. Whatever its inroads in the visual codes of television (Brechtian devices in prime-time programming, modernist jump-cuts in soap-powder commercials, etc.), the much neglected *aural* codes of music are a different matter. While modernist techniques are accepted by the gatekeepers of high culture, in the market-place of commerce the sounds of dissonance are not so welcome. Today's rap music, like punk rock before it, encounters extraordinary difficulty in gaining airplay and media exposure precisely because its *sounds*, as much as its sentiments, are not conducive to a commercial environment. The music is, in classic modernist tradition, *disruptive*. (Andrew Goodwin, 'Popular Music and Postmodern Theory', *Cultural Studies*, 5, 1991, pp. 174–90 (pp. 176–7, 181–2).)

We are plunged back into the long-running classification debate: modernism or postmodernism? For Goodwin, much of what is put forward as examples of postmodernism in popular music is, in reality, eclecticism – which is not necessarily postmodern in itself. Moreover, the eclecticism of pop does not extend to include modernism, the dissonance of which, in rock or pop, usually results in the loss of a mass audience. There is, in other words, a high/low distinction in rock and pop, as in the arts in general. 'Postmodern rock' nevertheless remains an intriguing possibility that Goodwin wants to explore further. What he demands of the latter is a sense of 'political resistance', and he can identify some candidates – The Smiths, The Cure, New Order (Ibid., p. 187). On the whole, however, he feels that the arguments for postmodernism in rock and pop have been overstated, and that popular music awaits a more fully developed theory of its particular blend of aesthetic and cultural considerations.

Some critics postulate a more intimate connection between rock music and the postmodern, with the former exemplifying the breakdown of the categories of high and low culture in a postmodern age (although, as we have just noted, some commentators believe that the rock and pop world has its own version of the high/low divide):

> The historical moment of postmodernism is also the moment of the birth of rock culture, which is, like television (and unlike film), therefore implicated in many postmodern themes: the role of the multinational communications industry; the development of technologically-based leisure activities; the integration of different media forms; the significance of imagery; the fusion of art theory and sales technique. Pop songs are the soundtrack of postmodern daily life, inescapable in lifts and airports, pubs and restaurants, streets and shopping centres and sports grounds. We can't, in turn, understand the post-war history of pop without reference to the impact of Jameson's 'new kind of society'. (Simon Frith and Howard Horne, *Art into Pop*, London and New York: Methuen, 1987, p. 5.)

As we have noted, Jameson prefers to see the changes itemised by Frith and Horne as features of late capitalism rather than postmodernism, but they are in agreement that we now inhabit a 'new kind of society' that has impacted on all of our cultural forms. Rock and pop, Frith and Horne maintain, are uniquely placed to help us understand what it means to be postmodern. They emphasise the art school background of rock and pop in terms of the British music scene of the mid- to later twentieth century, which in itself constitutes a characteristically postmodern 'intertextual' network.

In another exploration of the breakdown between high and low culture in the musical realm, Jon Stratton identifies a specifically postmodern 'moment' in the history of rock that aligns it with developments in art-music:

> The history of rock and roll, from its working-class beginnings to its acceptance by a middle-class audience and to its more recent overlays with the increasingly rational, increasingly conservative high cultural musical tradition, demonstrates the reconstruction of aesthetic practice and pleasure in the postmodern world of consumption capitalism. It is in this context that we can identify three significant moments of emergence of post-war popular music. The first moment, in the period around 1954, is constituted around the production of a musical formulation which has been classified as rock and roll. The second moment occurred in the period between about 1964 and 1968 when rock and roll shifted from its articulation within a working-class discourse to a discourse which included a middle-class audience. The third moment occurred around 1975 to 1978 when

> rock and roll, in the specific form of punk and the plurality of post-punk rock forms, was integrated in its material practices within the coterminous concerns of the so-called high cultural avant-garde. This occurred within a cultural formulation which denies the specificity of difference between high culture and popular culture and, it should be added, working class and middle class as well ...
>
> ... [P]opular music practice at the third moment began to demonstrate a homology with the practices of the high cultural avant-garde in an increasing blurring of previously established distinctions. The traditional equation of high culture/classical music and popular culture/popular music is being eroded.
>
> Artists as diverse as [Brian] Eno, Philip Glass, Laurie Anderson and Jean-Luc Ponty bear this out. At the same time, new philosophical assumptions are needed to form the basis of the postmodernist aesthetic. Within rock and roll, for example, the new emphasis on style, spectacular commentary as an aesthetic practice, has provided the basis for a recuperation of elements within the rock and roll music tradition ranging from Peggy Lee to The Monkees who had previously been discarded as too lacking in emotion in terms of rock and roll's originary (and working-class) aesthetic of emotive involvement. (Jon Stratton, 'Beyond Art; Postmodernism and the Case of Popular Music', *Theory, Culture and Society*, 6, 1989, pp. 31–57 (pp. 32, 33).)

There has certainly been much more interaction between the classical and popular music worlds than hitherto, the work of the minimalist composer Philip Glass being particularly notable in this respect. Glass has written two 'symphonies' ('Low' and 'Heroes') based on albums by David Bowie in collaboration with Brian Eno. Glass's own remarks on the inspiration for these works indicates how the terms 'classic' and 'popular' have begun to lose their sense of definition in a postmodern world:

> 'Heroes,' like the 'Low' symphony of several years ago, is based on the work of David Bowie and Brian Eno. In a series of innovative recordings made in the late 70s, David and Brian combined influences from world music, experimental avant-garde and rock & roll and thereby redefined the future of popular music. The continuing influence of these works has secured their stature as part of the new 'classics' of our time. (Philip Glass, Sleeve Notes (1996) to 'Heroes' Symphony, Point Music, 1997.)

The fact that the score for 'Heroes' was soon turned into a ballet, an art form heavily associated with the classical music tradition, is evidence of yet more characteristically postmodern blurring of the boundaries between high art and popular culture.

Arguments have been put forward also for a feminist musical aesthetics utilising the insights of postmodern cultural enquiry. In a thought-provoking analysis of how aesthetic value has been determined in Western art music (mainly by reference to modernist, male-oriented criteria), Claire Detels puts the case for a new critical model:

> [I]t appears the time may now be ripe for the emergence of a feminist musical aesthetics, featuring a new paradigm that can support the new feminist musical criticism by changing the terms of the musico-aesthetic debate, similar to the way in which new feminist paradigms and theoretical concepts have changed the aesthetic debate in the literary and visual arts. The paradigm I am proposing is that of *soft boundaries and relatedness*, wherein the covert valuation of 'hard' (i.e., clearly distinct) boundaries in traditional aesthetic definitions and judgments about music is superseded by the recognition of the need to consider relatedness of music and musical entities across 'soft' (i.e., permeable) boundaries, including relatedness to social context and function. The soft boundary of the paradigm is not a hard-and-fast line or rule for defining and judging music as in traditional aesthetics but is similar to Heidegger's sense of boundary: 'that from which something *begins its essential unfolding*'.[30] As a result, the implicit critical focus of the paradigm is on how the unfolding proceeds within and across permeable boundaries, rather than on the definition and reification of the boundaries themselves. Or, in other words, the focus is necessarily the whole musical experience rather than any particularized musical entities.
>
> In its attention to relationship ... the paradigm of soft boundaries and relatedness has ties to contemporary postmodern and feminist theory, hence its characterization here as a postmodern feminist paradigm. The ties to postmodernism are most obvious for, as Jerome Klinkowitz has stated, the key to the postmodern habit of thought is 'that the authentic phenomenon in any event is not *fact* but *relationship*'.[31] The reorientation from fact to relationship has roots in existential and pragmatist philosophy, but it has received particular emphasis in the French poststructuralist theory of, for example, Michel Foucault, Jean-François Lyotard, and Jacques Derrida,

> wherein the traditional 'logocentric' claims to epistemological universality and objectivity have been deconstructed and replaced by a recognition of the validity of multiple perspectives of reality, each related to its own context. Thus, postmodernism has become the philosophy of pluralism and relativity, or, as Lyotard puts it, that which 'denies the solace of good forms'.[32] In the case of music, that denial must extend to supposed norms of musical structure ...
>
> Ideas borrowed from poststructural theory strongly suggest the value of softer, less hierarchical boundaries among the constituencies of artistic experience – in the case of music, the composer, performer, audience, critics, and community. For instance, the deconstructionist view of the literary work as 'text', of writing as 'textuality', and of reading as involving a co-creative 'intertextuality' is a model that, in effect, softens the boundaries among writer, reader, and community, and emphasizes not the fixing of absolute or hierarchical value but the play of meanings among fluid constituencies. ...
>
> [S]omething more than insightful criticism on the margins of musicology is needed if the conservative practices of our institutions of musical education are to be affected. For example, despite multiculturalist success in introducing jazz, popular music, and world music into the academic curriculum, the teaching methods for music history continue to ignore connections of musical style to culture, in favor of the otherwise long discredited 'Great Man [*sic*]' approach, where most of what is emphasized, tested, and recalled is data about composers, almost entirely male, in the traditional canon of Western art-music. (Claire Detels, 'Soft Boundaries and Relatedness: Paradigm for a Postmodern Feminist Musical Aesthetics', in Margaret Ferguson and Jennifer Wicke, eds, *Feminism and Postmodernism*, Durham, NC and London: Duke University Press, 1994, pp. 200–20 (pp. 201–2, 211, 215–16).)

Detels's analysis offers a strong challenge to the existing critical paradigm in Western art-music, which seems particularly susceptible to the application of postmodern theory. Here is an area in which strict hierarchies are still in force, in which composers and performers are standardly treated as heroic figures whose 'genius' and virtuosity are to be consumed by a largely passive audience (the concert and recital circuit, grand opera, recordings). It is also an area that, until relatively recently, has been very heavily male-dominated, thus reinforcing the gender stereotypes upon which our culture is constructed. The 'Great Man' approach derided by Detels still underpins public perceptions of the Western art-music tradition, in which figures like Bach, Mozart and Beethoven are accorded almost god-like status. Western art-music stands in particular need of deconstruction, but to some extent similar attitudes can be found in the rock and jazz worlds as well, given that these are just as much part of our capitalist, consumer-driven culture in which 'genius' is marketed as a commodity. Although Glass has succeeded in reaching a larger market than most composers of his type, Detels bemoans the fact that 'our musical culture' is stuck in a 'professional ghetto' from which it only fitfully connects with the public at large (Ibid., p. 220). A postmodernist-feminist aesthetics will be the first step on the road to a new paradigm from which we will all benefit – professional musicians and public alike. Detels is firmly in the optimist camp when it comes to the postmodern ethos.

The fascination with the postmodern that Steven Connor noted in the field of literary studies is clearly prevalent in the other critical disciplines as well. For opponents of the postmodern, it is a fatal attraction that undermines what they see as the whole point of criticism: making informed value judgements to put into the public arena for debate. A critic once remarked of literary theory, that it was not a theory of literature as such, but an 'alternative metaphysics'.[33] That is an objection that detractors would undoubtedly raise about the impact of the postmodern on criticism of the arts in general – that is, its proponents are less interested in being critics than in being postmodernists. While there can be some truth in that accusation, we have also observed how the postmodern has led to a reassessment of 'the proper relation', as Thomas Docherty put it (see Chapter one of this critical history), between aesthetics and politics. The arts can be seen as an area in which traditional cultural assumptions are being subjected to rigorous challenge, and critics can hardly avoid being drawn into those debates. To engage with the postmodern in the arts is to engage with politics, and to become aware that the two really cannot be separated. Irony is more than a stylistic device; it is both a response to, and an integral element of, cultural crisis.

We have also observed how postmodernism invites us to ponder what is the proper relation to our cultural past – an issue of considerable ideological resonance. The past is currently more of a factor in creative activity than it has been for several generations and, at best, this can suggest a real sense of dialogue with our heritage that is certainly culturally defensible. The notion of cultural superiority that the modernist movement so often communicated in its pronouncements is largely missing in postmodern artistic practice, and one could argue that this is a positive development – that it signals a better sense of proportion as to our own place in history. Postmodernism has also opened up the possibility of new readings of the art of the past; these are, again, generally of a politically informed nature, and can enable us to see the productions of, for example, the seventeenth and eighteenth centuries in a new light. Whatever the proper relation between aesthetics and politics may be, postmodernism has ensured that it remains a hot topic for debate.

Conclusion

What have we learned from this critical history of postmodern culture? We have certainly learned that postmodernism is an immensely wide-ranging phenomenon with the capacity to infiltrate nearly every area of our lives – right down to the practice of medicine and religion, and even how we watch television. Whether you agree with its sentiments or not, you cannot escape postmodernism. It is something all of us have to confront in some way or other. We have learned also that postmodernism is still very much news, despite various reports that it has already run its course. Those who feel it was a temporary, late twentieth-century phenomenon, there and gone within two or three decades, have been over-hasty in consigning it to history. Far from declining into a footnote, it continues to generate heated debate in the academy and to divide intellectual disciplines into opposing camps, as well as to inspire creative activity across all the arts. It has altered the ground rules of what counts as art, how the art world itself operates, and how the public and the creative artist interact. In the process, the high art/popular culture boundary has been comprehensively breached, thus helping to undermine élitism in our society.

In political terms, the postmodern is still very much with us, even if recent events have called into question its claim that metanarrative is a declining force in human affairs. The growth of religious fundamentalism, as we have noted at various points in this critical history, contradicts the postmodern analysis of our condition as being marked by the progressive withering away of metanarratives – but it also makes us aware of the postmodern's very real virtues. Uncritical obedience of authority can only too easily become a factor of our political lives, and postmodernism's critique of authority is an extremely valuable one that deserves to be continued. At the very least, it may help to keep metanarratives more honest than they might otherwise be, or have been in the past. In that sense, perhaps postmodernism is more of an ideologically oppositional movement than commentators such as Zygmunt Bauman have given it credit for – an alternative where he could not see one.

Religious fundamentalism may be more of a pre-modern than a modern metanarrative, but it shares with the modern an obsession with control, and it is against all such attempts at control, over thought as well as action, that postmodernism's critique is directed. In this case, looking back in irony is a politically significant activity, as well as a politically desirable one for most of us in a largely secular culture. Irony can certainly be justified as a response to this particular cultural crisis.

The area of greatest contention that we have identified over the course of our enquiries is that of value judgement. Postmodernism tends to claim that we have no basis for making value judgements. There is a school of thought within the movement that regards value judgement as one of the defining features of the hierarchical and authoritarian culture that is being rejected, hence a practice to be rejected utterly in its turn. Critics, even those who admit that modernity has its share of faults, cannot accept the avoidance of value judgement that the postmodern seems to entail. Keith Tester spoke for that constituency in general when he insisted that 'some ability to evaluate is necessary' (Chapter three), and value judgement remains a sticking point in any engagement with the postmodern. Yet we have seen that the postmodern involves various value judgements – if only of the implicit variety. The rejection of modernity and its works is at base a moral one. Modernity exploits and represses individuals both in the West and the Third World; therefore it is to be dismantled for the benefit of humanity at large. As we observed Derrida arguing with some passion in *Specters of Marx*, 'never have violence, inequality, exclusion, famine and thus economic oppression affected as many human beings in the history of the earth and humanity' (Chapter two). Postmodernism assumes moral failings in modernity, and that demands an act of value judgement. While some of its more extreme voices may sound as if they are being iconoclastic for sheer iconoclasm's sake, there is a core of moral principle in postmodernism that deserves to be acknowledged – and respected.

What postmodernism's detractors claim, however, is that you cannot make such value judgements if you are also simultaneously preaching relativism. Judgements reached without use of criteria agreed in advance may satisfy a thinker like Lyotard, but not his opponents, who will regard such decisions as being arbitrary at best. For the latter, a system so dangerously dependent on the whims of individuals in key positions makes a mockery of justice. The radical pretensions of postmodernism will continue to be treated with scepticism by traditional thinkers, of both the left and the right, as long as that charge of relativism can be levelled against postmodernism. What is certain is that the debate's significance far transcends the philosophical realm. At stake is our entire relationship to authority, and there is no doubt that authority is currently under scrutiny to an almost unprecedented degree in recent cultural history. In the West, at least, authority is no longer taken on trust.

There looks to be a lot of mileage left in this reassessment of authority's place in our lives – as well as of what counts as authority. Everything or nothing, replenishment or exhaustion, brave new world or return to the dark ages, the debate rolls on. Irony and crisis: postmodernism's critical history is still being written.

NOTES

INTRODUCTION

1 Jean-François Lyotard, *The Postmodern Condition: A Report on Knowledge*, trans. Geoff Bennington and Brian Massumi, Manchester: Manchester University Press, 1984, p. xxiv.
2 Charles Jencks, *The Language of Post-Modern Architecture*, 6th edn, London: Academy Editions, 1991, p. 13.

CHAPTER ONE

1 See Jencks, *The Language of Post-Modern Architecture*, p. 20. Margaret A. Rose attaches little significance to its use at this point, however (see Margaret A. Rose, *The Post-Modern and the Post-Industrial: A Critical Analysis*, Cambridge: Cambridge University Press, 1991, n. 1, p. 180).
2 Rudolf Pannwitz uses the term to refer to the new kind of individual emerging in European culture in *Die Krisis der Europäischen Kultur*, in which it suggests something like a fascist mentality (see Steven Best and Douglas Kellner, *Postmodern Theory: Critical Interrogations*, New York: Guilford Press, 1991, pp. 5–6).
3 Bernard Iddings Bell, *Postmodernism and Other Essays*, Milwaukee, WI: Morehouse, 1926; and *Religion for Living: A Book for Postmodernists*, London: John Gifford, 1939.
4 Bell, *Religion for Living*, p. xvi.
5 Bernard Rosenberg, 'Mass Culture in America', in Bernard Rosenberg and David Manning White, eds, *Mass Culture: The Popular Arts in America*, Glencoe, IL: Free Press, 1957, pp. 3–12 (p. 5).
6 Peter F. Drucker, *The Landmarks of Tomorrow: A Report on the New Post-Modern World*, London: Heinemann, 1957, p. ix.
7 Jencks, *The Language of Post-Modern Architecture*, p. 14.
8 [*Editorial note:*] In Hegel's philosophical scheme, a 'World Spirit' evolves through human history, until it achieves self-realisation. When it reaches this state, civilisation is assumed to have attained its highest form of expression, and history, as we have known it, ends (see, for example, G.W.F. Hegel, *Phenomenology of Spirit*, trans. A.V. Miller, Oxford: Oxford University Press, 1977). A 'negative Hegelianism', such as Bell is implying is to be found in the work of Foucault, prophesies an irreversible decline of human civilisation.
9 Arthur Penty had already been writing regular articles on the subject of post-industrialism in the *Daily Herald* newspaper before the First World War. These were subsequently published in book form as *Old Worlds for New: A Study of the Post-Industrial State*, London: George Allen and Unwin, 1917.
10 Ingeborg Hoesterey, 'Introduction: Postmodernism as Discursive Event', in Ingeborg Hoesterey, ed., *Zeitgeist in Babel: The Postmodernist Controversy*, Bloomington and Indianapolis, IN: Indiana University Press, 1991, pp. ix–xv (p. xv).

CHAPTER TWO

1 Immanuel Kant, *Critique of Pure Reason*, trans. Norman Kemp Smith, 2nd edn, London and Basingstoke: Macmillan, 1933; and *Critique of Practical Reason*, trans. and ed. Mary McGregor, Cambridge: Cambridge University Press, 1997.
2 J.P. Stern, *Nietzsche*, 2nd edn, London: Fontana, 1985, p. 115.
3 [*Editorial note:*] In Kant's *Critique of Pure Reason*, 'transcendental apperception' is the element in self-consciousness that unifies our thoughts, making experience of the world possible.
4 See Jean-Paul Sartre, *Existentialism and Humanism*, trans. Philip Mairet, London: Methuen, 1948. A literal translation from the French would be *Existentialism is a Humanism*, which implies a far closer connection than the English translation, although Sartre was later to change his mind on this notion.

5 For an example of the school's work, see Harold Bloom, et al., *Deconstruction and Criticism*, London and Henley: Routledge and Kegan Paul, 1979.

6 New Criticism was one of the most influential methods of literary criticism in the twentieth century. It treated literary works as self-contained artefacts that were to be analysed in terms of their internal unity and needed no reference to factors in the external world. The greater the degree of unity (such as consistent patterns of imagery in a poem), the more successful the literary work was held to be. Such a method was in sharp contrast to sociologically based forms of criticism, such as Marxism, which insisted that literary works had to be analysed as part of the wider socio-political culture of their time.

7 [*Editorial note:*] To be 'deterritorialised' is to lead a nomadic life in which one has no allegiance to any specific piece of territory (such as that bounded by the nation state). Since politics is largely based on the defence of territory, this would lead to a collapse of the political system as we know it.

8 Readers wishing to follow up this exchange in more detail are referred to my edited collection *Post-Marxism: A Reader*, Edinburgh: Edinburgh University Press, 1998. For the controversy surrounding post-Marxism in general, see my *Post-Marxism: An Intellectual History*, London and New York: Routledge, 2000.

9 Jürgen Habermas, 'Modernity: An Unfinished Project', trans. Nicholas Walker, in Maurizio Passerin d'Entrèves and Seyla Benhabib, eds, *Habermas and the Unfinished Project of Modernity: Critical Essays on 'The Philosophical Discourse of Modernity'*, Cambridge and Oxford: Polity Press and Blackwell, 1996, pp. 38–55 (p. 53).

CHAPTER THREE

1 [*Editorial note:*] That is, not needing to be known with certainty. Fallibilism takes a pragmatic attitude to knowledge, not requiring absolute proof.

2 [*Editorial note:*] Dana Polan, 'Post-modernism as Machine', paper given to the Australian Screen Studies Association, Sydney, December 1986.

3 [*Editorial note:*] Social constructivism regards both our knowledge and conception of reality as being dependent upon the particular relations and practices of our society. Symbolic interactionism claims that we adopt a series of agreed roles in social situations. We act as the role demands, having learned to see ourselves as others see us. The theory grew out of the work of the Chicago School of sociology (see also note 10 of this chapter).

4 [*Editorial note:*] See Mike Featherstone, *Consumer Culture and Postmodernism*, London: Sage, 1991, and Scott Lash, *Sociology of Postmodernism*, London and New York: Routledge, 1990. Extracts from both these works appear later in this chapter.

5 [*Editorial note:*] See Georg Simmel, 'The Philosophy of Fashion' (1905), trans. Mark Ritter and David Frisby, in David Frisby and Mike Featherstone, eds, *Simmel On Culture: Selected Writings*, London: Sage, 1997, pp. 187–217 (p. 192).

6 [*Editorial note:*] Benjamin believed that traditional works of art (such as paintings) had an 'aura' about them that expressed their sense of uniqueness as artefacts. The work's history and cultural status went towards creating, and maintaining, that aura. Many modern art forms, however, such as film and photography, did not have this sense of aura, since they could be copied. The original therefore had no special status. If on the one hand the aura was lost, on the other this made the art form more democratic, as it was more widely accessible. See Benjamin's essay, 'The Work of Art in the Age of Mechanical Reproduction' (1936), in the collection *Illuminations*, ed. Hannah Arendt, trans. Harry Zohn,

London and Glasgow: Collins/Fontana, 1973.

7 [*Editorial note:*] 'Hyper-criticism' refers to theories such as Marxism, which held that the dominant ideology affected all practices within a society. Whatever happened within the media and popular culture, for example, was to be regarded as infected by the values of the dominant ideology. If one accepted the Marxist line on this, then all forms of criticism turned into ideological critiques.

8 'Cultural populism' is defined by McGuigan as the assumption that popular culture is more important than 'high' culture.

9 [*Editorial note:*] See Marshall Berman, *All That is Solid Melts into Air: The Experience of Modernity*, London: Verso, 1982.

10 [*Editorial note:*] Rather confusingly, there are two Chicago 'Schools' – one in sociology and the other in architecture – both of which grew up in the late nineteenth century and both of which had research interests in the city as a social entity. The sociological school was famed for its work on social psychology, which led to the development of the theory of symbolic interactionism. The architectural school is identified with the development of the skyscraper, which became an integral part of the rebuilding programme in central Chicago after the Great Fire of 1871. It seems likeliest that Davis is referring to the architectural school here. The Frankfurt School was a group of philosophers and social scientists attached to the Institute of Social Research at the University of Frankfurt in the 1920s and 30s, which subsequently relocated to New York after the Nazi take-over in Germany in 1933. Leading members of the School, such as Theodor W. Adorno, Max Horkheimer (see Chapter two) and Herbert Marcuse, developed an analytical method called 'Critical Theory', which had its base in Marxism.

11 [*Editorial note:*] 'Postfordism' describes the move from a heavy-manufacturing, production-line-based economy (Fordism), to a more flexible, often service-led, model of the kind that post-industrial theorists such as Daniel Bell (see Chapter one) advocate. Fordism is identified with modernity.

12 [*Editorial note:*] See Michel Foucault, *The Order of Things: An Archaeology of the Human Sciences*, trans. Alan Sheridan-Smith, London: Tavistock, 1970.

13 [*Editorial note:*] See Fredric Jameson, 'Postmodernism and Consumer Society', in Hal Foster, ed., *The Anti-Aesthetic*, Port Townsend, WA: Bay Press, 1983, pp. 111–25 (later republished as *Postmodern Culture*, London and Concord, MA: Pluto Press, 1985).

14 [*Editorial note:*] Jean Baudrillard, 'The Ecstasy of Communication', in Foster, *The Anti-Aesthetic*, pp. 126–34.

15 [*Editorial note:*] Jean Baudrillard, 'Forgetting Foucault', trans. Nicole Dufresne, *Humanities in Society*, 3, 1980, pp. 87–111.

16 [*Editorial note:*] As devised by the French playwright of the absurd, Alfred Jarry (best-known work, *Ubu Roi*), pataphysics 'is the science of imaginary solutions'.

17 [*Editorial note:*] In deconstructionist theory, 'supplementarity' describes how meaning fails ever to be complete. Just as the *Oxford English Dictionary* requires a supplement at its end (that is, it is not complete in itself as it stands), so all words require to be supplemented by others – and are, in turn, supplements of other words. The process of supplementation never ends. The word 'supplement' itself means an addition to the original, such that it is both part of, and *not* part of, the original (as in the *OED* example). Deconstructionists play upon this ambiguity, which they take as evidence of a more general ambiguity within language.

18 [*Editorial note:*] E. Young, 'On the Naming of the Rose: Interests and

Multiple Meanings as Elements of Organisational Culture', *Organisation Studies*, 10, 1989, pp. 187–206.

19 See, for example, S. Clegg, *Modern Organizations: Organization Studies in the Postmodern World*, London: Sage, 1990; John Hassard and Denis Pym, eds, *The Theory and Philosophy of Organisations: Critical Issues and New Perspectives*, London: Routledge, 1990; M. Alvesson and H. Wilmott, eds, *Critical Management Studies*, London: Sage, 1992; M. Alvesson, *Cultural Perspectives on Organisations*, Cambridge: Cambridge University Press, 1993; R.D. Stacey, D. Griffin, and P. Shaw, *Complexity and Management: Fad or Radical Challenge to Systems Thinking?*, London and New York: Routledge, 2000.

20 [*Editorial note:*] Milbank's term of 'hyper-reason' seems to imply reason taken to ridiculous extremes, its only role being to prove that arbitrary power underpins all human activities.

21 Jean-François Lyotard, *The Inhuman: Reflections on Time*, trans. Geoffrey Bennington and Rachel Bowlby, Cambridge and Oxford: Polity Press and Blackwell, 1991. This work is covered in more detail in Chapter four.

22 For another critical view of this aspect of contemporary life, see James Gleick, *Faster: The Acceleration of Just About Everything*, London: Little, Brown, 1999.

23 [*Editorial note:*] Deconstructionists argue that meaning is never complete or fixed; it is instead always 'differed' and 'deferred'. The meaning of a word at any one point differs from a range of other meanings it had in the past (and will have in the future), and is deferred from reaching completion. Walker is arguing that this same process of 'deferral' is at work when it comes to the principle of state sovereignty, which likewise is never finally fixed.

24 'First nations' refer to the original inhabitants of colonised countries, such as America, Canada and Australia.

25 [*Editorial note:*] See Anthony Giddens, *Profiles and Critiques in Social Theory*, London: Macmillan, 1982, p. 227.

26 [*Editorial note:*] See Samuel P. Huntington, *The Clash of Civilizations and the Remaking of World Order*, New York: Simon and Schuster, 1996.

27 [*Editorial note:*] Said's article, 'Islam and the West are Inadequate Banners', published in the *Guardian*-owned *Observer* newspaper on 16 September 2001 (and later in expanded form as 'Collective Passion' in Egypt's *Al-Ahram Weekly*), shows the kind of sentiments to which Warraq is objecting. Referring to 'formulaic expressions of grief and patriotism' on the part of America's political class, Said goes on to assert that 'to most people in the Islamic and Arab worlds the official US is synonymous with arrogant power, known for its sanctimoniously munificent support not only of Israel but of numerous repressive Arab regimes, and its inattentiveness even to the possibility of dialogue with secular movements and people who have real grievances' (p. 27, main section).

CHAPTER FOUR

1 Imre Lakatos, 'Falsification and the Methodology of Scientific Research Programmes', in Imre Lakatos and Alan Musgrave, eds, *Criticism and the Growth of Knowledge*, Cambridge: Cambridge University Press, 1970, pp. 91–196 (p. 178).

2 See the extract from Žižek's *The Sublime Object of Ideology* in Chapter two of this critical history (pp. 85–6).

3 Thomas Kuhn deals with this topic in detail in *The Copernican Revolution: Planetary Astronomy in the Development of Western Thought*, Cambridge, MA and London: Harvard University Press, 1957.

4 [*Editorial note:*] See Louise B. Young, *The Unfinished Universe*, New York: Simon and Schuster, 1986.

5 The belief that the order and design

in our world cannot be accidental, and that they can only be explained as the work of a divine creator. It was a popular argument in the eighteenth and nineteenth centuries among Christian theologians, and is still occasionally used by philosophers of religion nowadays.

6 [*Thom's note:*] 'According to some purists, the French term "Morphogenèse" is used only to designate the appearance of new organic forms in the course of evolution. In English the word "Morphogenesis" is more widely used, since it designates, among other things, the development of the adult organism from the embryo. ... Here we shall employ the term morphogenesis ... in the widest sense, to denote any process creating (or destroying) forms.' (René Thom, *Mathematical Models of Morphogenesis*, trans. W.M. Brookes and D. Rand, Chichester: Ellis Horwood, 1983, pp. 13, 14.)

7 One of the current favourites to lead us to such a unified theory is 'superstring theory'; see, for example, the account given in Brian Greene, *The Elegant Universe: Superstrings, Hidden Dimensions, and the Quest for the Ultimate Theory*, London: Jonathan Cape, 1999, in which it is argued that we are on the very verge of success in this quest.

8 [*Editorial note:*] Descartes held that human beings consisted of a mind and a body, contingently connected (through the pineal gland), and that the mind could exist independently of the body. Mind, therefore, was not strictly speaking part of nature. Descartes also argued that there was a crucial difference between humans and the rest of the animal kingdom, and that animals could be considered, in some sense, mere machines. Again, this makes a distinction between humanity and the natural world.

9 [*Editorial note:*] 'Photonics' is the term given to the use of light to carry information – as in optical fibres and lasers. More popularly, it refers to the optical transmission technologies applied to 'Information Technology' (IT) – the Internet, phones, video and so on (definition supplied by Dr Brett Wilson, UMIST, Manchester).

10 [*Editorial note:*] Frederick Winslow Taylor's *The Principles of Scientific Management* (1911), New York: Dover, 1997, put forward theories designed to improve manufacturing workers' output. Taylorism notoriously treated workers much like machines.

11 [*Editorial note:*] See Marshall McLuhan, *Understanding Media: The Extensions of Man*, London: Routledge and Kegan Paul, 1964.

12 Alan Sokal, 'Transgressing the Boundaries: Towards a Transformative Hermeneutics of Quantum Gravity', *Social Text*, 46/47, 1996, pp. 217–52 (reprinted in Sokal and Bricmont, *Intellectual Impostures*, as Appendix A, pp. 199–240). Dismayed at how fashionable postmodernism was becoming in American academic life, Sokal decided to write a parody to show how gullible an academic audience could be when confronted by scientific jargon. The article purported to show that physical reality was merely 'a social and linguistic construct' (Ibid., p. 200).

CHAPTER FIVE

1 [*Editorial note:*] CIAM (*Congrès Internationaux d'Architecture Moderne*) was founded in 1928, with a declaration calling for a rationalisation and standardisation of methods in both architecture and the building trade.

2 [*Editorial note:*] The Bauhaus was a movement in architecture and design, which was founded in Germany in 1919. Its leading theorists, such as Walter Gropius, argued that the form of a building should reflect its function, which meant stripping it of all ornamentation or extraneous decorative elements. The same principle could be applied to design in general, as with furniture.

3 [*Editorial note:*] See Walter Gropius, *The New Architecture and the Bauhaus*, trans. P. Morton Schand, Cambridge, MA: MIT Press, 1965 (see also note 2).
4 [*Editorial note:*] See Sigmund Freud, 'The Uncanny' (1919), in *Studies in Para-Psychology*, New York: Collier, 1963, p. 31.
5 [*Editorial note:*] See Dick Higgins, *A Dialectic of Centuries: Notes Towards a Theory of the New Arts*, New York and Barton, VT: Printed Editions, 1978.
6 [*Editorial note:*] 'Metafiction' is a term much used by commentators on literary postmodernism, and refers to narratives that are self-reflexive – that is, they are as much concerned with the act of writing itself as the particular narrative being told. See also Patricia Waugh, *Metafiction: The Theory and Practice of Self-Conscious Fiction*, London and New York: Methuen, 1984.
7 [*Editorial note:*] A. Wilde, *Horizons of Assent: Modernism, Postmodernism, and the Ironic Imagination*, Philadelphia, PA: Pennsylvania University Press, 1987.
8 [*Editorial note:*] Carl D. Malmgren, *Fictional Space in the Modernist and Postmodernist American Novel*, Lewisburg, PA: Bucknell University Press, 1985.
9 [*Editorial note:*] Larry McCaffery, *The Metafictional Muse: The Works of Robert Coover, Donald Barthelme, and William H. Gass*, Pittsburgh, PA and London: University of Pittsburgh Press, 1982, p. 264.
10 'Postmodernism is not to be taken in a periodizing sense.' (Lyotard and Thébaud, *Just Gaming*, note (by Thébaud), p. 16.)
11 [*Editorial note:*] In Cage's piece, the performer sits in front of a piano for 4 minutes, 33 seconds without playing a note, then leaves the stage. The work consists of whatever incidental noise occurs in the recital room over this time-period.
12 John Barth, 'The Literature of Replenishment: Postmodernist Fiction', *Atlantic Monthly*, 245, 1980, pp. 65–71.
13 See, for example, the Preface to the reissued edition of Graff's *Literature Against Itself: Literary Ideas in Modern Society* (1979), Chicago: Ivan R. Dee, Inc., 1995, in which the author notes that, 'Much of my writing in the 1980s and 1990s has been devoted to sorting out the differences between the more useful and the more fatuous versions of postmodern theory and practice' (p. xii).
14 [*Editorial note:*] Pound adopted this phrase as his motto and later used it as the title for a collection of his essays, *Make it New*, London: Faber and Faber, 1934.
15 [*Editorial note:*] Charles Newman, *The Aura of Postmodernism: The Act of Fiction in an Age of Inflation*, Evanston, IL: Northwestern University Press, 1985, pp. 27–35.
16 [*Editorial note:*] In Lyotard, a 'phrase regime' is a discourse (or set of beliefs), with its own internal rules and conventions. Those rules and conventions may well be incommensurable with those of other phrase regimes, producing 'differends' (irreconcilable disputes).
17 See John Locke, *An Essay Concerning Human Understanding* (1690), ed. A.D. Woozley, London and Glasgow: Fontana/Collins, 1964, Book 2, Chapter 33.
18 [*Editorial note:*] 'Two related terms describing postmodernist fiction are *fabulation* and *surfiction*. Both terms imply an aggressive and playful luxuriation in the nonrepresentational, in which the writer takes delight in the artifice of writing rather than in using writing to describe or make contact with a perceived extra-fictional reality.' (Jeremy Hawthorn, *A Glossary of Contemporary Literary Theory*, London: Edward Arnold, 1992, p. 156.) Much so-called 'cyberpunk' fiction would qualify for this label (see, for example, the work of William Gibson).
19 [*Editorial note:*] Both Swift and Fielding see themselves as carrying on the tradition of earlier satirists and

comic writers. Cervantes's influence on Fielding is well documented, while in the case of Swift, his satire is informed by the efforts of such authors as Erasmus, Rabelais, and Thomas More. In addition, both writers are steeped in the classics, and the debates that flow from this body of work are well represented in their narratives.

20 [*Editorial note:*] The 'Neo-Geo' movement (also called 'simulationism') was active in New York in the 1980s. Influenced by French poststructuralist and postmodernist thought, its objective was to investigate the use of geometry in modern art on the pretext that geometric abstraction could be used as a means of social control (that is, it was expressing the logic of the larger social order). In 'colour-field' painting, 'the canvas is stained with thin, translucent color washes', such that they 'partly reflect the spirituality of Oriental mysticism' (H.W. Janson, *History of Art*, 5th edn, rev. Anthony F. Janson, London: Thames and Hudson, 1995, pp. 799, 794). Mark Rothko's paintings, often consisting of large washes of just two colours, exemplify the style. 'Op' art explores the act of vision by the use of optical illusions. The swirling patterns of lines in a Bridget Riley composition, for example, can suggest subtleties of movement.

21 [*Editorial note:*] As pointed out in note 8, Chapter one, Hegel postulated the existence of a 'World Spirit' evolving through human history until it achieved self-realisation, at which point history would end.

22 [*Editorial note:*] For Greenberg, one of the major theorists of modernism in art, modernism was largely a matter of formal features. He was an advocate of abstraction and 'flatness' in painting – that is, he saw modernism as a break with realist art and its extensive use of perspective. Greenberg also believed that painting should be self-referential, or 'painterly' (about the act of painting itself).

23 [*Editorial note:*] Denzin's definition of 'astral' is: 'Sent from the stars; the American woman revealed in the reflections sent from Hollywood stars.' (*Images of Postmodern Society*, p. 80.) In other words, the effect of the star system is to glamorise film characters.

24 [*Editorial note:*] *Mise-en-abîme* is a term derived from heraldry and refers to the practice of an image (on a shield, for example) containing a smaller replica of itself. In theory, the process could go on into infinity, and that notion of an infinite regress (as in the case of meaning) has been very attractive to postmodern theorists and creative artists. *Mise-en-abîme* is also used to describe the self-reflexive nature of much postmodern art, which is the main sense intended with Almodóvar.

25 [*Editorial note:*] See Pierre Sorlin, 'Ist es möglich, eine Geschichte des Kinos zu schreiben?' ('Is it Possible to Write a History of the Cinema?'), *Montage a/v*, 5, 1996, p. 27.

26 [*Editorial note:*] In the work of the Russian literary theorist Mikhail Bakhtin, 'heteroglossia' refers to the plurality of discourses (various voices, various viewpoints) that can be found in the novel form.

27 [*Editorial note:*] 'Diegesis' (the 'telling' of a narrative) is to be distinguished from 'mimesis' (the 'showing' of narrative, as in a play). It is a distinction that can be traced back to Plato, but in more recent theoretical usage the terms have come to refer to 'plot' and 'story' respectively. It is that latter sense of 'plot' that we find in Kellner.

28 [*Editorial note:*] 'Hermeneutics' is the term given to the art of explanation or exegesis (of Scripture, for example). To be 'anti-hermeneutic' would be to refuse to provide such clarification of meaning and, as Kellner indicates, it is an all too common practice among postmodern critics.

29 [*Editorial note:*] George Lipsitz, 'Cruising Around the Historical Bloc:

Postmodernism and Popular Music in East Los Angeles', *Cultural Critique*, 5, 1986/7, pp. 157–77.

30 [*Editorial note:*] Martin Heidegger, 'Building, Dwelling, Thinking', in *Basic Writings*, p. 356.

31 [*Editorial note:*] Jerome Klinkowitz, *Rosenberg, Barthes, Hassan: The Postmodern Habit of Thought*, Athens, GA and London: University of Georgia Press, 1988, p. 8.

32 [*Editorial note:*] Lyotard, *The Postmodern Condition*, p. 81.

33 Leonard Jackson, *The Poverty of Structuralism: Literature and Structuralist Theory*, London and New York: Longman, 1991, p. 1.

BIBLIOGRAPHY

Texts from which extracts have been taken

Adair, Gilbert, *The Postmodernist Always Rings Twice: Reflections on Culture in the 90s*, London: Fourth Estate, 1992.

Adorno, Theodor W., *Negative Dialectics*, trans. E. B. Ashton, London: Routledge and Kegan Paul, 1973.

— and Horkheimer, Max, *Dialectic of Enlightenment* (1944), trans. John Cumming, London and New York: Verso, 1979.

Ahmed, Akbar S., *Postmodernism and Islam: Predicament and Promise*, London and New York: Routledge, 1992.

Aitken, Ian, *European Film Theory and Cinema: A Critical Introduction*, Edinburgh: Edinburgh University Press, 2001.

Allen, Jeffner and Young, Iris Marion, eds, *The Thinking Muse: Feminism and Modern French Philosophy*, Bloomington and Indianapolis, IN: Indiana University Press, 1989.

Ang, Ien, *Living Room Wars: Rethinking Media Audiences for a Postmodern World*, London and New York: Routledge, 1996.

Appignanesi, Lisa, ed., *Postmodernism: ICA Documents 4 and 5*, London: Free Association Books, 1989.

Arac, Jonathan, Godzich, Wlad, and Martin, Wallace, eds, *The Yale Critics: Deconstruction in America*, Minneapolis, MN: University of Minnesota Press, 1983.

Barrow, John D., *Impossibility: The Limits of Science and the Science of Limits*, London: Vintage, 1999.

Barth, John, 'The Literature of Exhaustion', in Bradbury, Malcolm, ed., *The Novel Today: Writers on Modern Fiction*, Manchester: Manchester University Press, 1977.

Baudrillard, Jean, *America*, trans. Chris Turner, London and New York: Verso, 1988.

— *Cool Memories*, trans. Chris Turner, London and New York: Verso, 1990.

Bauman, Zygmunt, *Intimations of Postmodernity*, London: Routledge, 1992.

Bell, Daniel, *The Coming of Post-Industrial Society: A Venture in Social Forecasting*, Harmondsworth: Penguin, 1976.

— *The Cultural Contradictions of Capitalism*, London: Heinemann, 1976.

Belton, John, *American Cinema/American Culture*, New York: McGraw-Hill, 1994.

Berry, Philippa, and Wernick, Andrew, eds, *Shadow of Spirit: Postmodernism and Religion*, London and New York: Routledge, 1992.

Bertens, Hans, *The Idea of the Postmodern: A History*, London and New York: Routledge, 1995.

Bové, Paul, 'Variations on Authority: Some Deconstructive Transformations of the New Criticism', in Arac, Jonathan, Godzich, Wlad, and Martin, Wallace, eds, *The Yale Critics: Deconstruction in America*, Minneapolis, MN: University of Minnesota Press, 1983, pp. 3–19.

Boyne, Roy, and Rattansi, Ali, eds, *Postmodernism and Society*, Basingstoke and London: Macmillan, 1990.

Bradbury, Malcom, ed., *The Novel Today: Contemporary Writers on Modern Fiction*, Manchester: Manchester University Press, 1977.

Callinicos, Alex, *Against Postmodernism: A Marxist Perspective*, Cambridge and Oxford: Polity Press and Blackwell, 1990.

Carver, Terrell, *The Postmodern Marx*, Manchester: Manchester University Press, 1998.

Cohen, Ralph, 'Do Postmodern Genres Exist?', *Genre*, 20, 1987, pp. 241–57.

Collins, Jim, Radner, Hilary, and Collins, Ava Preacher, *Film Theory Goes to the Movies*, New York and London: Routledge, 1993.

Connor, Steven, *Postmodernist Culture: An Introduction to Theories of the Contemporary*, Oxford and Cambridge, MA: Blackwell, 1989.

Cooke, Philip, *Back to the Future: Modernity, Postmodernity and Locality*, London: Unwin Hyman, 1990.

Coveney, Peter, and Highfield, Roger, *Frontiers of Complexity: The Search for Order in a Chaotic World*, London: Faber and Faber, 1995.

Crook, Stephen, 'The End of Radical Social Theory?: Notes on Radicalism, Modernism, and Postmodernism', in Boyne, Roy, and Rattansi, Ali, eds, *Postmodernism and Society*, Basingstoke and London: Macmillan, 1990, pp. 46–75.

Crowther, Paul, *Critical Aesthetics and Postmodernism*, Oxford: Clarendon Press, 1993.

Danto, Arthur, *Beyond the Brillo Box: The Visual Arts in Post-Historical Perspective*, Berkeley, Los Angeles, CA and London: University of California Press, 1992.

Davies, Paul, *The Cosmic Blueprint: Order and Complexity at the Edge of Chaos*, Harmondsworth: Penguin, 1995.

Davis, Michael, *City of Quartz: Excavating the Future in Los Angeles*, London: Verso, 1990.

Deleuze, Gilles, and Guattari, Felix, *Anti-Oedipus: Capitalism and*

Schizophrenia, trans. Robert Hurley, Mark Seem, and Helen R. Lane, London: Athlone Press, 1983.

— *A Thousand Plateaus: Capitalism and Schizophrenia*, trans. Brian Massumi, London: Athlone Press, 1988.

Denzin, Norman K., *Images of Postmodern Society: Social Theory and Contemporary Society*, London: Sage, 1991.

Derrida, Jacques, *Positions*, trans. Alan Bass, London: Athlone Press, 1981.

— *Limited Inc*, trans. Samuel Weber and J. Mehlman, Evanston, IL: Northwestern University Press, 1988.

— *Specters of Marx: The State of the Debt, the Work of Mourning, and the New International*, trans. Peggy Kamuf, New York and London: Routledge, 1994.

Detels, Claire, 'Soft Boundaries and Relatedness: Paradigm for a Postmodern Feminist Musical Aesthetics', in Ferguson, Margaret, and Wicke, Jennifer, eds, *Feminism and Postmodernism*, Durham, NC and London: Duke University Press, 1994, pp. 200–20.

Dickens, David R., and Fontana, Andrea, eds, *Postmodernism and Social Inquiry*, London: UCL Press, 1994.

Docherty, Thomas, ed., *Postmodernism: A Reader*, Hemel Hempstead: Harvester Wheatsheaf, 1993.

Donoghue, Denis, *The Pure Good of Theory*, Oxford and Cambridge, MA: Blackwell, 1992.

Dunn, Robert, 'Postmodernism: Populism, Mass Culture, and Avant-garde', *Theory, Culture and Society*, 8, 1991, pp. 111–35.

Eagleton, Terry, *The Ideology of the Aesthetic*, Oxford and Cambridge, MA: Blackwell, 1990.

Eco, Umberto, *Reflections on 'The Name of the Rose'*, trans. William Weaver, London: Secker and Warburg, 1984.

Eisenman, Peter, 'Blue Line Text', *Architectural Design*, 58, 1988, pp. 6–9.

Ellul, Jacques, *The Technological Society*, trans. John Wilkinson, New York: Alfred A. Knopf, 1964.

Elsaesser, Thomas, 'Specularity and Engulfment: Francis Ford Coppola's *Bram Stoker's Dracula*', in Neale, Steven, and Smith, Murray, eds, *Contemporary Hollywood Cinema*, London and New York: Routledge, 1998, pp. 191–208.

Etzioni, Amitai, *The Active Society: A Theory of Societal and Political Processes*, London and New York: Free Press, 1968.

Farganis, Sondra, 'Postmodernism and Feminism', in Dickens, David R., and Fontana, Andrea, eds, *Postmodernism and Social Inquiry*, London: UCL Press, 1994.

Featherstone, Mike, *Consumer Culture and Postmodernism*, London: Sage, 1991.

Ferguson, Margaret, and Wicke, Jennifer, eds, *Feminism and Postmodernism*, Durham, NC and London: Duke University Press, 1994.

Fiske, John, *Media Matters: Everyday Culture and Political Change*, 2nd edn, Minneapolis, MN and London: University of Minnesota Press, 1994.

Foster, Hal, ed., *Postmodern Culture*, London and Concord, MA: Pluto Press, 1985 (originally published as *The Anti-Aesthetic*, Port Townsend, WA: Bay Press, 1983).

Foucault, Michel, *Madness and Civilization: A History of Insanity in the Age of Reason*, trans. Richard Howard, London: Tavistock, 1967.

— *The History of Sexuality: Volume 2. The Use of Pleasure*, trans. Robert Hurley, Harmondsworth: Penguin, 1987.

Frampton, Kenneth, 'Some Reflections on Postmodernism and Architecture', in Appignanesi, Lisa, ed., *Postmodernism: ICA Documents 4 and 5*, London: Free Association Books, 1989, pp. 75–87.

— *Modern Architecture: A Critical History*, 3rd edn, London: Thames and Hudson, 1992.

Fraser, Nancy, and Nicholson, Linda J., 'Social Criticism without Philosophy: An Encounter between Feminism and Postmodernism', in Ross, Andrew, ed., *Universal Abandon?: The Politics of Postmodernism*, Edinburgh: Edinburgh University Press, 1989, pp. 83–104.

Frith, Simon, and Horne, Howard, *Art into Pop*, London and New York: Methuen, 1987.

Fuentes, Victor, 'Almodóvar's Postmodern Cinema: A Work in Progress ...', trans. Kathleen M. Vernon and Barbara Morris, in Vernon, Kathleen M., and Morris, Barbara, eds, *Post-Franco, Postmodern: The Films of Pedro Almodóvar*, Westport, CT and London: Greenwood Press, 1995, pp. 155–70.

Fukuyama, Francis, *The End of History and the Last Man*, London: Hamish Hamilton, 1992.

— 'The West Has Won', *The Guardian*, 11 October 2001, p. 21.

Gamble, Sarah, 'Postfeminism', in Gamble, Sarah, ed., *The Routledge Companion to Feminism and Postfeminism*, London and New York: Routledge, 2001, pp. 43–54.

— *The Routledge Companion to Feminism and Postfeminism*, London and New York: Routledge, 2001 (originally published as *The Icon Critical Dictionary of Feminism and Postfeminism*, Cambridge: Icon Books, 1998).

Gasché, Rodolphe, *The Tain of the Mirror: Derrida and the Philosophy of Reflection*, Cambridge, MA and London: Harvard Univerity Press, 1986.

Gellner, Ernest, *Postmodernism, Reason and Religion*, London and New York: Routledge, 1992.

Geras, Norman, 'Post-Marxism?', *New Left Review*, 163, 1987, pp. 40–82.

Gergen, K., 'Organization Theory in the Postmodern Era', in Reed, M., and Hughes, M., eds, *Rethinking Organization*, London: Sage, 1992, pp. 207–26.

Glass, Philip, Sleeve Notes (1996) to 'Heroes' Symphony, Point Music, 1997.

Gleick, James, *Chaos: Making a New Science*, London: Sphere Books, 1988.

Goodwin, Andrew, 'Popular Music and Postmodern Theory', *Cultural Studies*, 5, 1991, pp. 174–90.

Graff, Gerald, 'The Myth of the Postmodernist Breakthrough', *Tri-Quarterly*, 26, 1973, pp. 383–417.

Habermas, Jürgen, 'Modernity versus Postmodernity', *New German Critique*, 22, 1981, pp. 3–14.

— *The Philosophical Discourse of Modernity: Twelve Lectures*, trans. Frederick Lawrence, Cambridge and Oxford: Polity Press and Blackwell, 1987.

— *The New Conservatism: Cultural Criticism and the Historians' Debate*, ed. and trans. Shierry Weber Nicholsen, Cambridge and Oxford: Polity Press and Blackwell, 1989.

— 'Work and Weltanschauung: The Heidegger Controversy from a German Perspective', trans. John McCumber, *Critical Inquiry*, 15, 1989, pp. 431–56.

Halley, Peter, *Collected Essays 1981–1987*, Zurich and New York: Bruno Bischofberger Gallery and Sonnabend Gallery, 1988.

Haraway, Donna J, *Simians, Cyborgs, and Women: The Reinvention of Nature*, New York: Routledge, 1991.

Harding, Sandra, 'Feminism, Science, and the Anti-Enlightenment Critiques', in Nicholson, Linda J., ed., *Feminism/Postmodernism*, London and New York: Routledge, 1990, pp. 83–106.

Harrison, James, 'Doctors Have a Duty to Remain True Patient Advocates', *British Medical Journal*, 314, 5 April 1997, p. 1044.

Harvey, David, *The Condition of Postmodernity: An Enquiry into the Origins of Cultural Change*, Cambridge, MA and Oxford: Blackwell, 1990.

Hassan, Ihab, *The Dismemberment of Orpheus: Towards a Postmodern Literature*, New York: Oxford University Press, 1971.
Hassard, John, and Parker, Martin, eds, *Postmodernism and Organisations*, London: Sage, 1993.
Hebdige, Dick, *Hiding in the Light: On Images and Things*, London and New York: Routledge, 1988.
Heidegger, Martin, *Basic Writings: Martin Heidegger*, ed. David Farell Krell, 2nd edn, London: Routledge, 1993.
Hekman, Susan J., *Gender and Knowledge: Elements of a Postmodern Feminism*, Cambridge and Oxford: Polity Press and Blackwell, 1990.
Heller, Agnes, and Fehér, Ferenc, *The Postmodern Political Condition*, Cambridge and Oxford: Polity Press and Blackwell, 1988.
Hodgkin, Paul, 'Medicine, Postmodernism, and the End of Certainty', *British Medical Journal*, 313, 21 December 1996, pp. 1568–9.
Hudnut, Joseph, 'The Post-modern House', *Architectural Record*, 97, 1945, pp. 70–5.
— *Architecture and the Spirit of Man*, Cambridge, MA: Harvard University Press, 1949.
Hutcheon, Linda, *A Poetics of Postmodernism: History, Theory, Fiction*, New York and London: Routledge, 1988.
— *The Politics of Postmodernism*, London and New York: Routledge, 1989.
Huyssen, Andreas, *After the Great Divide: Modernism, Mass Culture and Postmodernism*, Basingstoke and London: Macmillan, 1988.
Jameson, Fredric, *Signatures of the Visible*, New York and London: Routledge, 1990.
— *Postmodernism, or, The Cultural Logic of Late Capitalism*, London and New York: Verso, 1991.
Jasper, David, ed., *Postmodernism, Literature and the Future of Theology*, Basingstoke and London: Macmillan, 1993.
Jencks, Charles, *The Language of Post-Modern Architecture*, 6th edn, London: Academy Editions, 1991.
— *What is Post-Modernism?*, 4th edn, London: Academy Editions, 1996.
Joyce, Patrick, 'History and Post-Modernism', *Past and Present*, 133, November 1991, pp. 204–9.
Kant, Immanuel, *The Critique of Judgement* (1790), trans. James Creed Meredith, Oxford: Clarendon Press, 1952.
Kaplan, E. Ann, ed., *Rocking Around the Clock: Music Television, Postmodernism, and Consumer Culture*, New York and London: Routledge, 1987.
— *Postmodernism and its Discontents: Theories, Practices*, London and New York: Verso, 1988.

Kellner, Douglas, *Jean Baudrillard: From Marxism to Postmodernism and Beyond*, Cambridge and Oxford: Polity Press and Blackwell, 1989.

— *Media and Culture: Cultural Studies, Identity and Politics Between the Modern and the Postmodern*, London and New York: Routledge, 1995.

Kelly, Catriona, 'History and Post-Modernism', *Past and Present*, 133, November 1991, pp. 209–13.

Klein, Herbert, 'The Art of Being Tristram', in Pierce, David, and de Voogd, Peter, eds, *Laurence Sterne in Modernism and Postmodernism*, Amsterdam and Atlanta, GA: Editions Rodopi, 1996, pp. 123–32.

Klemm, David E., 'Back to Literature – and Theology?', in Jasper, David, ed., *Postmodernism, Literature and the Future of Theology*, Basingstoke and London: Macmillan, 1993, pp. 180–90.

Kolb, David, *Postmodern Sophistications: Philosophy, Architecture, and Tradition*, Chicago and London: University of Chicago Press, 1990.

Kroker, Arthur, *The Possessed Individual: Technology and Postmodernity*, Basingstoke and London: Macmillan, 1990.

Kuhn, Thomas, *The Structure of Scientific Revolutions*, 2nd edn, Chicago and London: University of Chicago Press, 1970.

Kuspit, Donald, 'The Contradictory Character of Postmodernism', in Silverman, Hugh J., ed., *Postmodernism – Philosophy and the Arts*, New York and London: Routledge, 1990, pp. 53–68.

Laclau, Ernesto, and Mouffe, Chantal, *Hegemony and Socialist Strategy: Towards a Radical Democratic Politics*, London: Verso, 1985.

Lash, Scott, 'Postmodernism as Humanism?: Urban Space and Social Theory', in Turner, Bryan S., ed., *Theories of Modernity and Postmodernity*, London: Sage, 1990, pp. 62–74.

— *Sociology of Postmodernism*, London and New York: Routledge, 1990.

Lewin, Roger, *Complexity: Life on the Edge of Chaos*, London: Phoenix, 1993.

Lewis, Barry, 'Postmodernism and Literature (or: Word Salad Days, 1960–90)', in Sim, Stuart, ed., *The Routledge Companion to Postmodernism*, London and New York: Routledge, 2001, pp. 121–33.

Lewontin, R.C., *The Doctrine of DNA: Biology as Ideology*, Harmondsworth: Penguin, 1993.

Linklater, Andrew, *Beyond Realism and Marxism: Critical Theory and International Relations*, Basingstoke and London: Macmillan, 1990.

Linstead, Steve, 'Deconstruction in the Study of Organizations', in Hassard, John, and Parker, Martin, eds, *Postmodernism and Organisations*, London: Sage, 1993, pp. 49–70.

Lovibond, Sabina, 'Feminism and Postmodernism', in Boyne, Roy, and

Rattansi, Ali, eds, *Postmodernism and Society*, Basingstoke and London: Macmillan, 1990, pp. 154–86.

Lyotard, Jean-François, *The Postmodern Condition: A Report on Knowledge*, trans. Geoff Bennington and Brian Massumi, Manchester: Manchester University Press, 1984.

— 'Rewriting Modernity', *SubStance*, 54, 1987, pp. 8–9.

— *The Inhuman: Reflections on Time*, trans. Geoffrey Bennington and Rachel Bowlby, Cambridge and Oxford: Polity Press and Blackwell, 1991.

— *Lessons on the Analytic of the Sublime*, trans. Elizabeth Rottenberg, Stanford, CA: Stanford University Press, 1994.

— and Thébaud, Jean-Loup, *Just Gaming*, trans. Wlad Godzich, Manchester: Manchester University Press, 1985.

McDonald, Christie, ed., *Texts and Discussions with Jacques Derrida: The Ear of the Other. Otobiography, Transference, Translation*, trans. Peggy Kamuf, Lincoln, NA and London: University of Nebraska Press, 1985.

McGowan, John, *Postmodernism and its Critics*, Ithaca, NY and London: Cornell University Press, 1991.

McGuigan, Jim, *Cultural Populism*, London and New York: Routledge, 1992.

McHale, Brian, *Postmodernist Fiction*, New York and London: Methuen, 1987.

— *Constructing Postmodernism*, London and New York: Routledge, 1992.

McRobbie, Angela, *Postmodernism and Popular Culture*, London and New York: Routledge, 1994.

Milbank, John, 'Problematizing the Secular: The Post-postmodern Agenda', in Berry, Philippa, and Wernick, Andrew, eds, *Shadow of Spirit: Postmodernism and Religion*, London and New York: Routledge, 1992, pp. 30–44.

Mills, C. Wright, *The Sociological Imagination*, New York: Oxford University Press, 1959.

Montag, Warren, 'What is at Stake in the Debate on Postmodernism?', in Kaplan, E. Ann, ed., *Postmodernism and its Discontents: Theories, Practices*, London and New York: Verso, 1988, pp. 88–103.

Morris, Meaghan, *The Pirate's Fiancée: Feminism, Reading, Postmodernism*, London and New York: Verso, 1988.

Neale, Steven, and Smith, Murray, eds, *Contemporary Hollywood Cinema*, London and New York: Routledge, 1998.

Newman, Oscar, *Defensible Space: People and Design in the Violent City*, London: Architectural Press, 1973.

Nicholson, Linda J., ed., *Feminism/Postmodernism*, New York and London: Routledge, 1990.
Nietzsche, Friedrich, *On the Genealogy of Morals: A Polemic* (1887), trans. Douglas Smith, Oxford and New York: Oxford University Press, 1996.
— *The Birth of Tragedy and Other Writings* (1873), trans. Ronald Spiers, eds, Raymond Geuss and Ronald Spiers, Cambridge: Cambridge University Press, 1999.
Norris, Christopher, *What's Wrong with Postmodernism: Critical Theory and the Ends of Philosophy*, Hemel Hempstead: Harvester Wheatsheaf, 1990.
Oliva, Achille Bonito, *Trans-avantgarde International*, trans. Dwight Gast and Gwen Jones, Milan: Giancarlo Politi Editore, 1982.
Owens, Craig, 'The Discourse of Others: Feminists and Postmodernism', in Foster, Hal, ed., *Postmodern Culture*, London and Concord, MA: Pluto Press, 1985, pp. 57–82.
Pierce, David, and de Voogd, Peter, eds, *Laurence Sterne in Modernism and Postmodernism*, Amsterdam and Atlanta, GA: Editions Rodopi, 1996.
Plant, Sadie, *Zeros + Ones: Digital Women + The New Technoculture*, London: Fourth Estate, 1998.
Portoghesi, Paolo, *Postmodern: The Architecture of the Postindustrial Society*, trans. Ellen Shapiro, New York: Rizzoli International, 1983.
Prigogine, Ilya, and Stengers, Isabelle, *Order Out of Chaos: Man's New Dialogue with Nature*, London: Heinemann, 1984.
Pyle, Forest, 'Making Cyborgs, Making Humans: Of Terminators and Blade Runners', in Collins, Jim, Radner, Hilary, and Collins, Ava Preacher, eds, *Film Theory Goes to the Movies*, New York and London: Routledge, 1993, pp. 227–41.
Readings, Bill, *Introducing Lyotard: Art and Politics*, London and New York: Routledge, 1991.
Reed, M., and Hughes, M., eds, *Rethinking Organization: New Directions in Organizational Theory and Analysis*, London: Sage, 1992.
Rojek, Chris, and Turner, Bryan S., eds, *Forget Baudrillard?*, London and New York: Routledge, 1993.
Rorty, Richard, 'Postmodernist Bourgeois Liberalism', *Journal of Philosophy*, 80, 1983, pp. 583–9.
— *Contingency, Irony, and Solidarity*, Cambridge: Cambridge University Press, 1989.
Rose, Margaret, *The Post-modern and the Post-industrial: A Critical Analysis*, Cambridge: Cambridge University Press, 1991.

Ross, Andrew, ed., *Universal Abandon?: The Politics of Postmodernism*, Edinburgh: Edinburgh University Press, 1989.

Ruland, Richard, and Bradbury, Malcolm, *From Puritanism to Postmodernism: A History of American Literature*, London and New York: Routledge, 1991.

Said, Edward W., *Orientalism: Western Conceptions of the Orient*, 2nd edn, Harmondsworth: Penguin, 1995.

Sarup, Madan, *An Introductory Guide to Post-structuralism and Postmodernism*, Hemel Hempstead: Harvester Wheatsheaf, 1988.

Searle, John R., 'Reiterating the Differences: A Reply to Derrida', *Glyph*, 1, 1977, pp. 198–208.

Shildrick, Margrit, *Leaky Bodies and Boundaries: Feminism, Postmodernism and (Bio)Ethics*, London and New York: Routledge, 1997.

Silverman, Hugh, ed., *Postmodernism – Philosophy and the Arts*, London and New York: Routledge, 1990.

Sim, Stuart, *Contemporary Continental Philosophy: The New Scepticism*, Aldershot and Burlington, VT: Ashgate Press, 2000.

— ed., *The Routledge Companion to Postmodernism*, London and New York: Routledge, 2001 (originally published as *The Icon Critical Dictionary of Postmodern Thought*, Cambridge: Icon Books, 1998).

— and Walker, David, *Bunyan and Authority: The Rhetoric of Dissent and the Legitimation Crisis in Seventeenth-century England*, Bern and New York: Peter Lang, 2000.

Smart, Barry, *Modern Conditions: Postmodern Controversies*, London and New York: Routledge, 1992.

Soja, Edward W., *Postmodern Geographies: The Reassertion of Space in Critical Social Theory*, London: Verso, 1989.

Sokal, Alan, and Bricmont, Jean, *Intellectual Impostures: Postmodern Philosophers' Abuse of Science*, London: Profile Books, 1998.

Stam, Robert, and Miller, Toby, eds, *Film and Theory: An Anthology*, Malden, MA and Oxford: Blackwell, 2000.

Stone, Lawrence, 'History and Post-Modernism', *Past and Present*, 131, May 1991, pp. 217–18.

Stratton, Jon, 'Beyond Art: Postmodernism and the Case of Popular Music', *Theory, Culture and Society*, 6, 1989, pp. 31–57.

Tester, Keith, *The Life and Times of Post-modernity*, London and New York: Routledge, 1993.

Tijssen, Lieteke van Vucht, 'Women between Modernity and Postmodernity', in Turner, Bryan S., ed., *Theories of Modernity and Postmodernity*, London: Sage, 1990, pp. 147–63.

Toulmin, Stephen, *The Return to Cosmology: Postmodern Science and the Theology of Nature*, Berkeley, Los Angeles, CA and London: University of California Press, 1982.

Toynbee, Arnold, *A Study of History*, vols. I–VI, abridged by D.C. Somervell, New York and Oxford: Oxford University Press, 1947.

— *A Study of History*, vol. IX, London: Oxford University Press, 1954.

Turner, Bryan S., ed., *Theories of Modernity and Postmodernity*, London: Sage, 1990.

— 'Cruising America', in Rojek, Chris, and Turner, Bryan S., eds, *Forget Baudrillard?*, London and New York: Routledge, 1993, pp. 146–61.

Vattimo, Gianni, *The End of Modernity: Nihilism and Hermeneutics in Postmodern Culture*, trans. Jon R. Snyder, Cambridge and Oxford: Polity Press and Blackwell, 1988.

Venturi, Robert, Izenour, Steven, and Brown, Denise Scott, *Learning from Las Vegas: The Forgotten Symbolism of Architectural Form*, 2nd edn, Cambridge, MA and London: MIT Press, 1977.

Vernon, James, *Politics and the People: A Study in English Political Culture, c. 1815–1867*, Cambridge: Cambridge University Press, 1993.

Vernon, Kathleen M., and Morris, Barbara, eds, *Post-Franco, Postmodern: The Films of Pedro Almodóvar*, Westport, CT and London: Greenwood Press, 1995.

Virilio, Paul, *Speed and Politics: An Essay on Dromology*, trans. Mark Polizzotti, New York: Semiotext(e), 1986.

Walker, R.B.J., *Inside/Outside: International Relations as Political Theory*, Cambridge: Cambridge University Press, 1993.

Warraq, Ibn, 'Islam – the Final Taboo: Honest Intellectuals Must Shed their Spiritual Turbans', *The Guardian*, 'Saturday Review', 10 November 2001, p. 12.

West, David, *An Introduction to Continental Philosophy*, Cambridge and Oxford: Polity Press and Blackwell, 1996.

White, Hayden, *Metahistory: The Historical Imagination in Nineteenth-Century Europe*, Baltimore, MD and London: Johns Hopkins University Press, 1973.

Woods, Tim, *Beginning Postmodernism*, Manchester and New York: Manchester University Press, 1999.

Young, Iris Marion, 'The Ideal of Community and the Politics of Difference', *Social Theory and Practice*, 12, 1986, pp. 1–26.

Žižek, Slavoj, *The Sublime Object of Ideology*, London and New York: Verso, 1989.

Other texts cited

Alvesson, M., *Cultural Perspectives on Organisations*, Cambridge, Cambridge University Press, 1993.

— and Wilmott, H., eds, *Critical Management Studies*, London: Sage, 1992.

Barth, John, 'The Literature of Replenishment: Postmodernist Fiction', *Atlantic Monthly*, 245, 1980, pp. 65–71.

Baudrillard, Jean, 'The Ecstasy of Communication', in Hal Foster, ed., *The Anti-Aesthetic,* Port Townsend, WA: Bay Press, 1983, pp. 126–34 (later republished as *Postmodern Culture*, London and Concord, MA: Pluto Press, 1985).

— 'Forgetting Foucault', trans. Nicole Dufresne, *Humanities in Society*, 3, 1980, pp. 87–111.

Bell, Bernard Iddings, *Postmodernism and Other Essays*, Milwaukee, WI: Morehouse, 1926.

— *Religion for Living: A Book for Postmodernists*, London: John Gifford, 1939.

Benjamin, Walter, *Illuminations*, ed. Hannah Arendt, trans. Harry Zohn, London and Glasgow: Collins/Fontana, 1973.

Berman, Marshall, *All That is Solid Melts into Air: The Experience of Modernity*, London: Verso, 1982.

Best, Steven, and Kellner, Douglas, *Postmodern Theory: Critical Interrogations*, New York: Guilford Press, 1991.

Bloom, Harold, et al., *Deconstruction and Criticism*, London and Henley: Routledge and Kegan Paul, 1979.

Clegg, S., *Modern Organizations: Organization Studies in the Postmodern World*, London: Sage, 1990.

Coomaraswamy, Ananda K., and Penty, Arthur J., eds, *Essays in Post Industrialism: A Symposium of Prophecy Concerning the Future of Society*, London, 1914.

Coppock, Vicki, Haydon, Deena, and Richter, Ingrid, *The Illusions of 'Post-feminism': New Women, Old Myths*, London: Taylor and Francis, 1995.

Derrida, Jacques, *Of Grammatology*, trans. Gayatri Chakravorty Spivak, Baltimore, MD and London: Johns Hopkins University Press, 1976.

Drucker, Peter F., *The Landmarks of Tomorrow: A Report on the New Post-Modern World*, London: Heinemann, 1957.

Foucault, Michel, *The Archaeology of Knowledge*, trans. A.M. Sheridan Smith, London: Tavistock, 1972.

— *Discipline and Punish: The Birth of the Prison*, trans. Alan Sheridan, Harmondsworth: Penguin, 1979.

— *The Order of Things: An Archaeology of the Human Sciences*, trans. Alan Sheridan-Smith, London: Tavistock, 1970.

Freud, Sigmund, 'The Uncanny' (1919), in *Studies in Para-Psychology*, New York: Collier, 1963.

Frisby, David, and Featherstone, Mike, eds, *Simmel on Culture: Selected Writings*, London: Sage, 1997.

Giddens, Anthony, *Profiles and Critiques in Social Theory*, London: Macmillan, 1982.

Gleick, James, *Faster: The Acceleration of Just About Everything*, London, Little, Brown, 1999.

Graff, Gerald, *Literature Against Itself: Literary Ideas in Modern Society* (1979), Chicago: Ivan R. Dee, Inc., 1995.

Greene, Brian, *The Elegant Universe: Superstrings, Hidden Dimensions, and the Quest for the Ultimate Theory*, London: Jonathan Cape, 1999.

Gropius, Walter, *The New Architecture and the Bauhaus*, trans. P. Morton Schand, Cambridge, MA: MIT Press, 1965.

Habermas, Jürgen, 'Modernity: An Unfinished Project', trans. Nicholas Walker, in Passerin d'Entrèves, Maurizio and Benhabib, Seyla, eds, *Habermas and the Unfinished Project of Modernity: Critical Essays on 'The Philosophical Discourse of Modernity'*, Cambridge and Oxford: Polity Press and Blackwell, 1996, pp. 38–55.

Hassard, John, and Pym, Denis, eds, *The Theory and Philosophy of Organisations: Critical Issues and New Perspectives*, London: Routledge, 1990.

Hawthorn, Jeremy, *A Glossary of Contemporary Literary Theory*, London: Edward Arnold, 1992.

Hegel, G.W.F., *Phenomenology of Spirit* (1807), trans. A.V. Miller, Oxford: Oxford University Press, 1977.

Hoesterey, Ingeborg, ed., *Zeitgeist in Babel: The Postmodernist Controversy*, Bloomington and Indianapolis, IN: Indiana University Press, 1991.

Huntington, Samuel P., *The Clash of Civilizations and the Remaking of World Order*, New York: Simon and Schuster, 1996.

Jackson, Leonard, *The Poverty of Structuralism: Literature and Structuralist Theory*, London and New York: Longman, 1991.

Jameson, Fredric, 'Postmodernism and Consumer Society', in Hal Foster, ed., *The Anti-Aesthetic*, Port Townsend, WA: Bay Press, 1983, pp. 111–25 (later republished as *Postmodern Culture*, London and Concord, MA: Pluto Press, 1985).

Janson, H.W., *History of Art*, 5th edn, rev. Anthony F. Janson, London: Thames and Hudson, 1995.

Kant, Immanuel, *Critique of Pure Reason* (1781, 1787), trans. Norman Kemp Smith, 2nd edn, London and Basingstoke: Macmillan, 1933.

— *Critique of Practical Reason* (1788), trans. and ed. Mary McGregor, Cambridge: Cambridge University Press, 1997.

Klinkowitz, Jerome, *Rosenberg, Barthes, Hassan: The Habit of Postmodern Thought*, Athens, GA and London: University of Georgia Press, 1988.

Kuhn, Thomas, *The Copernican Revolution: Planetary Astronomy in the Development of Western Thought*, Cambridge, MA and London: Harvard University Press, 1957.

Lakatos, Imre, 'Falsification and the Methodology of Scientific Research Programmes', in Lakatos, Imre, and Musgrave, Alan, eds, *Criticism and the Growth of Knowledge*, Cambridge: Cambridge University Press, 1970, pp. 91–196.

— and Musgrave, Alan, eds, *Criticism and the Growth of Knowledge*, Cambridge, Cambridge University Press, 1970.

Lipsitz, George, 'Cruising Around the Historical Bloc: Postmodernism and Popular Music in East Los Angeles', *Cultural Critique*, 5, 1986/7, pp. 157–77.

Locke, John, *An Essay Concerning Human Understanding* (1690), ed. A. D. Woozley, London and Glasgow: Fontana/Collins, 1964.

Lyotard, Jean-François, van Reijen, Willem, and Veerman, Dick, 'An Interview with Jean-François Lyotard', *Theory, Culture and Society*, 5, 1988, pp. 277–309.

Malmgren, Carl D., *Fictional Space in the Modernist and Postmodernist American Novel*, Lewisburg, PA: Bucknell University Press, 1985.

Marx, Karl, and Engels, Friedrich, *The Communist Manifesto*, ed. Frederic L. Bender, New York and London: W. W. Norton, 1988.

McCaffery, Larry, *The Metafictional Muse: The Works of Robert Coover, Donald Barthelme, and William H. Gass*, Pittsburgh, PA and London: University of Pittsburgh Press, 1982.

McLuhan, Marshall, *Understanding Media: The Extensions of Man*, London: Routledge and Kegan Paul, 1964.

Newman, Charles, *The Aura of Postmodernism: The Act of Fiction in an Age of Inflation*, Evanston, IL: Northwestern University Press, 1985.

Ortega y Gasset, José, *The Dehumanization of Art and Other Essays on Art, Culture and Literature*, trans. Helene Weyl et al., Princeton, NJ: Princeton University Press, 1968.

Passerin d'Entrèves, Maurizio, and Benhabib, Seyla, eds, *Habermas and the Unfinished Project of Modernity: Critical Essays on 'The Philosophical*

Discourse of Modernity', Cambridge and Oxford: Polity Press and Blackwell, 1996.
Penty, Arthur J., *Old Worlds for New: A Study of the Post-Industrial State*, London: George Allen and Unwin, 1917.
Polan, Dana, 'Postmodernism as Machine', paper given to the Australian Screen Studies Association, Sydney, December 1986.
Pound, Ezra, *Make it New*, London: Faber and Faber, 1934.
Rabinow, P., ed., *The Foucault Reader*, New York: Random House, 1984.
Rosenberg, Bernard, 'Mass Culture in America', in Rosenberg, Bernard, and White, David Manning, eds, *Mass Culture: The Popular Arts in America*, Glencoe, IL: Free Press, 1957, pp. 3–12.
Rosenberg, Bernard, and White, David Manning, eds, *Mass Culture: The Popular Arts in America*, Glencoe, IL: Free Press, 1957.
Said, Edward, 'Islam and the West are Inadequate Banners', *The Observer*, 16 September 2000, p. 27, main section.
Sartre, Jean-Paul, *Existentialism and Humanism*, trans. Philip Mairet, London: Methuen, 1948.
Sim, Stuart, ed., *Post-Marxism: A Reader*, Edinburgh: Edinburgh University Press, 1998.
— *Post-Marxism: An Intellectual History*, London and New York: Routledge, 2000.
Simmel, Georg, 'The Philosophy of Fashion', trans. Mark Ritter and David Frisby, in David Frisby and Mike Featherstone, eds, *Simmel on Culture: Selected Writings*, London: Sage, 1997, pp. 187–217.
Sokal, Alan, 'Transgressing the Boundaries: Towards a Transformative Hermeneutics of Quantum Gravity', *Social Text*, 46/47, 1996, pp. 217–52.
Sorlin, Pierre, 'Ist es möglich, eine Geschichte des Kinos zu schreiben?', *Montage a/v*, 5, 1996.
Stacey, R. D., Griffin, D., and Shaw, P., *Complexity and Management: Fad or Radical Challenge to Systems Thinking?*, London and New York: Routledge, 2000.
Stern, J. P., *Nietzsche*, 2nd edn, London: Fontana, 1985.
Taylor, Frederick Winslow, *The Principles of Scientific Management* (1911), New York: Dover, 1997.
Thom, René, *Mathematical Models of Morphogenesis*, trans. W. M. Brookes and D. Rand, Chichester: Ellis Horwood, 1983.
Waugh, Patricia, *Metafiction: The Theory and Practice of Self-Conscious Fiction*, London and New York: Methuen, 1984.
Wilde, A., *Horizons of Assent: Modernism, Postmodernism, and the Ironic*

Imagination, Philadelphia, PA: Pennsylvania University Press, 1987.

Young, E., 'On the Naming of the Rose: Interests and Multiple Meanings as Elements of Organisational Culture', *Organisation Studies*, 10, 1989, pp. 187–206.

Young, Louise B., *The Unfinished Universe*, New York: Simon and Schuster, 1986.

GLOSSARY OF CRITICAL TERMS

Antifoundationalism: Philosophical discourse in the West depends on certain principles to prove the truth of its pronouncements. The law of identity (a = a; a thing is equal to itself) has arguably been the crucial principle involved. Without that it is difficult to see how anything at all could be proved or how we could ever have certain knowledge. In modern times, however, the law of identity has been called into question – for example, by developments in particle physics, where in some instances a particle appears not to be identical to itself – and many philosophers have in consequence come to doubt the foundations of their subject. Such philosophers have been dubbed antifoundationalists (poststructuralists and postmodernists being prominent among them), and they tend to argue that, since we have no means of proving anything with certainty, truth is a relative concept. The ramifications of that debate extend well beyond the boundaries of philosophy (see also **relativism).**

Decentred subject: Over the course of the last century or so, various theories have been put forward to suggest that the self is far less of a unity than had traditionally been supposed. Freudian psychoanalysis, for example, saw us as being largely at the mercy of drives buried within our unconscious, and that notion of the individual subject not being in control of his or her own destiny has become deeply engrained within cultural theory. Poststructuralist theorists in general argue that the self is a very fluid entity and that unity is an illusion. There is no essence to the individual self: that is, something within us that remains constant over time, as Western culture had generally maintained from about the Renaissance period onwards – and with increasing emphasis from the Enlightenment. Our personal identity is instead in a continual state of flux – 'decentred', as it were. As was noted in **antifoundationalism**, recent science has provided a fruitful source of evidence for such views. To be decentred can be taken in a positive sense, to mean that we can escape from cultural conventions, such as those regarding gender identity. Feminist theorists in particular have pursued this line with some considerable enthusiasm.

Deconstruction: This is a movement deriving from the work of Jacques Derrida, one of the major figures in **poststructuralism**. Derrida argues that language is marked by instability and ambiguity, and that words never achieve full meaning: at any one point, meaning is to be considered in a state of flux. Following on from Ferdinand de Saussure's theories of language, in which **signifiers** (words) are held to be only arbitrarily connected to **signifieds** (concepts), Derrida has devised a range of methods to make this arbitrariness apparent. Word-play and punning, for example, are extensively used by deconstructionist theorists to demonstrate how words can have multiple meanings, as well as chains of association to other words (through similar sound qualities, for example) that could continue indefinitely. Words are not fixed in their meaning, therefore, but always hint at other contexts. By challenging the notion of fixed meaning, Derrida is calling into question one of the most fundamental assumptions underpinning discourse in the West, and deconstruction does have subversive aims in this regard. (See also **differance** and **metaphysics of presence**).

Dialectics/Dialectical materialism: Dialectical thought proceeds by way of conflict between opposing terms, challenging us to find a method of resolution for the contradictions involved. Hegel's dialectic, for example, is based on the notion that each thesis creates an antithesis, and that the conflict between the two generates a higher stage of development, or new thesis, at which point the process begins over again. In Hegel's philosophy of history, the 'World Spirit' progresses through various stages of societal development (Asiatic through feudal to modern, for example) until it achieves self-realisation. Marx's dialectical materialism builds on Hegel's model of dialectics, but places the process more firmly in the material world. For Marx, the dialectic that is working through history resolves itself into a class struggle, whereby each new form of social existence engenders within itself the means of its own overcoming. Thus feudalism (thesis) creates the conditions for the rise of the bourgeoisie (antithesis), and the conflict between the feudal ruling class and the bourgeoisie ends with the victory of the more progressive bourgeois class (new thesis). The next stage in the process is the emergence of the industrial proletariat out of bourgeois society, which Marx argues will culminate in the dictatorship of the proletariat. Dialectical materialism was developed further by various thinkers after Marx's death (Lenin, for example), becoming the official ideology of the Soviet bloc. For Marxist theorists, dialectical materialism constitutes the 'science of society'.

Differance: Jacques Derrida argues that meaning is never stable and that it is always in a process of fluctuation. Words are to be construed as fields of meaning rather than fixed entities, with new meanings constantly being added and echoes, or in Derrida's terminology, *traces*, of an indeterminable number of other meanings always present at any one time. Derrida also speaks of there being a *surplus* of meaning at any one time, and asserts that we can never capture the full meaning of any word, the traces of which fan out indefinitely. The process by which words are prevented from reaching full meaning is what Derrida calls differance, and it is perpetually active within discourse. Differance means that words are always *deferred* from reaching full meaning, and *differed* from their previous appearances.

Differend: Jean-François Lyotard's term for a dispute between individuals (or groups) using different phrase regimes (or **discourses**). Each phrase regime has its own internal rules and procedures, rendering them incommensurable with each other. A territorial dispute between the original inhabitants of a colonised country (Australia, say) and its colonisers is unlikely to be settled to the satisfaction of both parties, since their phrase regimes are mutually exclusive. Although both can claim ownership over the land, both cannot exercise it simultaneously. In most instances, differends are 'resolved' by the stronger party imposing its will on the weaker (as will generally be the case when territorial disputes such as the aforementioned occur). Lyotard thinks that such disputes should make us re-examine our phrase regimes.

Discourse: In the work of Michel Foucault, discourse comes to take on the meaning of a self-contained system with its own internal rules and procedures. We can speak of the discourse of art or philosophy, for example, or even more specialised discourses within these general areas, such as the discourse of abstract expressionism in modern painting (yet another discourse in its own right). The term carries the connotations of genre, discipline and **paradigm** combined, and is related to another one of Foucault's key concepts, **episteme** (a historical period plus all its practices and beliefs). Within an episteme, we would find a range of particular discourses. Discourses can be repressive, in the sense of sanctioning certain practices that the individual discourse supports at the expense of others.

Double coding: Charles Jencks's critique of modern architecture claimed that it had lost touch with the general public, who tended to find modern buildings, with their severe lines and lack of decoration, alienating. He argued that architects were under an obligation to 'double code' their buildings – that is, to ensure they included features that appealed to the general public as well as to the professional architectural community. In architectural terms, this has generally come to mean deploying a mixture of old and new styles in the same building. Double coding has since become a key element of postmodern artistic practice, which makes a conscious effort to work on two levels, the popular and the intellectual, as Jencks had recommended.

Epistemology/Episteme: Epistemology is the branch of philosophy concerned with theories of knowledge. Broadly speaking, there are two main schools of thought on how we gain knowledge: the empiricist (which claims that knowledge derives from sense-experience), and the rationalist (which claims that knowledge is the product of the operation of our reason). In the former camp we could place such philosophers as the 'British Empiricists' John Locke and David Hume; in the latter, Plato and René Descartes. Empiricism and rationalism are at opposite ends of a spectrum and it is possible to construct a position in between – as in the case of Immanuel Kant, who argued that while knowledge came from sense-experience, the form that sense-experience took was dictated by the way our reasoning faculty worked. Episteme is a phrase much used by the poststructuralist cultural theorist and historian Michel Foucault, for whom it signifies a historical period and the entire range of cultural practices and beliefs contained within it. Ultimately, such practices and beliefs are validated with reference to the dominant ideology of the time, which determines what does and does not count as knowledge for the culture in question.

Hegemony: A concept devised by Marxist theorists to explain why bourgeois societies managed to maintain control over the working class, despite this not being in the latter's best interest. For Marxist theorists such as Antonio Gramsci and Louis Althusser, it was a matter of the bourgeois society infiltrating its values into the institutions of a society, including the world of the media and the arts, such that the population at large accepted these as the 'natural' values of their culture and aspired to them. The success of this project meant that the general socialist revolution predicted by Marxist theory was delayed, and that capitalism had found a way to overcome, for the time being anyhow, its periodic crises. The concept has been attacked by post-Marxists, notably the writing team of Ernesto Laclau and Chantal Mouffe, as a form of special pleading designed to disguise deficiencies in Marxist theory itself.

Hermeneutics: The interpretation of texts to bring out their hidden or obscure meanings. The practice derives from biblical scholarship, which sought to reveal the true meaning (as the theologian in question conceived it) that lay behind the Bible's vast store of stories and images.

Certain morals could be drawn from these stories and images, which could then be passed on – in sermon form, for example – to the lay public. In our own time, the term generally applies to the close analysis of texts according to a particular critical method or theory. What Marxists draw from a text is its hidden meanings regarding class relations, while feminist hermeneutics concentrates on what texts have to disclose about gender relations and patriarchy.

Humanism/Liberal humanism: Humanism can be traced back at least to classical times, although in its modern guise it is a product of the Renaissance (including, significantly, that period's rediscovery of classical learning). From the Renaissance onwards, there is an increasing interest in the individual (mankind as the 'measure of all things', its proper object of study), and it becomes the role of culture to provide the means for that individual to develop his or her latent talents. Self-expression and self-realisation become key goals for Western culture, a development for which the Enlightenment provides yet more impetus (see also **subject**). Humanism need not entail liberal politics and democratic political structures (it did not in Renaissance times, for example), but since the Enlightenment it has tended to encompass such ideals. 'Liberal' can be interpreted here in a fairly wide sense, to mean a commitment to individual rights, such as equal treatment before the law, mass suffrage and so on. Broadly speaking, one could define most Western democracies as liberal humanist in outlook, even if many of the political parties involved would be wary of the term 'liberal', and might seek to qualify it in a variety of ways. At least in theory, such societies claim to guarantee individual freedom.

Intertextuality: This is the notion that texts are inextricably interconnected with each other, with each individual text containing references to, or echoes of, a wide range of other texts and so on in an ever more complex network. For the French cultural theorist and feminist Julia Kristeva, for example, each text is a mosaic composed of quotations drawn from innumerable other texts. From such a perspective, every text is in dialogue with the collected body of writing in our culture – a notion wittily captured by Umberto Eco's remark in his novel *The Name of the Rose*, that 'books speak of books: it is as if they spoke among themselves' (trans. William Weaver, London: Picador, 1984, p. 286).

Logocentrism/Phallogocentrism: Logocentrism is Jacques Derrida's term for the belief in Western culture that words communicate fixed meanings in discourse between individuals. The assumption being made is that the full meaning of the word is 'present' to us, in our minds, as we deliver it, and that it can then be received in that same form by the addressee. For Derrida, this involves a commitment to what he calls the **metaphysics of presence**, which in his view is built on an illusion. Derrida's own position is that meaning is unstable and constantly undergoing change (see also **deconstruction**). Phallogocentrism, a term also coined by Derrida, combines the notions of phallocentrism and logocentrism. It has been adopted by feminists, for whom it sums up the bias towards patriarchal authority in Western culture in which male discourse is taken to have greater weight than female – that is, it is considered to have greater 'presence' and to be closer to the truth. The movement to develop a specifically feminine form of writing, *écriture féminine* (see the work of the French feminists Luce Irigaray and Hélène Cixous, for example), is designed to counter this perceived phallogocentrist bias.

Metaphysics of presence: The **deconstructionist** Jacques Derrida argues that all discourse in Western culture is based in a belief that the meanings of words are fully 'present' to us, in our minds, as we communicate them to others (see also **logocentrism**). For Derrida, on the other hand, the meaning of words is in a continual state of ferment and can never be pinned down precisely. The notion of 'presence' implies that words and meanings have stability, and that no significant 'slippage' ever occurs. On that basis, we can communicate to each other with a confidence that the meaning of our phrases will be received as we intended them to be. Derrida contends that this is an illusion, and that words and meanings are riven with instability instead. Meaning, as far as he is concerned, is always indeterminate.

Narrative/Metanarrative/Grand narrative: Recent cultural theory regards the construction of narrative as a basic human trait, extending the concept to take in such activities as politics, which is viewed as a series of narratives vying for our attention. According to thinkers such as Jean-François Lyotard, ideology aspires to the condition of metanarrative or grand narrative (*grand récit*) – which is to say that given ideologies claim to be ultimate authorities, and seek to exclude all competitors. In the case of Marxism, this means that it regards its own narrative as the solution to all the world's socio-political problems, and treats all other ideologies as false (see also **dialectical materialism**). Lyotard, along with the postmodern movement in general, is suspicious of such claims to universal applicability, and champions the cause of 'little narrative' (*petit récit*) instead. Little narratives do not aspire to universal status and tend to be put together to counter specific abuses of power, after which they dissolve. The *ad hoc* groupings of workers and students generated by the 1968 *événements* in Paris are an excellent example of how little narrative is supposed to work. Lyotard sees narrative as a positive characteristic of human existence, which only becomes problematical when it tries to suppress other narratives – that is, when it turns into metanarrative or grand narrative.

Nomadism: In the work of Gilles Deleuze and Felix Guattari, nomadism becomes a metaphor for opting out of existing political systems; it is as much an attitude of mind as a way of life. Nomadism represents a rejection of central authority, since nomads wander around freely, disregarding national borders and the claims of the nation state in their travels. Since they belong to no particular place, they are said to be 'deterritorialised', which becomes a political ideal for Deleuze and Guattari. Nomads neither need, nor obey, central authority: a lifestyle that runs counter to modern practice, with its emphasis on the nation state and its assumed right to exercise control over the subjects within its bounded territory. In a more general sense, nomadism means to dissent from established patterns of thought within one's culture (see particularly Gilles Deleuze and Felix Guattari, *A Thousand Plateaus: Capitalism and Schizophrenia*, trans. Brian Massumi, London: Athlone Press, 1988).

Ontology: The branch of philosophy that studies the nature of being. There is a large literature on this going back to classical times, and it has been a matter of endless fascination to the philosophical community. Arguably the most important enquiry into the nature of being in recent times is that of Martin Heidegger, who in *Being and Time* (1927) put forward the notion that we were 'thrown' into being. Being was thus a contingent state for which there was no reason, and our recognition of this induced a state of anxiety within us. Jean-Paul Sartre's *Being and Nothingness* (1943) follows on from Heidegger in picturing a world in which we are forced to face up to the contingency of an existence into which we have been 'abandoned'. In Sartre's world, being is always at risk of annihilation by non-being, and this omnipresent threat induces a response of either anguish or 'bad faith' (a denial of the reality of our situation). The positive side of contingency is that we have the freedom to choose how to act, since there is no predetermined pattern to our existence. The ontological condition of humankind is one of the major themes of modernist literature, which often pictures this as one of alienation.

Other: The relationship between self and other has been a long-term concern of Western philosophy, and how we view the other, whether as friend or threat, depends largely on the concept of self we espouse. The more sharply defined our sense of self, the more we are likely to fear the encroachment of the other – which in extreme cases would extend to the entire human race (see also **subject/subjectivity**). In poststructuralist and postmodern debate, the 'other' has come to take on the more specialised meaning of those excluded by the dominant ideology. Thus in Michel Foucault, the 'other' becomes such groups as homosexuals, the insane and prisoners, all of whom have failed to conform to the norms laid down by society and as a result find themselves marginalised. Jean-François Lyotard uses the term 'the jews' to refer to all those groups (not just the Jewish race itself) who are demonised by Western culture. To be 'other' in these contexts is invariably to be perceived as a threat to the dominant ideology.

Paganism: In Jean-François Lyotard's work, paganism describes a culture in which there is no centralised authority, and where all judgements are made on a pragmatic basis. In a pagan society we judge 'without criteria', taking each case on its merits. A good legal judgement will be one that in retrospect is found to have had a good outcome for society, rather than one that simply applies rules mechanically without regard for the particular circumstances of the case in question. Lyotard is adamant throughout his later writings that to judge *with* pre-established criteria (a legal code, for example) is to remain within the framework of grand narrative – that is, traditional authority. Paganism is his preferred alternative to that form of society, which he feels has lost its credibility. Objectors are more likely to note that judging without criteria turns justice into a somewhat arbitrary concept – certainly one that is more open to abuse than in our current system (see particularly Jean-François Lyotard and Jean-Loup Thébaud, *Just Gaming*, trans. Wlad Godzich, Manchester: Manchester University Press, 1985).

Paradigm/Paradigm shift: A paradigm can be regarded as a system of belief that holds sway over any area of discourse at a particular time. Thus one can speak of a cultural paradigm (modernism or postmodernism, for example), or a critical paradigm (**structuralism** or **poststructuralism**). The term was popularised by the philosopher of science Thomas Kuhn, for whom the history of science consisted of a series of paradigms, which in each instance eventually came to be superseded by new ones with greater explanatory and predictive power. At such points, a scientific revolution occurred. Newtonian physics gave way to Einsteinian relativity, and the latter in its turn to quantum mechanics. A crucial aspect of scientific revolutions is that the competing paradigms (old and new) are incommensurable with each other: you can believe one or the other, but not both. When the weight of opinion is towards the new, we can speak of a paradigm shift.

Relativism: The belief that truth is a relative rather than an absolute concept. Mainstream philosophy has operated on the premise that there are such things as truths that can be known with certainty. Mathematics would be one area that provides a profusion of examples. Behind mathematics lies logic and its basic laws, such as the law of identity (a = a; that is, a thing equals itself), which to most philosophers provides a firm basis for truth. In modern physics, however, the law of identity has come under attack, given that there are many instances in particle physics where a particle appears *not* to be identical to itself. Such findings have helped to fuel the cause of **antifoundationalism**, which adopts a resolutely relativist perspective. Even before the advent of modern physics, the notion of truth as an absolute concept had come under attack. For the nineteenth-century philosopher Friedrich Nietzsche, for example, truths merely represented the values of the ruling classes, and were to be regarded as no more than worn-out metaphors. Relativists tend to point out that there is no ultimate foundation for theories of truth, while their opponents can always counter that relativists undermine their own argument by assuming the truth of statements like, 'truth is a relative concept'. Again, as was noted in the case of antifoundationalism, the ramifications of this debate extend well beyond the boundaries of philosophy.

Rhizome: In the work of Gilles Deleuze and Felix Guattari, the rhizome becomes the model for networks of communication between human beings. As found in nature, rhizomes (tubers or mosses, for example), have the ability to grow connections between any two points on their surface. A system that works in that manner, Deleuze and Guattari argue, bypasses the need for any central controlling mechanism. To develop structures that operate in a rhizomatic manner – the Internet being an outstanding example – would be to destabilise central authority. For these thinkers, rhizomatic structures point the way to a new, more democratic, kind of politics. It is in the nature of rhizomatic structures that the authorities find it very difficult to prevent their spread (see particularly Gilles Deleuze and Felix Guattari, *A Thousand Plateaus: Capitalism and Schizophrenia*, trans. Brian Massumi, London: Athlone Press, 1988).

Sign/Signifier/Signified: In the linguistic theories of Ferdinand de Saussure, language is a self-contained system with its own internal rules and procedures, or 'grammar'. Language operates by means of 'signs', which are made up of a 'signifier' (word) and 'signified' (concept). The combination of the word 'dog' and the concept 'dog' in our minds, for example, constitutes a sign to which we respond. We can then be said to have understood the meaning of the utterance. The connection between signifier and signified is arbitrary (there are, after all, different words for 'dog' across different languages), but it generally requires the agreement of the rest of the language community in question before any change is made. For deconstructionist theorists, however, the arbitrariness of the connection is an argument against the notion of meaning being stable (see also **deconstruction**, **differance** and **metaphysics of presence**). Saussure regarded his theory of language as the beginning of the development of a 'science' for the study of signs: 'semiology' as he termed it.

Structuralism/Poststructuralism: Structuralism is heavily based on the linguistic theories of Ferdinand de Saussure, and treats all systems as if they were languages with their own internal 'grammar' (see also **sign/signifier/signified**). The point of structuralist analysis is to catalogue the grammar of each system, such that we can understand its internal workings, or 'structure'. Each literary genre has its own signifiers and signifieds, for example, which are combined into signs to which the audience responds in a fairly predictable manner. Structuralism seeks to identify common structures and patterns within all systems, including human behaviour, and regards itself as carrying forward Saussure's ideas for the development of a discipline of semiology, whereby all sign-systems can be classified. Poststructuralism is a reaction against structuralism and its analytical methods, which had come to dominate cultural theory by the mid-twentieth century (it was certainly the critical **paradigm** in the France of the period). For poststructuralists, structuralist analysis had become too predictable and was failing to yield up new insights. Figures like Jacques Derrida argued that structuralism assumed that meaning was buried within a system, just waiting for structuralist analysis to tease it out. That implied to him a commitment to stable meaning, which his own theory of **deconstruction** was designed to contest. Poststructuralism involves a range of opinions and methods, but there is general agreement among its many theorists that structuralism is just too 'neat' a form of analysis (it always finds the grammar it seeks), and that it includes assumptions about the nature of meaning that they find untenable. What poststructuralists particularly dislike is the structuralist claim to offer universal explanations (of how all systems work, for example). To the poststructuralist mind, this constitutes authoritarianism in action, and thus a prime target for their own anti-authoritarian project.

Subject/Subjectivity: In modern culture the subject – that is, the individual human being – is given a central role. Subjects are thought to have a unique essence and to constitute a unity over time. Modern culture purports to provide the means for such subjects to develop their abilities and talents, and encourages self-realisation and self-expression. Whether in artistic or business terms, entrepreneurial activity is prized. The assumption is made that by developing one's abilities and talents, one can come to exert more control over one's environment, and thus one's destiny. Subjectivity refers to the intense sense of selfhood that comes about as a result of this cultural programme. Postmodern thought rejects this model of the individual, and espouses the concept of the **decentred subject** instead, arguing that the self is a much more fluid, less unified, entity than modernity assumes.

Telos/Teleology: Teleology carries the notion of being designed for some specific purpose and, more crucially, of being *determined* to carry that process through. It is derived from the Greek word '*telos*', meaning 'end', which has now been adapted into English. Hegel's view of history is teleological, because it assumes that the 'World Spirit' is constantly evolving towards a state of self-realisation – at which point the end of history as we know it will have arrived. It can do no other than work towards that objective, that being the purpose of its existence, and it will continue, no matter what difficulties it may encounter, until success is achieved. Marx's view of history as a process of class struggle driving towards the establishment of the dictatorship of the proletariat is often seen as similarly teleological (see also **dialectics/dialectical materialism**).

ACKNOWLEDGEMENTS

The author and publisher wish to thank the following for their permission to reprint copyright material:

Jencks, 1991. Used by permission of Charles Jencks • Jencks, 1996. © 1996 John Wiley & Sons Ltd. Used by permission of John Wiley & Sons Ltd. • Ellul, 1964. © 1964 Alfred A. Knopf. Used by permission of Alfred A. Knopf, a division of Random House, Inc. • Eisenman, 1988. Used by permission of *Architectural Design* and Peter Eisenman • Newman, 1973. Used by permission of Oscar Newman • Sim, 2000. Used by permission of Ashgate Publishing Ltd. • Derrida, 1981. © 1972 Les Editions de Minuit. © 1981 University of Chicago/Athlone Press. Used by permission of Athlone, a division of Continuum Publishing, and University of Chicago Press • Harrison, 1997. Hodgkin, 1996. Used by permission of the *British Medical Journal* • Nietzsche, 1999. Rorty, 1989. Rose, 1991. Vernon, 1993. Walker, 1993. Used by permission of Cambridge University Press • McGowan, 1991. Used by permission of Cornell University Press • Habermas, 1989b. Used by permission of *Critical Inquiry* • Goodwin, 1991. Used by permission of Andrew Goodwin • Detels, 1994. © 1994 Duke University Press. Used by permission of Duke University Press • Aitken, 2001. Fraser, 1989. Nicholson, 1989. Used by permission of Edinburgh University Press • Plant, 1998. © 1997 Sadie Plant. Used by permission of HarperCollins Publishers Ltd. and Doubleday, a division of Random House, Inc. • Frampton, 1989. Used by permission of Free Association Books • Etzioni, 1968. Used by permission of Amitai Etzioni • Cohen, 1987. Used by permission of Ralph Cohen • Searle, 1977. Used by permission of John R. Searle • Fuentes, 1995. Used by permission of Greenwood Press • Gasché, 1986. © 1986 by the President and Fellows of Harvard College. Used by permission of Harvard University Press • Bell, 1976b. Used by permission of Heinemann Educational • Prigogine and Stengers, 1984. Used by permission of The Random House Group Ltd. and Ilya Prigogine • Allen and Young, 1989. Used by permission of Jeffner Allen • White, 1973. Used by permission of Johns Hopkins University Press • Rorty, 1983. Used by permission of the *Journal of Philosophy* • Crook, 1990. Lovibond, 1990. Huyssen, 1988. Klemm, 1993. Kroker, 1990. Linklater, 1990. Used by permission of Palgrave Macmillan • Carver, 1998. Woods, 1999. Used by permission of Manchester University Press • Lyotard and Thébaud, 1985. Bové, 1983. Fiske, 1994. • Used by permission of University of Minnesota Press • Lyotard, 1984. Used by permission of Manchester University Press and University of Minnesota Press • Belton, 1994. Hudnut, 1945. Used by permission of The McGraw-Hill Companies • Venturi, Izenour and Brown, 1977. Used by permission of MIT Press • Geras, 1987. Used by permission of *New Left Review* • Derrida, 1988. Used by permission of Northwestern University Press • Hassan, 1971. © 1982 University of Wisconsin Press. Used by permission of The University of Wisconsin Press • Mills, 1959. Toynbee, 1947. Used by permission of Oxford University Press, Inc. • Barrow, 1999. Nietzsche, 1996. Toynbee, 1954. Crowther, 1993. Kant, 1952. Used by permission of Oxford University Press • Joyce, 1991. Kelly, 1991. Stone, 1991. Used by permission of Oxford University Press • Docherty, 1993. Norris, 1990. Sarup, 1988. Used by permission of Pearson Education • Foucault, 1987. © 1984 Editions Gallimard. Translation © 1985 Random House, Inc. Used by permission of Editions Gallimard • Said, 1985. © 1978 Edward W. Said. Used by permission of Pantheon Books, a division of Random House, Inc. • Sim and Walker, 2000.

© 2000 Peter Lang Publishing, Inc. Used by permission of Peter Lang Publishing, Inc. • Glass, 1996. Used by permission of Dunvagen Music Publishers, Inc. • Stam and Miller, 2000. Callinicos, 1990. Habermas, 1989a. Habermas, 1987. Hekman, 1990. Heller and Fehér, 1988. Kellner, 1989. Lyotard, 1991. Vattimo, 1988. West, 1996. Connor, 1989. Donoghue, 1992. Eagleton, 1990. Harvey, 1990. Used by permission of Blackwell Publishing • Sokal and Bricmont, 1998. Used by permission of Profile Books • Klein, 1996. Used by permission of Rodopi • Cooke, 1990. Foucault, 1967. Farganis, 1994. Adorno, 1973. Ahmed, 1992. Ang, 1996. Bauman, 1992. Bertens, 1995. Elsaesser, 1998. Gamble, 2001. Gellner, 1992. Hebdige, 1988. Heidegger, 1993. Hutcheon, 1989. Hutcheon, 1988. Kaplan, 1987. Kellner, 1995. Lash, 1990b. Lewis, 2001. McGuigan, 1992. McHale, 1992. McRobbie, 1994. Milbank, 1992. Readings, 1991. Ruland and Bradbury, 1991. Shildrick, 1997. Smart, 1992. Tester, 1993. Turner, 1993. Frith and Horne, 1987. McHale, 1987. Used by permission of Routledge • Denzin, 1991. Featherstone, 1991. Gergen, 1992. Linstead, 1993. Lash, 1990a. Tijssen, 1990. Dunn, 1991. Stratton, 1989. Used by permission of Sage Publications • Virilio, 1986. Used by permission of Semiotexte Ltd. • Young, 1986. Used by permission of *Social Theory and Practice* • Lyotard, 1994. Used by permission of Stanford University Press • Frampton, 1992. Used by permission of Thames and Hudson • Warraq, 2001. © Ibn Warraq. Used by permission of *The Guardian* • Graff, 1973. © 1995 Gerald Graff. Used by permission of Gerald Graff • Danto, 1992. © 1992 Arthur C. Danto. Used by permission of Farrar, Straus and Giroux, LLC and Georges Borchardt, Inc., Literary Agency • Toulmin, 1982. © 1983 The Regents of the University of California. Used by permission of University of California Press • Kolb, 1990. Kuhn, 1970. Used by permission of University of Chicago Press • McDonald, 1985. © 1985 Schocken Books. Used by permission of Random House Inc. and Schocken Books, a division of Random House, Inc. • Adorno and Horkheimer, 1979. Baudrillard, 1988. Baudrillard, 1990. Davis, 1990. Laclau and Mouffe, 1985. Montag, 1988. Morris, 1988. Soja, 1989. Žižek, 1989. Used by permission of Verso • Fukuyama, 1992. © 1992 Francis Fukuyama. Davies, 1995. © 1995 Paul Davies. Lewontin, 1993. © 1991 R.C. Lewontin and the Canadian Broadcasting Corporation. Used by permission of Penguin Books • Owens, 1985. Used by permission of Pluto Press • Eco, 1984. Gleick, 1988. Originally published by William Heinemann. Used by permission of The Random House Group Ltd. • Deleuze and Guattari, 1988. © 1980 Les Editions de Minuit. © 1987 University of Minnesota/Athlone Press. Deleuze, and Guattari, 1983. © 1972 Les Editions de Minuit. © 1983 University of Minnesota/Athlone Press. Used by permission of Athlone, a division of Continuum Publishing • Coveney and Highfield, 1995. Used by permission of Faber and Faber • Habermas, 1981. Used by permission of *New German Critique* and Telos Press Ltd.

Every effort has been made to contact the copyright holders of material quoted in this book. However, there are instances where we have been unable to trace or contact copyright holders before our printing deadline. If notified, the publisher will be pleased to acknowledge the use of copyright material.

Thanks go to Dr Helene Brandon for various Internet searches, as well as for help in selecting the medical extracts (Chapter four); Dr David Walker for help with the history material (Chapter three); Angelique du Toit with the business studies material (Chapter three); and to Duncan Heath at Icon Books for support and advice throughout the project.

INDEX